access to history

Russia and its Rulers 1855–1964 for OCR

ANDREW HOLLAND

SECOND EDITION

HODDER
EDUCATION
AN HACHETTE UK COMPANY

15

The Publishers would like to thank the following for permission to reproduce copyright material:

Photo credits: p14t Library of Congress, LC-USZ62-128131; **p14b** Library of Congress, LC-USZ62-128133; **p15** Library of Congress, LC-DIG-hec-04921; **p19** Library of Congress, LC-DIG-ggbain-30798; **p20** https://commons.wikimedia.org/wiki/Category:Joseph_Stalin_in_photographs#/media/File:Stalin_Joseph.jpg; **p23** Bundesarchiv, Bild 183-B0628-0015-035/Heinz Junge/CC-BY-SA 3.0; **p46** Heritage Image Partnership Ltd/Alamy Stock Photo; **p47** Thomas Johnson/Sygma/Corbis; **p80** Granger, NYC./Alamy Stock Photo; **p105** https://commons.wikimedia.org/wiki/File:Nikolai_Dmitriev-Orenburgsky_The_Fire_in_the_village.jpg.

Acknowledgements: Allen Lane, *An Economic History of the U.S.S.R.* by A. Nove, 1969. Allen & Unwin, *A History of Russian Railways* by J.N. Westwood, 1964. Blackwell, *Europe Reshaped* by J. Grenville, 1999. Heinemann, *Russia and its Rulers 1855–1964* by Mike Wells, 2008. Hodder Education, *Reaction and Revolution: Russia 1881–1924* by Michael Lynch, 2004; *Origins and Development of Authoritarian and Single-party States* by Michael Lynch, 2013. Oxford University Press, *Endurance and Endeavour: Russian History 1812–2001* by J.N. Westwood, 1993, 2002; *Russia 1855–1919: From Tsars to Commissars* by Peter Oxley, 2001. Routledge, *Russia and the USSR, 1855–1991* by Stephen J. Lee, 2006. The Free Press, *Khrushchev: The Man and his Era* by William Taubman, 2003.

Every effort has been made to trace all copyright holders, but if any have been inadvertently overlooked the Publishers will be pleased to make the necessary arrangements at the first opportunity.

Although every effort has been made to ensure that website addresses are correct at time of going to press, Hodder Education cannot be held responsible for the content of any website mentioned in this book. It is sometimes possible to find a relocated web page by typing in the address of the home page for a website in the URL window of your browser.

Hachette UK's policy is to use papers that are natural, renewable and recyclable products and made from wood grown in sustainable forests. The logging and manufacturing processes are expected to conform to the environmental regulations of the country of origin.

Orders: please contact Bookpoint Ltd, 130 Milton Park, Abingdon, Oxon OX14 4SB. Telephone: +44 (0)1235 827720. Fax: +44 (0)1235 400454. Lines are open 9.00a.m.–5.00p.m., Monday to Saturday, with a 24-hour message answering service. Visit our website at www.hoddereducation.co.uk

© 2016 Andrew Holland
Second edition © Andrew Holland

First published in 2010 by
Hodder Education
An Hachette UK Company
Carmelite House, 50 Victoria Embankment
London EC4Y 0DZ

Impression number	10	9	8	7	6	5	4	3	2
Year		2020	2019	2018	2017	2016			

Cover photo © Swim Ink 2, LLC/Corbis
Produced, illustrated and typeset in Palatino LT Std by Gray Publishing, Tunbridge Wells
Printed and bound by CPI Group (UK) Ltd, Croydon CR0 4YY

A catalogue record for this title is available from the British Library

ISBN 978 1471838941

Contents

Dedication

Keith Randell (1943–2002)

The *Access to History* series was conceived and developed by Keith, who created a series to 'cater for students as they are, not as we might wish them to be'. He leaves a living legacy of a series that for over 20 years has provided a trusted, stimulating and well-loved accompaniment to post-16 study. Our aim with these new editions is to continue to offer students the best possible support for their studies.

Introduction

This introduction gives you an overview of the following:
★ The OCR A level course
★ How you will be assessed on this unit
★ The different features of this book and how they will aid your learning

The OCR A level course

This study will form part of your overall History course for the OCR specification, of which there are three unit groups and a topic-based essay. The unit groups comprise:

- British period study and enquiry (unit group 1)
- non-British period study (unit group 2)
- thematic study and historical interpretations (unit group 3).

This book has been written to support your study of the thematic study and historical interpretations unit Y318, Russia and its Rulers 1855–1964.

This unit considers how far the nature of government in the Russian Empire and the USSR changed from 1855 to 1964. How different leaders used ideologies, structures and tools to govern will be looked at; there is a particular focus on how the mechanisms of government altered to deal with different types of opposition that emerged. Following on from this is consideration of the ways in which regimes, wars and revolutions impacted on the politics, economy and society of the Russian Empire and the USSR. The unit finishes with a section on the reasons for and extent of change to the composition of the Russian Empire and the USSR.

There is also an in-depth analysis of the three interpretation depth studies:

- Alexander II's domestic reforms
- The Provisional Government
- Khrushchev in power 1956–64

How you will be assessed on this unit

Each of the three unit groups has an examination paper, whereas the topic-based essay is marked internally but externally moderated.

Unit group 1	Unit group 2	Unit group 3
The British period study is assessed through two essays from which you answer one, and the enquiry is assessed through a source-based question. This counts for 25 per cent of your overall marks	The non-British period study is assessed through a short essay and one longer essay. This counts for fifteen per cent of your overall marks	The thematic and historical interpretations are assessed through two essays which cover at least 100 years, and one in-depth question based on two interpretations of a key event, individual or issue that forms a major part of the theme. This counts for 40 per cent of your overall marks

For the topic-based essay you will complete a 3000–4000-word essay on a topic of your choice. This counts for twenty per cent of your overall marks.

Examination questions for unit group 3

You will be entered for a specific unit for your A level, and your examination paper will contain only the questions relating to that unit. There will be two sections in the examination paper. Section A is the historical interpretations and Section B is the thematic essay.

In Section A there will be two interpretations about one of the depth studies and one question. The question will be worth 30 marks.

In Section B there will be three thematic essay questions, each worth 25 marks, and you will have to answer two of them. As this is a thematic paper the questions may be drawn from more than one key topic.

Section A questions

Section A questions will be worded as follows:

Evaluate the interpretations in both of the passages and explain which you think is more convincing as an explanation of X. [30]

For example:

Evaluate the interpretations in both of the passages and explain which you think is more convincing as an explanation of the reasons for the Emancipation Edict of 1861.

Section B questions

Examples of questions using some of the more common command terms, and specific requirements for answering each term, can be found at the end of each chapter. The command terms are important. A key to success is the ability to display understanding of what these terms mean and what you are being asked to do.

Command term	Description
Assess	Weigh up the relative importance of a range of themes and reach a supported judgement as to which is the most important across the whole period
To what extent/ how far	Consider the relative importance of the named issue or theme and weigh up its role by comparing it (comparative evaluation) with other issues or themes and reach a balanced judgement as to its relative importance across the whole period
How successful	Consider a range of issues or themes and make a judgement as to how successful each was before reaching an overall judgement about success by comparing each issue or theme

Answering the questions

The A level examination is two and a half hours long. Section A carries slightly more marks than each question in Section B and, therefore, particularly as you will need time to read the interpretations, it would be sensible to spend about one hour on Section A and 45 minutes on each essay in Section B. Before you start any of the questions, make a brief plan. Advice on planning both the historical interpretations question and the thematic essay is given on pages 70–1 and 73–5.

The answers you write will be marked against the relevant mark scheme. It would be useful to familiarise yourself with this before the examination so that you are aware of the criteria against which your work will be marked. Question specific mark schemes offer guidance, but they cannot cover everything. You may write something that is relevant and accurate but not in the question specific mark scheme: you will still gain credit for it. You will be rewarded for well-argued and supported responses that show evidence of synthesis across the period (see pages 121–5). Marks will not be deducted for information that is incorrect, but you should remember that incorrect knowledge may undermine your argument.

The different features of this book and how they will aid your learning

The book starts with a chronological overview of Russia and its rulers from 1855 to 1964. The topic will then be explored throughout the four main thematic chapters in the book. This is intended to act as a reference point that can be referred to throughout your study of the main themes.

Each main thematic chapter in the book covers one of the key topics listed in the OCR specification:

- Chapter 1 will look at the nature of Russian government.
- Chapter 2 focuses on the impact of dictatorial regimes on the economy and society of the Russian Empire and the USSR.
- Chapter 3 examines the impact of war and revolution on the development of the Russian Empire and the USSR.
- Chapter 4 deals with changes to the Russian Empire, the role of nationalities and the emergence of satellite states.

Each chapter also has a section on the three named depth studies and provides more detail and, where relevant, discussion of any historical debates about that study in relation to the theme of the chapter.

At the end of the book is a timeline of the major events (pages 228–30) and suggestions for further reading.

The headings below outline the main features of each main thematic chapter.

Chapter overviews

Chapters start with a brief overview of the theme and a series of bullet points which list the main issues discussed. The structure of the chapter is outlined and a timeline lists the key dates for the events discussed in the chapter.

Chapter sections

The chapters are divided into sections, each addressing one of the bullet points listed in the overview. The section addresses a key question or questions, and is further broken down into a series of sub-headings to help your understanding of the topic. By the end of each section you should be able to answer the key question. Your understanding will be reinforced by a summary diagram for each section.

Profiles

These are brief sections detailing the life and key dates of important people in relation to the topic studied.

Key figures

Concise summaries are given of important people in relation to certain events to do with the topic studied.

Key terms

The key terms that you need to understand in order to grasp the important concepts and issues surrounding the topic are emboldened in the chapter the first time they are used in the book, and are defined in the margin and the glossary at the end of the book.

Key debates

Historians often disagree about the causes or significance of historical events and the role and impact of individuals. Key debates are listed at the start of the chapter and are discussed in the historical interpretations section at the end. Not only will this introduce you to some of the key historical debates about the period you are studying, but by using your historical knowledge and the information in the chapter you will be able to test the views of the historians, which will help you to prepare for the Section A examination question.

Chapter summaries

At the end of each chapter there will be a summary of the key points covered in the chapter, which will help with revision.

Refresher questions

There will be a series of refresher questions at the end of each chapter. These will not be examination-style questions, but will be designed to ensure that you have a clear understanding of the main points and issues raised in the chapter.

Study skills

Each chapter has a study skills section. In each section one part will develop the skills needed for the thematic essay and the other part will develop the skills needed for the historical interpretations question. There will often be examples of strong and weak paragraphs and the opportunity for you to practise the skills on relevant questions and interpretations.

Russia 1855–1964: an overview

This book covers the period from 1855 to 1964 in Russian history, from the ascension of Tsar Alexander II to the end of the rule of communist leader Nikita Khrushchev. It focuses on the nature of Russian government and its impact on the Russian economy and society. In particular, emphasis is placed on the degree of change and continuity between the autocracies of the tsars and the dictatorships of the communists.

In order to discern patterns of change and continuity over the period in question, it is important to consider the similarities and differences between each ruler and not just before and after the 1917 Revolution (when autocracy was replaced with communism). Also, getting too embroiled in the details of particular events and developments, such as the 1917 Revolution, will impede identification of the patterns of change and continuity. Most people will know something about Rasputin, the murder of Nicholas II and his family, the events of October 1917, the atrocities committed by Stalin and the Cold War. However, the purpose of this book is to encourage the reader to synthesise such knowledge so that judgements can be made about more general patterns of change and continuity. This is especially important when studying this particular period of Russian history. It is easy to assume that the events of 1917 acted as a major turning point in the development of Russian government. A more thoughtful analysis of the history, though, will reveal that there is a case for arguing that there was more continuity than change in the way Russia was ruled.

A chronological summary of the main periods of rule

Alexander II (1855–81)

Challenges

Before Alexander II came to the throne, serious social unrest over living and working conditions had been mounting. The effects of the Crimean War added to this discontent (see Chapter 3 for details about the causes, course and consequences of the war). Among the higher echelons of Russian society, there was also concern that Russia was falling behind Western Europe and would soon become a second-rate power.

Domestic policies

The tsar implemented a package of reforms, the majority of which naturally stemmed from the emancipation of the serfs in 1861. Changes were made to local government, the military, the legal system, education and the economy which seemed to constitute the start of a more liberal age. But this did not prevent Alexander II from resorting to repression to keep opponents in line. One of the ironies of this period was that as the people became more liberated, they showed an inclination to threaten the security of the ruling elite and were subsequently clamped down on again.

Alexander III (1881–94)

Challenges

The assassination of Alexander II in 1881 illustrated the degree of opposition that had mounted during his reign and that threatened autocracy. Alexander III also had to deal with land ownership issues that resulted from the emancipation of the serfs and clamours for more rapid industrialisation.

Domestic policies

A 'reaction' to the liberal policies of Alexander II occurred. Many of the reforms prior to 1881 were reversed or altered. Of particular note was the 1881 Statute of State Security which sanctioned greater use of repression. Russification was also introduced to control the discontent among national minority groups. All of this was a marked departure from the freedoms granted by the previous ruler. On a more positive note, the tsar appointed Sergei Witte as finance minister to modernise the Russian economy. However, Alexander never lived to witness the full impact of Witte's efforts as he died prematurely from kidney disease in 1894.

Nicholas II (1894–1917)

Challenges

Unlike his father and grandfather, Nicholas did not have the personal qualities required to be a successful ruler. Opposition to his rule proliferated and became more organised in the form of the radicals (the Social Democratic Workers' Party – the SDs – and the Socialist Revolutionary Party – the SRs) and the liberals (Kadets and Octobrists – see Chapter 1 for more details about these groups). The Bolsheviks, a division of the SDs, went on to seize power from the Provisional Government and to murder Nicholas and his family. To distract the attention of the people from growing economic problems, Nicholas engaged in a disastrous war with Japan (1904–5). The consequences of this fuelled the so-called revolution of 1905 (see Chapter 3 for more details about the war and the link with revolution). Nicholas also committed Russia to fight in the First World War, although initially this was welcomed by the bulk of the population. However, he never got to grips with the enormous challenges this posed. With hindsight, it would appear that his decision to take personal control of the armed forces, thus leaving his wife (and Rasputin) in charge of domestic affairs, was a huge mistake. In 1917, he was forced to abdicate and his regime was replaced by the Provisional Government (see Chapter 1 for more details of this event).

Domestic policies

- *Economic reforms*. Nicholas encouraged Witte to continue with his plan to modernise the Russian economy, with a particular emphasis on the expansion of heavy industries and the railways. Agricultural issues were addressed mainly through the efforts of Stolypin and his land reforms.

- *Political reforms*. As a result of the serious popular unrest of 1905, Nicholas ordered the setting up of a representative political chamber called the *Duma*. Although this appeared to be a step on the road to a constitutional monarchy, Nicholas came to distrust the *Duma* to the extent that he severely restricted its composition and powers.
- *Social reforms*. In the field of social reform, there was some reversion to the ideas espoused by Alexander II. Education was expanded and there was a relaxation in censorship. Nevertheless, Nicholas showed little intention of diverting from autocracy and his general attitude towards the Russian people did not marry well with their changing wants and needs.

The Provisional Government (March 1917 to October 1917)

Challenges

Although the Provisional Government was only ever intended to be a temporary arrangement, it could not disguise the fact that it was unelected, unrepresentative and essentially the 'old guard' in disguise. From the beginning it was also pushed into accepting a power share with the Petrograd soviet. This meant that the Provisional Government had to rely on members of the soviet to provide support if reforms were to be pushed through. The two biggest problems it faced were demands for fairer land distribution and Russia's war performance. Neither was tackled with any confidence, which led to the opposition gaining momentum and eventually taking over.

Domestic policies

The Provisional Government attempted to halt social unrest by imposing a number of liberal measures:

- The police department was disbanded and all policing was to be carried out by local militias.
- Old-style regional governors and officials were replaced with a new wave of administrators.
- Many political prisoners (for example, Trotsky) were released or given an amnesty to return to Russia.
- Newspapers, books and pamphlets increased in circulation. The net effect was to allow Russian people to voice their opinions more strongly about how they wanted their country to be run in the future.
- From the beginning, the Provisional Government had promised and planned for the creation of a democratically elected Constituent Assembly. In the end, their promises did little to appease agitators and the new liberal climate simply allowed dissent to mount.

The inherent weaknesses of the government plus the context it was operating in provided an opportunity for the Bolsheviks to take over.

Lenin (1917–24)

Challenges

Lenin faced two immediate problems after he seized power. First, he had to confront opposition. Second, he needed to tackle Russia's involvement in the First World War. After he had dealt with these issues he had to move on to consolidate Bolshevik power and win acceptance of the new regime from the rest of the world.

Domestic policies

Lenin solved the war problem by authorising the signing of the Treaty of Brest-Litovsk in March 1918. This was essentially a peace treaty with Germany and the terms for Russia were harsh. Bolshevik authority was quickly established through the setting up of the Soviet of People's Commissars or *Sovnarkom*. This elite cabinet set out its stall by issuing a number of decrees. A number of these focused on banning opposition and were to be enforced through the use of a new secret police force, the *Cheka*. But opposition either went underground or was difficult to control because of the geographical size of Russia.

The strength and spread of opposition resulted in a Civil War which the Bolsheviks won using the Red Army, the *Cheka* and the policy of War Communism (see Chapter 3 for more details about the war, including the nature and extent of opposition to the Bolsheviks). War Communism was despised and, when the war was over, it was replaced with the New Economic Policy (NEP). The NEP was the main plank in Lenin's strategy to stabilise Russia and modernise the economy. After Lenin died, a power struggle ensued. One of the issues debated was the viability and efficacy of the NEP. The right wanted it to continue whereas the left wanted it to be replaced. When Stalin emerged victorious from the struggle he quickly imposed a personalised style of rule and a raft of economic and social policies that mirrored his brand of communism.

Stalin (1928–53)

Challenges

Stalin had to deal with the legacy of Lenin, who had been revered, and the fact that there were those in the party who mistrusted Stalin's intentions. There were also the ongoing problems related to agriculture, industry and national minorities. From 1939 to 1945, Russia became involved in the Second World War and was invaded by Nazi Germany. Before his death in 1953, he had yet another war to confront – the Cold War. However, the most challenging aspects of the Cold War had to be dealt with by Khrushchev, who took over from Stalin.

Domestic policies

There was clear continuity in the way that Stalin dealt with opposition. He used the secret police (NKVD) to arrest people, who ended up being jailed, exiled or executed. Such arrests happened in waves and were known as purges. Show trials and other forms of propaganda were used to control the behaviour of the people. The scale of repression was far greater than under any other leader but the importance of it lay in the terror that it created. The fear of the Stalinist regime was of a magnitude that meant that Stalin had absolute control of people's lives.

The problem of agriculture was tackled through the imposition of collectivisation and dekulakisation, which was also intertwined with repression. Agricultural policies were geared towards aiding the development of heavy industry; those employed in growing numbers in factories, mines and industrial plants relied totally on peasants for their food.

Stalin's industrial policy focused on centralised planning (Five-Year Plans) and a move away from any semblance of the free market. This too was integrated with repression; workers who did not reach targets were usually punished severely. Whether these policies were the main factor in helping Russia to repel the Nazis during the Second World War is a matter for debate. What is fairly clear is that after the war Stalin was seen as a hero and he strengthened his position as a prominent world leader.

Khrushchev (1953–64)

Challenges

Although Stalin had become a hero of the Russian people he was still associated with the Great Terror and years of unprecedented repression. Khrushchev therefore had to stamp his own personality on Russian government and change the image of Russia created by Stalin. The latter was especially important given the nature of international relations in the post-war era. Agriculture was still considered to be in something of a mess but heavy industry had progressed, albeit to the detriment of living standards. From Khrushchev's perspective, one of the most important problems facing politicians was the deterioration in working and living conditions. The last thing he wanted was mass social unrest.

Domestic policies

Although Stalin was acclaimed as a war hero, he had gained support through fear and high-level repression. The non-communist world took advantage of this by proclaiming Russia to be the great enemy of the 'free' world. Khrushchev attempted to deal with this by denouncing the rule of his predecessor (de-Stalinisation).

Nevertheless, he carried on with the centralised planning of the economy but with more focus on the enhancement of light and consumer industries. The mainstay of his agricultural policy was the Virgin Land campaign, which was aimed at increasing the amount of land under the plough. A number of important social improvement programmes were put into operation, especially in the field of housing. However, the Khrushchev era continued to witness the use of repression to maintain law and order. Political prisoners were released and the *Gulag* was mostly made redundant but Russian citizens were still subject to rule through autocracy.

CHAPTER 1

The nature of government

The main aim of this chapter is to provide a clear picture of how the nature and structure of Russian government changed in the face of opposition from 1855 to 1964. It also considers the use of repression and reform by Russian leaders as tools to deal with opposition. A key area of debate to consider when looking at the nature of Russian government is the extent to which the communist leaders were 'Red tsars' (that is, the degree of similarity between the way in which the tsars and communists ruled).

In particular, this chapter examines the main characteristics of Russian government from 1855 to 1964, which can be categorised under the following headings:

★ Ideologies: autocracy, dictatorship and totalitarianism

★ Developments in central administration (structures and institutions)

★ Changes in local government

★ Methods of repression and enforcement

★ The extent and impact of reform

★ The nature, extent and effectiveness of opposition both before and after 1917

★ Attitude of the tsars, Provisional Government and communists to political change

★ The extent of political change

It also considers the debates surrounding the three in-depth topics:

★ How 'liberal' was Russian government from 1855 to 1881?

★ To what extent was the Provisional Government doomed to fail from the start?

★ How far did de-Stalinisation represent a genuine break from the past?

Key dates

1855	Alexander II became tsar	1918	Treaty of Brest-Litovsk signed
1861	Emancipation Edict announced	1924	Death of Lenin; power struggle ensued
1881	Assassination of Alexander II	1927	Stalin controlled Party Congress and expelled main rivals
1894	Death of Alexander III; Nicholas II became tsar	1936	New constitution issued
1898	Social Democratic Workers' Party formed	1953	Death of Stalin
1906	First *Duma* set up; Fundamental Laws passed	1953–6	Khrushchev took control of Russia; de-Stalinisation (1956 onwards)
1917	Abdication of Nicholas II; formation of Provisional Government; revolutions	1964	Khrushchev removed from power

1 Ideologies: autocracy, dictatorship and totalitarianism

▶ *How far could all Russian governments from 1855 to 1964 be described as autocratic?*

Autocracy

From 1855 to March 1917, Russia was governed as an **autocracy**. Tsars had absolute power which was said to be ordained by God. All Russians had to obey the will of the tsar or suffer punishment. The historian J.N. Westwood (2002) has indicated that there were three strands to tsarist autocracy:

- The 'tsar expected willing and total submission of his subjects'. This was a system based on religious faith, and did not require the tsar to be made accountable to the people through elections (or **constitutional government**).
- The tsar was obliged to act as a 'moral judge' on behalf of God. He had a **paternalistic** duty to protect his subjects and control their behaviour for the good of the nation as a whole. He was supported in this role by the **Russian Orthodox Church**.
- Autocracy was viewed as a practical necessity. The Russian Empire was so vast and diverse that it was better if one person had total control over imperial affairs. According to supporters of the tsarist regime, such as Konstantin Pobedonostsev (see profile on page 13), a **liberal democracy** and constitutional government would have been disastrous for Russia, as it would have led to too many people demanding too many different policies. Besides, as the vast majority of the population were illiterate peasants, democracy would have resulted in the governance of Russia by those who lacked 'the ability to reason'.

Continuity in the belief in autocracy

Although there was variation in how autocratic power was used by the tsars throughout the period, the significance of autocracy was continuously enforced through manifestos, speeches and policies.

Nicholas I used propaganda and slogans such as '**Orthodoxy, Autocracy and Nationality**' to promote tsarism. This was reinforced with legislation such as the **Fundamental Laws** of 1832, whose introduction stated:

> *The emperor of all the Russians is an autocratic and unlimited monarch: God himself ordains that all must bow to his supreme power, not only out of fear but also out of conscience.*

Konstantin Pobedonostsev

1827	Born
1841	Enrolled at the St Petersburg School of Jurisprudence
1859	Started teaching at Moscow State University and went on to gain a professorship (1860–65)
1864	Judicial reforms; he had helped in the preparation of these
1865	Became tutor to Alexander II's sons (Nicholas and Alexander)
1868	Appointed as a senator
1873	Condemned the jury system; showed signs of being more reactionary
1874	Became a member of the Council of Empire
1880	Appointed chief procurator of the Holy Synod
1907	Died

Konstantin Pobedonostsev was educated in Russian law in preparation for a career in the Russian civil service. After graduating from the St Petersburg School of Jurisprudence he joined the Moscow department of the Senate and quickly rose up the civil service ranks. One of his earliest achievements in government was to help the tsar to draft the judicial reforms of 1864. Pobedonostsev achieved renown as a legal adviser and writer on Russian law. Between 1868 and 1880, he published the three volumes of *A Course of Civil Law*; this proved to be a core text for all aspiring lawyers.

Pobedonostsev left the civil service to pursue a post as professor of civil law. This was relatively short lived as he was encouraged to become the tutor to the tsar's sons, Nicholas and Alexander. Nicholas died in 1865 but Alexander when on to succeed his father as tsar. Pobedonostsev is said to have been a major influence on Alexander III's policy making and manifesto. He was rewarded, in 1880, by being appointed as chief procurator of the Holy Synod. This allowed him to advise the tsar on religious matters, and to have influence in the Church, and over educational and social issues.

Pobedonostsev was a conservative and reactionary for much of his adult life. He was an advocate of autocracy and an enemy of liberal democracy. The clamour for greater freedom was said, by Pobedonostsev, to be influenced by 'the dangerous delusions of nihilistic youth'. As a devoutly religious man he venerated the Russian Orthodox Church; this also helps to explain his anti-Jewish sentiments. His influence, though, faded during the reign of Nicholas II until his death in 1907.

Alexander II did not waver from this sentiment despite showing reformist tendencies. After an assassination attempt was made on him in 1866, he adhered very strongly to the concept of autocracy. His successor and son, Alexander III, blamed moves towards liberalism for his father's eventual assassination in 1881.

Nicholas II – after making 'liberal' concessions in 1905 – introduced another set of Fundamental Laws (1906) which reiterated the need for the preservation of autocracy. The 1906 legislation stated that:

> *The All-Russian Emperor possesses the supreme autocratic power. Not only fear and conscience, but God himself, commands obedience to his authority. The Russian Empire is governed by firmly established laws that have been properly enacted.*

Thus, all of the tsars consistently promoted and justified autocracy. Even when reforms were enacted, it was clear that ultimate power and control, as sanctioned by God, rested in the hands of the tsar.

Alexander II

1818	Born into the Romanov dynasty
1855	Became tsar as a result of the death of his father, Nicholas I
1856	Made peace with enemies in Crimean War. Announced shortly afterwards that 'it is better to begin abolishing serfdom from above than to wait for it to begin to abolish itself from below'
1857	Created the Secret Committee on Peasant Affairs, which was designed to plan for the emancipation of the serfs (freeing serfs from control by their 'owners')
1861	Introduced the Great Emancipation Statute
1863	Reformed the education system by allowing the existence of private schools, making alterations to the curriculum and establishing an inspectorate
1864	Formed the Zemstva (regional councils) to improve local government. Changes to legal structures and processes were also made in the same year
1865	Issued new guidelines for publishers and writers which allowed for greater freedom to express new and challenging ideas
1866	Ended reform programme after first serious attempt on his life
1877	Organised the 'Trial of the 50', the trial of key political opponents
1881	Assassinated by the members of political terrorist group called the 'People's Will'

The Russian people seemed to welcome Alexander II to the throne and were generally happy with his reforms. However, the radicals were not impressed as Russia continued to be governed through autocracy. Ironically, Alexander was about to sign an agreement just before his death that would probably have resulted in a more democratic government.

Alexander III

1845	Born into the Romanov dynasty
1881	Became tsar as a result of the assassination of his father. Immediately passed the Statute Concerning measures for the Production of State Security and the Social Order. The Russification programme was also launched in the same year, starting with pogroms against Jews
1883	Established the Peasant Land Bank to provide cheap loans for the purchase of land
1884	Made further adjustments to the provision of education
1887	Ordered the execution of Lenin's brother (see profile of Lenin on page 19) and four others who plotted to execute the tsar
1889	Land Captains were appointed to monitor and control the behaviour of the peasants
1891	Forced to deal with terrible famine
1894	Died of nephritis (a kidney disorder) at the age of 49

Alexander III was a military man who believed strongly in autocracy. His period of rule is often seen as one of reaction and repression in response to the more relaxed liberal period of governance under his father. He was intent on returning stability to Russia and on ensuring that social unrest and opposition to tsarism did not get out of hand. His reign proved to be relatively peaceful and some very positive economic reforms were carried out.

Changes in the way autocracy was implemented

There were differences in the way in which the tsars performed their autocratic role. Before an assassination attempt on his life in 1866, Alexander II opted for a string of reforms which appeared to represent a dilution of autocracy (see profile on page 14).

In contrast, Alexander III quickly resorted to a more repressive form of autocracy. Opposition such as the **People's Will** was ruthlessly suppressed, and many of the changes instigated by the previous tsar were reversed. This **'Reaction'** was heavily influenced by Pobedonostsev, who argued that constitutional government or 'parliamentarianism' was unworkable.

Nicholas II continued in the same vein as his father. Constitutional reforms were implemented in 1905, but these were forced on the tsar as a result of economic crisis and the disastrous consequences of the Russo-Japanese War (1904–5) (see pages 139–42). The **Fundamental Laws of 1906** diluted the effect of the reforms, and by 1917 the *Duma* was little more than a talking shop frequented by politicians committed to autocracy.

Thus, the tsars used their autocratic power differently according to their differing circumstances. But political, economic and social reforms were never made with the intention of the tsar relinquishing any degree of control.

 **KEY TERMS**

People's Will A terrorist group consisting of members of the educated classes who were upset by Alexander II's refusal to continue with his reform programme after the mid-1860s.

'Reaction' Alexander III reacted to the liberal reforms put together by his father by reversing them and introducing more repressive measures.

Fundamental Laws of 1906 Regulations that reinforced the position of the tsar. Law 5, for example, stated that 'Supreme autocratic power belongs to the Emperor of all Russia'.

Nicholas II

1868	Born into the Romanov dynasty
1894	Took over as tsar on the death of his father, Alexander III. In the same year he married the Princess Alexandra, the German granddaughter of Queen Victoria
1905	Announced the October Manifesto and new constitution
1906	Introduced the first *Duma*
1913	Organised the tercentenary celebrations of Romanov family rule
1914	Took Russia into the First World War by signing the general mobilisation order
1915	Ordered Russian armed forces to be placed under the personal command of the tsar
1917	Return to Petrograd halted by rebels. Senior military officials and members of the *Duma* advised Nicholas to stand down. Abdicated to 'save' Russia
1918	Murdered, along with his family, in Ekaterinburg

Although Nicholas II attempted political reforms to appease opposition, his mishandling of Russia's involvement in the First World War led to his downfall and the end of the Romanov dynasty. Nicholas seemed to lack the political knowledge, understanding and skill of his father. If he had worked more cooperatively with the opposition groups in the *Duma* he may have survived. However, his stubborn attitude resulted in strict adherence to autocracy which proved unacceptable to other prominent members of Russian government.

Dictatorship

The Russian concept of dictatorship was partly derived from the writings of Karl Marx and Friedrich Engels (see profiles on pages 17 and 18). By the late 1840s, their work was known among a minority of Russian radicals, but it was not until the 1880s that their ideas had really taken root within the Russian intelligentsia.

Marxism

There were three aspects of Marxism that seemed especially relevant to those who opposed autocracy.

Marx and the idea of superstructure

Marx believed that the foundation or base of society was maintained and established by a ruling elite; this base benefited the elite to the detriment of others. In tsarist Russia the foundation was agricultural serfdom, with a small amount of industrialisation. To maintain this, a superstructure of institutions was needed by the ruling class to establish order. Marx believed that this kind of system was unfair and bound to lead to conflict. In his eyes, the only way to change this was to destroy the base. Russian intellectuals took this to mean that serfdom and capitalism should be replaced by a more egalitarian society.

Marx and the labour theory of value

Marx adopted the 'labour theory of value' which claimed that under a **capitalist economy** the **proletariat** would never gain the full value of their efforts. A disproportionate amount of wages would be taken away to provide capitalists with profits far in excess of what was needed to maintain industrialisation. However, this would eventually prove unacceptable to workers as they increasingly realised that they were being exploited. Marx predicted that the result would be a worker uprising to overthrow the system – a revolution. Unsurprisingly, it was expected that this transformation would begin in the advanced industrialised European nations such as Germany and Britain. This was an issue that Russian radicals had to square with what was happening in their homeland; Russia was largely rural and 'backward' and, according to Marx, not the kind of place where a revolution would happen.

Marx and the dictatorship of the proletariat

Marx referred to the likely conflict between capitalists and workers as a class struggle. He argued that it was the final part of an ongoing series of struggles throughout history between different social groups. The conflict between capitalists and workers would be resolved when workers seized control of the means of production, distribution and exchange. Before full **communism** could emerge (a classless society), there would be a **dictatorship of the proletariat**, in which political control would be placed in the hands of the workers and those representing their interests. The Bolsheviks under Lenin and Stalin (see profiles on pages 19 and 20) modified these guidelines to suit the circumstances they found themselves in. Hence, by the end of the Civil War (1917–21), the governance of Russia was based on **Marxism–Leninism** and then, from 1927 to 1953, by **Marxism–Leninism–Stalinism**.

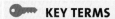 **KEY TERMS**

Capitalist economy An economy based on making as much profit as possible from industrial and commercial activity.

Proletariat Those who worked in industry and lived in urban areas.

Communism A form of rule which allowed for the control, by the 'people', of the means of production, distribution and exchange.

Dictatorship Absolute rule, usually by one person, with no legal, political, economic or social restrictions.

Dictatorship of the proletariat In theory, when the workers controlled political power. Lenin argued that before this could happen, workers would have to be ordered what to do by the Bolsheviks as they did not have the knowledge, understanding and skill to take full control of governing Russia.

Marxism–Leninism Lenin's interpretation of Marxism which argued that the move to worker control of the means of production, distribution and exchange could be speeded up.

Marxism–Leninism–Stalinism Stalin's version of Marxism–Leninism.

Marxism–Leninism

By the early 1890s, Lenin had fully embraced Marxism. Initially, both Lenin and **Martov** supported worker attempts to gain higher wages and better working conditions. However, when help was given to organise strikes in St Petersburg (1895, 1896, 1897), the authorities reacted by exiling the ringleaders. Consequently, when the Russian Social Democratic Workers' Party (RSDLP) was formed in 1898 to unite Russian Marxists, Lenin and others argued over strategy. Lenin believed that the authorities' reaction to the St Petersburg strikes proved that the 'superstructure' would always prevail to keep workers in their place. Instead of attempting to gain concessions within the capitalist system, Lenin thought it better to overthrow the existing ruling order by attacking the 'base'.

KEY FIGURE

Y.O. Martov (1873–1923)

Initially, friend of Lenin and co-editor of the radical newspaper *Iskra*. However, the two eventually fell out over what tactics to use to achieve their political aims.

Karl Marx

1818	Born in Trier, in the German Rhineland
1841	Started career as a journalist in Cologne, Germany
1843	Moved to Paris after being expelled from Germany because of his radical views
1845	Moved to Brussels after being expelled from Paris
1848	Returned to Germany to participate in the revolution as a reporter
1849	Settled in London and remained there for the rest of his life
1867	Publication of the first volume of *Das Kapital*
1881	Death of wife, Jenny Marx
1883	Died

Karl Marx was born on 5 May 1818 in Trier in western Germany. His father was a successful Jewish lawyer (although he converted to Christianity to help him progress in his career). Marx followed in his father's footsteps, studying law in Bonn and Berlin, but he also became interested in philosophy, especially the works of Hegel and Feuerbach. He then started a career as a journalist and decided to move to Paris, where he believed his writings would gain a wider audience. In Paris he met Friedrich Engels, the son of a wealthy factory owner, with whom he collaborated to develop ideas about revolutionary communism.

Marx's radicalism got him expelled from France; in 1845 he moved to Brussels, where he continued his partnership with Engels. Together they produced the famous *The Communist Manifesto* (published in 1848). The main message of the tract was that 'the history of all hitherto existing society was the history of class struggle'. The ultimate class struggle would be between capitalists and the proletariats (workers); revolutions would occur that would lead to governance of countries by workers ('dictatorships of the proletariat').

In 1849, Marx moved to London with his family and was again followed by Engels. Marx was plagued by illness and a lack of funds; he relied on the wealth and intellect of Engels to help him develop his ideas. In 1867, the first volume of *Das Kapital* was published. This set out some of Marx's key ideas on political economy, especially those concerning the labour theory of value (see page 16). The remaining volumes of the work came out after Marx's death having been edited by Engels.

In his later years, Marx became less productive as a writer. In 1881, he became depressed by the deaths of his wife, Jenny, and one of his daughters. He died on 14 March 1883 and was buried at Highgate Cemetery in London.

Friedrich Engels

1820	Born in Barmen, Germany
1842	Sent to Manchester
1844	*The Condition of the Working Class in England* published
1845	Moved to Brussels after being expelled from Paris
1849	Settled in London
1878	Married Lizzie Burns
1885	Second volume of *Das Kapital* published
1894	Third volume of *Das Kapital* published
1895	Died

Friedrich Engels was born in Barmen on 28 November 1820. His father was a wealthy German industrialist who owned factories producing cotton textiles in Manchester. In 1842, Engels was sent to Manchester by his father to gain an insight into the management of the Ermen & Engels factory. While he was there, the young Engels became appalled by the poor living and working conditions he observed in the city. His experience prompted him to write *The Condition of the Working Class in England*, published in 1844. This was an account of what Engels had observed and what he believed had caused such deprivation, the failings of capitalism. In the same year, he wrote articles for the radical journal *Franco-German Annals*, which was edited by Karl Marx. This started a lifelong collaboration and friendship between the two individuals. It functioned very well as Marx was the great thinker of radical ideas and Engels had a flair (and the money) to write material that appealed to a wide audience.

Engels moved to Paris and then Brussels with Marx, but, due to threats of imprisonment for their ideas, they eventually settled in the more liberal climate of London in 1849. When based in Brussels, both were influential in the setting up of an English Communist League (1846). More importantly, the two co-wrote a 12,000-word pamphlet that became *The Communist Manifesto* (published in 1848). The manifesto set out some of the principles of communism, as developed by Marx and Engels, and how the ideology was likely to lead to revolution.

While in England, Engels gave financial support to Marx and his family. He also introduced his friend to members of the Chartist movement. The move to England witnessed the two develop their ideas and more publications followed, including *The Peasant War in Germany* (1850), *Das Kapital*, volume 1 (1867) and *Anti-Dühring* (1878). When Marx died in 1883, Engels spent much of his time, until his own death, editing and writing up the last two volumes of *Das Kapital*.

KEY TERMS

Dialectical Relating to the ongoing changes in society from one stage to another.

Reds A general term for those who actively supported the Bolsheviks during the Civil War.

Whites A general term for those who actively opposed the Bolsheviks during the Civil War.

Lenin set out his 'revised' version of Marxism in a pamphlet entitled *What is to be Done?* (1902). He argued that the **dialectical** phase of Marxism could be speeded up in Russia. He proposed that a Party Central Committee led by professionals could govern in the interest of workers until the latter were ready to take control themselves. This was Lenin's interpretation of the dictatorship of the proletariat (that is, the core of Marxism–Leninism). Lenin's approach caused uproar within the RSDLP and by 1903 a deep split had emerged between Bolsheviks (Marxist–Leninists) and Mensheviks (other Marxists).

After the October Revolution of 1917 (see page 18 for details of the revolution), Lenin began to implement Marxism–Leninism. Opposition to Bolshevik ideology and rule resulted in the Russian Civil War. One school of thought is that Lenin welcomed the war as an opportunity to eradicate the bourgeoisie. Although the Bolshevik **Reds** defeated the **Whites**, this did not safeguard

V.I. Lenin

1870   Born as Vladimir Ilyich Ulyanov in Simbirsk, in the Urals. His father was a member of the lesser nobility and worked as a schools' inspector

1887   The execution of his brother strengthened Lenin's will to change the way Russia was ruled

1891   Graduated from university with a law degree

1895   Liaised with Plekhanov, a prominent revolutionary who had been exiled

1897   Was exiled to Siberia. Adopted the name of Lenin (after the River Lena in Siberia) as an alias

1898   Married Nadya Krupskaya

1900   Joined the Social Democrats (SDs) and went into a self-imposed exile abroad

1902   Published *What is to be Done?* (a collection of ideas about how Russia should be ruled)

1903   Led the Bolsheviks as a breakaway group in the SDs. From 1900 to 1903, he edited the main newspaper of the revolutionary movement (*Iskra* or *The Spark*)

1905   Returned to Russia to witness the 'revolution' but was not actively involved

1906–17 In exile overseas once more

1917   Returned to Russia after the Russian Revolution (February). Went on to lead Bolsheviks in displacement of the Provisional Government

1917–20 Strengthened Bolshevik rule and played an important role in ensuring the defeat of opposition during the Civil War

1921   Replaced War Communism with the New Economic Policy (see Chapters 2 and 3)

1922–3 Immobilised after a number of strokes

1924   Died

Although Lenin was often in exile he was a great influence on the revolutionary movement through his writings and actions. He was instrumental in the Bolshevik seizure of power and the establishment of communist rule in Russia. Some historians believe that Lenin laid a firm foundation for future communist leaders to build on. Thus, Stalin and Khrushchev are seen to continue with Leninist ideas and policies rather than to introduce the own brand of communism. Not all agree with this; they point to the highly repressive nature of Stalin's rule and the **de-Stalinisation** under Khrushchev as evidence that there was significant change in the way Russia was ruled by communists.

Marxism–Leninism. Within the party, debate continued over strategy. Lenin's toleration of the 'moderates' was evident when he replaced War Communism with the New Economic Policy (NEP). War Communism was associated with famine, whereas the NEP was more liberal and gave the people freedom to produce goods and services without restriction (see Chapter 2 for more details on these policies). More radical members of the party criticised these 'bourgeois' concessions, and demanded more central control. Others, such as **Trotsky**, pushed for a move towards a 'Permanent Revolution' which entailed spreading communism throughout the world and not just Russia. Trotsky's views were criticised by Stalin, who preferred a policy of establishing 'socialism in one country'. Stalin argued that the Communist Party could not influence the growth of communism elsewhere until it was firmly established within the Soviet Union.

 KEY TERM

De-Stalinisation The denunciation, by Khrushchev, of Stalin's policies.

 **KEY FIGURE**

Leon Trotsky (1879–1940)

A revolutionary, best known for his leading role in securing Bolshevik success during the Russian Civil War.

I.V. (Joseph) Stalin

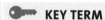

1879	Born as Iosif Vissarionovich Dzhugashvili in Georgia
1899	Expelled from Tbilisi Seminary (college for those training to be priests) for political views
1905	Started to represent local branches of Bolshevik Party (Georgia and South Russia) at conferences
1912	Elected to the Central Committee of the Bolsheviks
1913	Exiled to North Siberia
1917	Returned to Russia and became close ally of Lenin
1917–22	Became specialist in national minorities' issues (appointed Commissar for Nationalities in the first Soviet government). Active as a commander during the Civil War
1922	Appointed as General Secretary of the Communist Party
1923–7	Involved in a dispute with Trotsky, Kamenev and Zinoviev over who was to lead Russia after Lenin's death (see pages 54–5)
1927	Controlled Party Congress and expelled main rivals from the party
1928–33	Introduced the planned economy and the police state
1928	Adopted the first Five-Year Plan (see pages 87–8)
1929	Started collectivisation programme
1933–4	Allowed a 'thaw' in levels of control and repression
1936–8	Instigated the Great Terror and show trials
1939	Appointed Beria (see page 22) as head of the secret police. Also allowed the signing of the Nazi–Soviet Pact (see Chapter 3 for details)
1939–45	Led Russia in a war against Nazi Germany and successfully repelled German invasion
1945–53	Implemented internal reconstruction programme and devised strategies to cope with the initial stages of the **Cold War**
1953	Died (some historians have suggested that he was murdered)

Stalin is usually associated with a level of repression that was unprecedented in Russian history. He is also credited with industrialising Russia and ensuring that the Russian people were able to defeat Nazi Germany. However, there is much debate over the Stalinist era, with a number of historians claiming that Stalin's personal role in key developments has been exaggerated.

KEY TERM

Cold War A state of tension and hostility between the Soviet bloc and Western powers after the Second World War. However, the hostility did not spill over into actual fighting between the two power blocs.

These developments illustrate that Lenin, like the tsars, adjusted his ideology and policies to stave off opposition, but had no intention of veering away from his short-term goal of ruling, with the help of the party, as a dictator. Again, in comparison with the tsars, a policy of appeasement did not fully resolve the issue of opposition within the ruling elite. It took a far more radical approach to do this.

Totalitarianism

There is debate over the extent to which Stalin introduced a centralised form of dictatorial government that controlled every aspect of the behaviour of the citizens of the state (that is, totalitarianism). At the very least he appeared to formularise his own ideology based on Marxism–Leninism.

Marxism–Leninism–Stalinism

The death of Lenin in 1924 resulted in a power struggle within the party over how Russia would be governed. By 1927, Stalin had gained leadership of the Soviet Union through skilful manipulation of individuals and factions. He quickly promoted a refined version of Marxism–Leninism. There were two parts to Marxism–Leninism–Stalinism:

- Stalin argued that the 'base' of society could only be permanently changed by utilising a particular type of 'superstructure'. He went on to implement this through a **command economy** centred on **Five-Year Plans** and **collectivisation** (see pages 87–8 and 92–5 for details of these policies).
- The superstructure had to be highly personalised under the total control of one individual. This would prevent damaging infighting. Disagreement would be labelled **bourgeois**, and dealt with quickly. The use of propaganda (centring on the **cult of personality**) and repression would enforce Stalin's ideology.

Historians have explained this shift from a Lenin-style dictatorship to totalitarianism in a number of different ways:

- Some argue that Stalin's ideology provided a practical solution to the Soviet Union's problems through the implementation of Five-Year Plans and collectivisation.
- Others believe that Stalin manipulated Marxism–Leninism to serve his own **megalomania**, as shown by his repressive policies, and the imposition of the cult of personality (see page 54 for details about the power struggle).
- A recent view argues that Stalin was continuing the work of Lenin, who had already made the most significant and decisive reinterpretation of Marxism by establishing the Party Central Committee and other institutions designed to control the superstructure. Lenin had also used the *Cheka* to deal with opposition and stabilise central control of the economy.

Although Stalin's motives are unclear, it is evident that his version of absolute rule was taken to a new level. The result was wide-scale terror.

De-Stalinisation

After Stalin's death in 1953, a power struggle ensued. This gathered momentum after an emergency meeting of the **Council of Ministers**, the party **Central Committee** and the **Supreme Soviet of the USSR**. A rationalisation of Stalin's **Presidium** was agreed along with a clarification of the roles of leading communists. From this, four rivals emerged:

- *Malenkov.* He became chairman of the Council of Ministers and head of government. These positions were to be held alongside his role as **first secretary of the party**. However, he was demoted from party secretary

KEY TERMS

Command economy An economy that is controlled totally by the state.

Five-Year Plans These involved setting production targets which were to be achieved on a five-year cycle.

Collectivisation A communal system of farming whereby peasants shared resources to produce food, which was then distributed to ensure that local populations were adequately fed. Surpluses were sent to urban populations.

Bourgeois Anything associated with the wealth and status of the middle classes.

Cult of personality The use of propaganda to build a positive image of a leader so that the population offers total obedience to that leader.

Megalomania An individual's belief that they are very powerful and important.

Council of Ministers Senior politicians who drafted domestic policies.

Central Committee The chief decision-making group of the Russian Communist Party.

Supreme Soviet of the USSR The main law-making body in Soviet government.

Presidium A small group of ministers rather like the Cabinet in the British political system.

First secretary of the party The most important administrative officer in the Communist Party.

KEY TERMS

Duopoly Power in the hands of two people.

MVD The secret police that was the successor of the NKGB and the predecessor of the KGB.

Collective leadership Rule by a group whereby responsibilities are equally shared out.

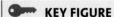

KEY FIGURE

Lavrentiy Beria (1899–1953)

Initially paved a political career through the post of Transcaucasia Party Secretary (1932–8). He replaced Yezhov as head of the secret police (NKVD) (1938–53) and became feared for his lack of scruples and his cold-heartedness.

two weeks after Stalin's death, since he was suspected of colluding with Beria in order to form a **duopoly** of power.

- *Beria.* He was appointed Minister of Internal Affairs (**MVD**), an office which absorbed the previously titled People's Commissariat for State Security (NKGB). Some believed that **Beria** had been involved in the murder of Stalin. He was soon denounced as a traitor, arrested and executed. After he was shot in 1953, the MVD was placed under the control of the party rather than one individual.
- *Khrushchev.* He gained the post of secretary of the Party Central Committee from Malenkov. On paper, this was not the most significant job, but in practice it meant that Khrushchev was in touch with the desires and needs of party members. It therefore gave him a useful power base.
- *Vorishilov.* He was appointed president of the USSR and was to act as a figurehead.

Immediately after Stalin's death there were moves to reorganise the political establishment and discard Stalinist sympathisers. The Presidium was reduced to ten members, and by 1956 a third of the Party Central Committee was new. A similar process happened in the republic and local party committees, where half of the secretaries were replaced.

Collective leadership

Underlying this was the notion that power should be placed in the hands of a collection of individuals – **collective leadership**. Initially, conflict between Malenkov and Khrushchev meant that this was difficult to achieve. Malenkov advocated more consumerism and Westernisation (similar to the demands of liberal reformers under the tsars and to Lenin's NEP). Opponents of this argued that it reflected the desires of the administration and not the people of Russia.

Khrushchev's response

Khrushchev offered the Virgin Land campaign as an alternative (see Chapter 2 for details). He believed that this would solve the most pressing problems and lead to greater internal wealth and stability. By 1955, under pressure from Khrushchev, Malenkov was forced to resign as prime minister, and was demoted to minister for power stations. He was replaced by Bulganin, who was far more sympathetic towards Khrushchev.

The move to de-Stalinisation

After the execution of Beria and demise of Malenkov, Khrushchev was keen to move Russia away from governance based on extreme repression. He believed that this had tarnished the USSR's image overseas, and was unhelpful at a time of increasing international tension. He also thought that many people would welcome an alternative to the repressive nature of Stalinist rule. Khrushchev thus launched a scathing attack on Stalin, which formed the start

Nikita Khrushchev

1894	Born in the Ukraine, the son of a peasant
1899–1917	Employed as an industrial worker in Donbas region. Elected to the local workers' council (soviet) in 1917
1918	Appointed as commissar (official) in the Red Army
1922–9	Very active as party member in the Ukraine
1929	Enrolled as a student at the Moscow Industrial Academy
1935–8	Successful as the first secretary of the Moscow party. Responsible for the planning and building of the Moscow metro system
1938	Moved on to become first secretary of the Ukraine party
1941	During the war, operated as key political commissar with special responsibility for Stalingrad
1944	Gained position as prime minister of the Ukraine
1949	Became first secretary of Moscow party again but also secretary to the Central Committee
1953–6	Started to dominate the party and won struggle for power against Malenkov and Beria. The Virgin Land campaign was started (see Chapter 2 for details)
1956	Launched a verbal attack on Stalinism during the Twentieth Party Congress. This marked the start of what has been called de-Stalinisation. Also, Russian troops were ordered to crush an uprising in Hungary
1957	Moved towards decentralising the control of the Russian economy. Ordered the launching of the first Soviet spacecraft, *Sputnik I*
1961–4	Faced with major Cold War crises (construction of Berlin Wall, Cuban Missile Crisis, nuclear arms race, space race)
1964	Removed from power
1971	Died

Khrushchev was a staunch believer in the communist ideal and was intent on proving that Stalinism was an unfortunate blip on the road to a much better life for all Russian peoples. Thus, he promised a raft of economic and social reforms designed to raise living standards to levels not previously experienced.

Unfortunately, he struggled, against the backdrop of the financially crippling Cold War, to find the money to carry out his plans. He also suffered as a result of what some rivals saw as a liberal attitude and the image he portrayed as a man of the people. In the end, it was relatively easy for his opponents to launch a campaign that secured his dismissal.

of de-Stalinisation. The denunciations began at the Twentieth Party Congress in 1956. Khrushchev made a speech on 'The Cult of the Individual and its Consequences'. The contents of the speech were never published (hence, it was 'secret') but the key points were leaked to Communist Party organisations so that they would be familiar with Khrushchev's position. The following criticisms were made of Stalin:

- He had never been accepted by Lenin as a potential leader.
- He had created a state that was unprepared for military conflict in 1941.
- He had committed a range of unforgivable crimes against the people.
- He had committed misdemeanours against 'outsiders' who should have been embraced by the Soviet leadership. For example, Stalin ordered the assassination of the Hungarian revolutionary leader, Béla Kun.

The impact of the 'Secret Speech'

Although the contents of the 'Secret Speech' were not officially disclosed until 1961, it still caused an outcry among senior party members.

The role of the Anti-Party Group

The 'Anti-Party Group', who opposed Khrushchev, attempted to abolish the post of first secretary of the party, which would have destroyed Khrushchev's power base. The chief protagonists, Molotov, Kagonovich and Malenkov, were quickly dealt with by Khrushchev, who pointed out that only the party Central Committee could change the party organisational structure. The actions of the three opponents were therefore illegal, and they were swiftly removed from the Presidium.

Key features of de-Stalinisation

The key features of de-Stalinisation were:

- The release of political prisoners from labour camps. This started soon after Stalin's death but gathered momentum from the time of the Secret Speech.
- A relaxation of censorship resulting in the publication of articles, novels and plays that criticised Stalin, including works by Ehrenburg, Pasternak, Solzhenitsyn and Yevtushenko.
- The erosion of the legacy of the cult of personality: pictures and statues of Stalin were removed from public places; Stalingrad was renamed Volgograd; and at the Twenty-second Party Congress in 1961, Stalin's body was removed from the Lenin mausoleum and buried in a concrete-filled hole beneath the wall of the Kremlin.

The reaction to de-Stalinisation

KEY TERM

Gulags Labour camps that were used mainly to house political dissidents and those suspected of being anti-communist.

After the initial shock of the Secret Speech, the reaction to de-Stalinisation bore a striking resemblance to that which occurred when Alexander II introduced his reforms. There were strikes (which included newly released prisoners from the ***Gulags***), riots and protests for even greater freedoms (especially from the satellite states such as Yugoslavia, Poland and Hungary, see pages 189 and 209–13). But Khrushchev resisted the temptation to use violence to deal with unrest. Order was maintained through the MVD, which was under the control of the party. However, Khrushchev still dismissed rebellious politicians at will (for example, Zhukov and Bulganin) and used physical force when deemed necessary (for example, tanks were sent into Hungary in 1956 to suppress the Nagy regime). Thus, Khrushchev, like Alexander II, did not intend to move too far from authoritarian rule; the one-party, one-leader state was to remain intact until the fall of the Soviet Union in 1991.

Summary diagram: Ideologies: autocracy, dictatorship and totalitarianism

Similarities	Differences
• Belief in the need for absolute control • Personalised power • The use of repression to maintain control • The use of reform to maintain control • Reluctance to allow openness and proliferation of freedoms	• Justifications for autocratic rule; tsars (God), communists (nature of the proletariat and historical inevitability) • Views on human nature; tsars (weaknesses inherent), communists (determined by social class and therefore environment) • Views on reform; tsars (not welcomed as they led to challenges to government), communists (not welcomed as they maintained the bourgeois system) • Views on representative government; tsars (threat because of dilution of power), communists (threat because parliaments were bourgeois)

---

2 Developments in central administration

▶ *How far did the structure of Russian government remain the same throughout the period from 1855 to 1917?*

Government under the tsars 1855–1917

When Alexander II came to the throne, he was left with a central government structure dating back to the beginning of the nineteenth century. From 1855 to 1905, the format and institutions of central government remained largely the same with only one significant, but temporary, addition made in 1861 (see Figure 1.1, page 26). This system appeared to function effectively, but economic and social change gave rise to the emergence of a number of political groups that clamoured for more representation through a constitutional form of government. More radical elements wanted a complete overthrow of the system and its replacement with a form of rule based on communist principles.

Pressure for change

The pressure for change started to accelerate during the disastrous Russo-Japanese War of 1904–5 (see pages 139–42). The year 1905 is often called one of revolution, since there were assassinations of key political figures, a massacre of a group of workers by state troops (**Bloody Sunday**), strikes, a naval mutiny (*Potemkin*) and other incidents of social unrest.

 **KEY TERMS**

Bloody Sunday
On 9 January 1905, a group of demonstrators marching on the Winter Palace, and led by Father Gapon, were shot at by soldiers. Over 200 people were killed and about 800 injured.

Potemkin A battleship on which a mutiny occurred. The incident was later made famous through the silent film *Battleship Potemkin* (1928).

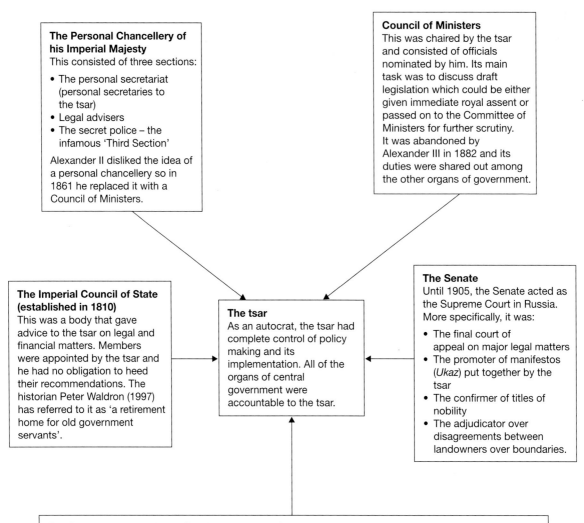

The Personal Chancellery of his Imperial Majesty
This consisted of three sections:

- The personal secretariat (personal secretaries to the tsar)
- Legal advisers
- The secret police – the infamous 'Third Section'

Alexander II disliked the idea of a personal chancellery so in 1861 he replaced it with a Council of Ministers.

Council of Ministers
This was chaired by the tsar and consisted of officials nominated by him. Its main task was to discuss draft legislation which could be either given immediate royal assent or passed on to the Committee of Ministers for further scrutiny. It was abandoned by Alexander III in 1882 and its duties were shared out among the other organs of government.

The Imperial Council of State (established in 1810)
This was a body that gave advice to the tsar on legal and financial matters. Members were appointed by the tsar and he had no obligation to heed their recommendations. The historian Peter Waldron (1997) has referred to it as 'a retirement home for old government servants'.

The tsar
As an autocrat, the tsar had complete control of policy making and its implementation. All of the organs of central government were accountable to the tsar.

The Senate
Until 1905, the Senate acted as the Supreme Court in Russia. More specifically, it was:

- The final court of appeal on major legal matters
- The promoter of manifestos (*Ukaz*) put together by the tsar
- The confirmer of titles of nobility
- The adjudicator over disagreements between landowners over boundaries.

The Committee of Ministers (established in 1861)
There were initially thirteen ministers (ten by the 1890s) who each had a responsibility for a particular aspect of the administration of Russian affairs. Each ministry was connected to departments that had very specific responsibilities, e.g. state horse breeding. Four of the ministerial posts were considered more important than the others:

- Minister of the interior: responsible for domestic affairs, particularly those concerning law and order
- Minister for war
- Minister of finance
- Chief procurator of the Holy Synod: responsible for all religious affairs.

Ministers had a purely administrative role. They did not formulate policies and were always answerable to the tsar. With hindsight, a major weakness of the Committee was that members seldom consulted each other and often pursued policies that conflicted. This was especially problematic when the minister of finance wanted to implement tighter budgetary control while other ministers planned to spend large amounts on reforms. The Committee was abolished in 1900. Its work was shared out between a newly formulated Council of Ministers, the *Duma* and the State Council (see Figure 1.2, page 27).

Figure 1.1 Central government institutions 1855–1905.

The response to the events of 1905

Nicholas II responded by releasing the **October Manifesto**, which confirmed that a more representative form of government would be established, centring on the *Duma*. Along with the Fundamental Laws, this theoretically created a very different kind of political structure.

KEY TERM

October Manifesto
Nicholas II's blueprint for a new form of elective government that revolved around the *Duma*.

The tsar
Despite the introduction of a democratically elected *Duma*, the tsar continued to rule as an autocrat. His position was actually reinforced by the passing of the Fundamental Laws of 1906.

↓

The Council of Ministers
This became the main law-making and administrative body. It was chaired by a prime minister (the first was Witte) who was selected by the tsar. It was like a parliamentary cabinet found in Western liberal democratic systems of government. Its membership consisted of officials similar to those who had served as ministers in the Committee of Ministers. It provided material for the upper and lower houses to debate. In theory, the results of such discussions would then be reported back to the tsar, who would then make a decision as to whether the Council of Ministers should implement a new law or policy. The Fundamental Laws (Article 87) allowed ministers to report directly to the tsar when the two houses were in recess. Thus, in reality, the tsar could bypass the State Council and *Duma* if he believed that they might try to prevent certain measures from being enacted. The two chambers would have found it impossible to undo any legislation once the tsar had given it his stamp of approval.

↓

The State Council (the nominated and elected upper chamber)
The main task of this body, previously the Imperial Council of State, was to act as a check on the activity of the *Dumas*. The latter had to agree with the State Council over the nature of possible reforms before they could be considered for approval by the tsar. Members of the council were either nominated by the tsar as under the old system, or elected as representatives of towns, the Church, guilds, universities, *Zemstva* (local government councils) and the nobility.

↓

The *Duma* (the elected lower chamber)
The *Duma* was to be an assembly of people elected from a variety of social groups who would meet to debate the affairs of state. Although it was not given the authority to pass laws it could block proposed legislation. The election process was made deliberately complex. It involved voting for 'others' who would then choose representatives from political parties to sit in the chamber. This 'electoral college' system was designed in a way that favoured those with property and discriminated against workers and peasants. However, as the first *Duma* proved, there was no guarantee that the result of elections would create a *Duma* that was in total support of the ruling elite. Elections to the *Duma* were to occur every five years, but the tsar had the authority to disband the *Duma*, which he did in 1906, 1907 and 1917.

↓

The Senate
The make-up and role of the Senate were pretty much as they were before the issuing of the Fundamental Laws.

Figure 1.2 The new government's structure after 1905.

 **KEY TERMS**

Polish question The question as to whether the Poles would be allowed self-rule.

Kadets The Constitutional Democrats, a liberal political group founded in 1905.

Labourists Those who were specifically interested in improving the working conditions of the proletariat.

Vyborg Manifesto A set of demands from militant *Duma* MPs asking the people of Finland not to pay taxes or serve in the armed forces until the *Duma* was restored.

Octobrists Supporters of the tsar and, in particular, his proposals made in the October Manifesto.

Justices of the peace Landowners appointed as officials to maintain law and order at a local level. They worked in conjunction with the police.

Land captains Landowners who were appointed, from 1889 onwards, mainly to supervise the work of the regional councils, or *Zemstva*, that had been introduced by Alexander II.

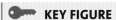 **KEY FIGURE**

Pyotr Stolypin (1862–1911)

In 1906, he was moved from the post of minister of the interior to prime minister (1906–11). Stolypin proved to be an authoritarian administrator although he was quick to respond to the changing political climate in Russia. He is best known for introducing the Peasants' Land Bank and land reforms (including the attempted break-up of the *mir*).

Dumas from 1906 to 1917

Between 1906 and 1917, four *Dumas* were elected, whose composition, duration and impact varied considerably. The progress of each is outlined below.

The first *Duma*, April to July 1906

Members of the first assembly participated in rigorous debate over matters of the empire, such as the **Polish question**. However, the most important discussions concerned land distribution. The government made a statement that compulsory redistribution was not an option. This angered the first *Duma*, whose more radical solution quickly gained press coverage. In response, Nicholas II claimed that the actions of the lower chamber were illegal, and disbanded it after two months.

Between the sitting of the first and second *Dumas*, a new approach to dealing with dissidents was adopted, sparked by the arrest, trial and imprisonment of key **Kadet** and **Labourist** Party members who had signed the **Vyborg Manifesto**. The new chairman of the Council of Ministers, **Stolypin**, thought that the process of dealing with dissenters was too cumbersome and 'soft'. He therefore ordered the trial system for civilian rioters to be accelerated by introducing field court-martials. The result was a series of quick trials and executions which gained the label of 'Stolypin's neckties'.

The second *Duma*, February to June 1907

The composition of the second *Duma* was greatly affected by Stolypin's policies. There were fewer Kadets and Labourists, but more Social Democrats (SDs), Socialist Revolutionaries (SRs), **Octobrists** and the far right. However, the tsar and Stolypin continued to mistrust the work of the *Duma* over land reform and the management of the Russian army. When a Social Democrat member of the *Duma* was framed for attempting to arrange an army mutiny, the tsar proclaimed that the *Duma* was subversive, dissolved it, and overhauled the electoral system.

The third *Duma*, November 1907 to June 1912

As a result of the electoral reforms, the third *Duma* mainly consisted of people loyal to the crown, such as wealthy property owners from the countryside and cities. There was also a significant reduction in nationalist members from non-Russian parts of the empire. However, as historian J.N. Westwood (2002) has pointed out, 'an unrepresentative *Duma* was not necessarily an ineffective *Duma*'. During the period, major reforms strengthened the army and navy. The judicial system was further improved with the reinstatement of **justices of the peace** and the abolition of **land captains**. For the first time, state-run insurance schemes for workers were introduced. All of this occurred because Nicholas II and his ministers showed more trust in the lower chamber. Even though

Stolypin did his best to destabilise the *Duma* by manipulating **Article 87** to create an even greater bias towards autocracy, the lower chamber served its full term of office.

The fourth *Duma*, November 1912 to February 1917

The final *Duma* was again dominated by politicians from the far right. Its rule coincided with brutal repression of civil disorder, such as when state police killed striking miners at the Lena Goldfields (1912). This outraged many *Duma* members. In 1914, the *Duma* made the following proclamation:

> *The Ministry of the Interior systematically scorns public opinion and ignores the repeated wishes of the new legislature. The Duma considered it pointless to express any new wishes in regard to internal policy. The Ministry's activities arouse dissatisfaction among the broad masses that have hitherto been peaceful. Such a situation threatens Russia with untold dangers.*

The final *Duma* became infamous for putting pressure on the tsar to abdicate; members subsequently formed the backbone of the short-lived Provisional Government. However, despite its critique of the tsarist government, the *Duma* remained an institution dominated by the 'old guard'.

Overall, it is clear that the *Duma* played an important role in instigating political, economic and social changes beneficial to many sectors of Russian society. Nevertheless, as historian Peter Waldron (1997) argues, collectively, the *Dumas* and the Council of Ministers 'made very little difference to the underlying nature of the Russian state'. *Duma* politicians on the left were largely ignored by the government, and the majority in the lower chamber remained loyal to the principle of autocracy.

The emergence of the Progressive Bloc

The progress of the fourth *Duma* was interrupted by the outbreak of the First World War in 1914. The *Duma* met a week after the start of the war, but its work was disrupted when a group of socialist members walked out at Nicholas II's decision to commit Russia to a war they considered unwinnable. By 1915, a **'Progressive Bloc'** of *Duma* representatives demanded a National Government to take charge of the war effort. Nicholas responded by suspending the *Duma* in August 1915, and personally taking charge of the armed forces.

The changing economic and social context

The *Duma* reopened in November 1916 but with the Progressive Bloc still prominent. By this time, economic and social conditions in Russia had deteriorated. **Real wages** had plummeted, food prices had rocketed upwards and fuel supplies had diminished. There was also concern over the role of the tsarina in the governance of the empire, partly because of her Germanic background, and partly because of her 'friendship' with the holy mystic

KEY TERMS

Article 87 A section of the 1906 Fundamental Laws that allowed for proposed legislation to be submitted directly to the tsar for his approval.

Progressive Bloc A group within the fourth *Duma* consisting of members of the Kadets, Octobrists, Nationalists and Party of Progressives, who challenged the authority of Nicholas II.

Real wages Wages after the impact of inflation is taken into account. That is, the amount of money available that allows the purchase of goods and services.

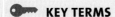

Grigori Rasputin (1869–1916)

A religious mystic who gave counsel to Nicholas II and his family. He was introduced to the tsar and tsarina (Alexandra) in 1905 to treat their son Aleksei (who suffered from haemophilia). When Nicholas took command of the military in 1915, Rasputin seemed to extend his influence over the tsarina.

KEY TERMS

Petrograd St Petersburg was renamed Petrograd in August 1914. The tsar ordered the renaming as he thought St Petersburg (Sankt-Peterburg) sounded German. And, of course, war had just broken out between Russia and Germany.

April Theses Lenin's outline of policies to be followed by the Bolsheviks after his return from exile in April 1917.

Rasputin. These developments would result in the abdication of the tsar and the end of Romanov rule. The key events in 1917 were as follows:

- 9 January: about 150,000 workers took to the streets of St Petersburg to celebrate the anniversary of Bloody Sunday.
- 18 February: a strike occurred at the Putilov Steel Works.
- 19 February: bread rationing was introduced.
- 23 February: marchers celebrating International Women's Day and workers from the Putilov plant combined to protest about poor working and living conditions.
- 25 February: a general strike took place with workers being fired on by troops. Rodzianko, president of the *Duma*, urged the tsar to 'change' his attitude towards governing.
- 26 February: the *Duma* defied the tsar's instruction to disband. A major turning point was the decision by troops (about half of the **Petrograd** Garrison) to join the protesters.
- 27 February: the Petrograd soviet was formed alongside the provisional *Duma* committee. This was the foundation of governance through a dual authority and a clear indication that the tsar was considered unfit to rule by a majority of senior politicians.
- 1 March: Soviet Order No. 1 was passed, which gave the Petrograd soviet total control over the Russian military.
- 2 March: under pressure from close advisers and family members, Nicholas II decided to abdicate. An official Provisional Government was formed to deal with the crisis until elections to a Constituent Assembly could be held (see the Depth Study on pages 65–8 for discussion of the Provisional Government).

This sudden turn of events had not been expected. In theory, the abdication of Nicholas and the formation of the Provisional Government marked the end of autocracy in Russia. In practice, the move towards greater democracy was short lived and the governance of Russia was soon dominated by a single individual: Lenin.

From March to September 1917, the Provisional Government struggled to deal with its opponents, especially the Bolsheviks. There were a number of reasons for this:

- The majority of members of other parties wanted a short-term government based on consensus, with the main aim of creating a Constituent Assembly. The leading Bolsheviks rejected this since it would favour 'old interests' to the detriment of workers and peasants.
- Changes made by the Provisional Government facilitated the revival of political groups such as the Bolsheviks whose leaders had been in exile. Stalin moved back to Petrograd from exile in Siberia in March 1917, and Lenin from Switzerland in April. Lenin moved quickly to publish his **April Theses**, in which he condemned the Provisional Government for being bourgeois, and called for a seizure of power by the soviet.

- Bolshevik leaders used propaganda to appeal for support from both workers and peasants.
- The Provisional Government struggled to deal with the Bolsheviks directly. Although leading Bolsheviks were exiled or imprisoned after the disturbances of the **July Days**, Kerensky strengthened their position by involving them in the resolution of the **Kornilov** affair (see page 68).

By the end of 1917, the Bolsheviks were responsible for the governance of Russia. The main events leading to the final Bolshevik takeover in 1917 were as follows:

- 8 September: the Bolsheviks were in control of the Petrograd soviet. By the middle of September they also controlled the Moscow soviet.
- 7 October: Lenin returned from exile.
- 10 October: the Bolsheviks began planning for a revolution.
- 23 October: Kerensky closed *Pravda* and *Izvestiya* (Bolshevik newspapers); a round-up of leading Bolsheviks was attempted.
- 24 October: the Petrograd soviet's Military Revolutionary Committee began to seize power under the command of Trotsky.
- 26 October: the members of the Provisional Government were arrested, except for Kerensky, who fled (later to settle in the USA).
- 27 October: the **All-Russian Congress of Soviets** (in sitting since 25 October) was informed by Lenin that the Bolsheviks had seized power.
- 2 November: the Bolsheviks had total control of Moscow.

Lenin and the Bolshevik government

The Bolsheviks introduced a new constitution in July 1918. Before then, there were a number of issues that they had to deal with to allow them to consolidate their position.

The Second All-Russian Congress of Soviets

The Second All-Russian Congress of Soviets met on 25 October. Right-wing SRs and Mensheviks, who favoured a coalition government, walked out of the congress in protest. This left the Bolsheviks with little opposition and a clear mandate to rule.

The 'Petrograd revolution'

The October Revolution was a Petrograd revolution. The Bolsheviks, therefore, had to spread their authority. They attempted to do this by creating more soviets in towns and cities across Russia. This proved difficult due to opposition from the 'old guard'; resistance throughout the empire was a major reason for the outbreak of a civil war that was to last until 1921.

The Constituent Assembly

In order to avoid opposition, the Bolsheviks allowed elections to a Constituent Assembly in November. Unsurprisingly, the Bolsheviks failed to win a majority,

KEY TERMS

July Days From 3 to 6 July 1917, there were widespread demonstrations in Petrograd against the Provisional Government. The rebellion proved to be disorganised and was easily put down by troops still loyal to the government. The rising showed the weaknesses of opposition to the government at this point, particularly the Bolsheviks.

All-Russian Congress of Soviets A meeting of delegates from soviets throughout Russia to decide on the policies to be adopted by the soviets.

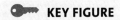

KEY FIGURE

Lavr Kornilov (1870–1918)
Appointed as the new commander-in-chief of the armed forces in July 1917. After the attempted coup he was arrested and imprisoned but as soon as he was released he formed the anti-Bolshevik Volunteer Army. He died fighting in the early stages of the Civil War.

coming second to the SRs. Lenin claimed that the Constituent Assembly was 'elected on the old register' and 'appeared as an expression of the old regime when the authority belonged to the bourgeoisie'. Lenin used this to justify shutting the assembly down after one day; there was no popular demonstration against this move. In January 1918, the Third All-Russian Congress of Soviets sanctioned the closure of the Constituent Assembly, and also proclaimed the establishment of the **Russian Soviet Federative Socialist Republic (RSFSR)**. The RSFSR was essentially the Great Russia of the old empire but was now to be ruled without a monarch (hence the use of the term republic).

The Decree on Land

Shortly after taking control from the Provisional Government, the Bolsheviks issued the Decree on Land. It sanctioned the requisition of private land by peasants, but stated that the division and redistribution could only be carried out by village soviets. It was very similar to what rival SRs had proposed for years, and therefore went some way to winning over the support of the Bolsheviks' opponents.

The issue of the war

The Bolsheviks issued a Decree on Peace, which called for an immediate truce and a peaceful settlement. This laid the foundation for an **armistice** that was signed on 2 December 1917. Although Germany insisted on harsh terms for a final settlement, Lenin still argued strongly in favour of a treaty. On 3 March 1918, the Soviet representative, Sokolnikov, signed the Treaty of Brest-Litovsk which ceded a huge portion of territory, amounting to about a third of European Russia, to Germany, including the Ukraine, Russia's most important grain-producing region. Russia also agreed to pay **reparations** of 3 billion roubles. Trotsky called the treaty a *diktat*.

The end of the war

By August 1918, Germany's campaign on the Western Front had collapsed and the German army soon withdrew from Russia completely. The Brest-Litovsk agreement became meaningless and Lenin now had the chance to rid the party of those who opposed him.

The organisation of the Bolshevik government

The organisation of the Bolshevik government took shape quickly after the Second All-Russian Congress of Soviets had disbanded. If the new regime had been a soviet government in the truest sense, it would have constituted a major break with the tsarist past, since genuine soviet rule would have revolved around the freedoms and liberties gained as a result of the revolts of February 1917. In reality, it introduced policies similar to those of the tsarist era, often in a very repressive form.

KEY TERMS

Russian Soviet Federative Socialist Republic (RSFSR) This resulted from the 1918 constitution. It constituted Russia and parts of Central Asia, most notably Kazakhstan, Uzbekistan and Turkmenia.

Armistice An agreement to stop fighting.

Reparations Payments that constitute compensation for the damage done during a war.

Diktat An order given by those in power; something that is non-negotiable.

The box below shows the new Bolshevik structure of government.

> ## The new Bolshevik structure of government
>
> ### The All-Russian Congress of Soviets and the Central Executive Committee
>
> The Congress and its organising committee (Executive Committee) were meant to be the mainstay of the new government. In theory, the commissars (see below) were answerable to the Executive Committee although the reality was different. When, in the summer of 1918, Mensheviks and SRs were expelled from the Executive Committee, it became dominated by Bolsheviks. Many of these were also 'people's commissars' and Russia was not far off being ruled as a 'one-party state'.
>
> ### The Council of People's Commissars (*Sovnarkom*)
>
> This consisted of 'people's commissars' (ministers) who had specific governmental responsibilities. Trotsky, for example, was placed in charge of foreign affairs and Stalin had to deal with nationalities. The chairman (prime minister) was Lenin. To begin with, the Council also consisted of left-wing SRs.
>
> ### The *Cheka*
>
> In December 1917, the All-Russian Extraordinary Commission for Combating Counter-Revolution and Sabotage was introduced (abbreviated to *Cheka*). It was headed by Dzerzhinski, a Polish communist. The main aim of the *Cheka* was to prevent the emergence and growth of counter-revolutionary movements. It therefore acted as a tool, rather than an organ, of government. It was disbanded in 1922 and replaced by the Main Political Administration (GPU/OGPU).

This new 'system' appeared to be democratic in so far as members of *Sovnarkom* were the product of a chain of elections:

- Village soviets chose representatives for district soviets.
- District soviets then elected members for the provincial soviets.
- Provincial soviets provided the membership of *Sovnarkom*.

However, the soviets were dominated by the Bolshevik Party, whose organisation resembled that of the new government:

- At local level, the party consisted of cells whose members would organise meetings (political workshops) to encourage grass-roots support.
- Cell members were elected to town or district committees.
- Committees then provided representatives to the annual party congress.
- The congress chose members to form the party Central Executive Committee (consisting of about a tenth of congress members).

The Central Executive Committee was responsible for the administration and operation of three political offices:

- The Politburo: a small, elite group of Bolsheviks responsible for formulating policy. The Politburo dominated the Central Committee and the running of the party.

- The Orgburo: this office organised party affairs.
- The Ogburo: this body was responsible for maintaining order and dealing with opposition.

The Bolsheviks promoted the party as one that was working to create an egalitarian society based on **democratic centralism**. Central control of Russian affairs would be in the hands of politicians elected by the Russian people (that is, the people of the RSFSR).

However, all the key government posts were held by senior Bolsheviks, and the administration was swamped with the '**leading cadres**' of the Bolshevik Party. During the Civil War years, any opposition towards a one-party state was eradicated, often with the help of the *Cheka*. Anyone wanting to get involved in politics had to either get permission to join the Bolshevik Party or become part of an opposition movement in exile.

As the party essentially became the government, membership to the former was increasingly seen as a privilege and a way to become more socially mobile. Thus, membership numbers grew significantly during the immediate post-Civil War period. In 1921, there were around 730,000 members, but by 1928 this had increased to about a million. Many found new careers and opportunities as part of the **Nomenklatura**, but the role of members depended mainly on their socio-economic background. By the time of Stalin's accession to power, the party had become very hierarchical:

- By the early 1930s, nearly ten per cent of the party was made up of *apparatchiki* (full-time, paid party organisers). These were educated members of society who served mainly as party secretaries.
- About 30 per cent of the party were employed as 'other' administrators. These too were educated people who, under the tsarist regime, had largely been part of the growing middle class.
- The rest of the party consisted of workers and/or peasants who, in their spare time, operated as party activists.

As the party and government became more centralised and nepotistic, the political regime became less democratic. Officials became more detached from grass-roots affairs, and workers showed less interest in politics. This was reinforced by the changing nature of the proletariat. More industrial workers were recruited from the ranks of the peasantry who were notorious for being apathetic towards party affairs. Recruitment campaigns such as the **Lenin Enrolment** attempted to address the issue, but they had minimal effect on the composition of the party.

Stalin and the USSR

Stalin wished to continue with democratic centralism since this was essential to the implementation of his economic policies and to dealing with internal enemies. Additionally, Stalin introduced a new constitution in 1936, which

KEY TERMS

Democratic centralism Under the Bolsheviks, the people would agree to being led by a cadre (group of key personnel) based in Moscow, until a genuine workers' government could be put in place.

Leading cadres The 'top' members of the Communist Party responsible for organising and educating the masses.

Nomenklatura 'Approved' officers, administrators and managers in the communist regime who possessed specialist skills.

Lenin Enrolment A campaign that aimed to encourage peasants to join the Bolshevik Party.

built on the earlier constitutions of 1918 and 1924, but also suggested that there would be more freedom for the peoples of the USSR (see Chapter 4 for details). Note that the constitution of 1918 created the RSFSR and that of 1924 the **USSR** (Union of Soviet Socialist Republics).

KEY TERM

USSR This resulted from the 1924 constitution. By this time, via a treaty of 1922, the Republics of the Ukraine, Belorussia and Transcaucasia (Azerbaijan, Armenia and Georgia) had joined with the RSFSR. Each republic was allowed its own government and other symbols of sovereignty such as national flags. However, such governments were still answerable to *Sovnarkom*.

Supreme Soviet of the USSR
This elected the Council of People's Commissars (*Sovnarkom*), was headed by a presidium and was given the sole power to make laws for the whole of the union. It was divided into two houses, partly to give the impression that a genuine federal form of government had been created.

Soviet of the Union
- Members were to be elected by electoral districts – one member per 30,000 people
- Elections were to take place every four years
- The Soviet of the Union therefore contained representatives of the peoples of the whole of the USSR.

Soviet of Nationalities
Membership consisted of:

- 25 members per union republic
- eleven members per autonomous republic
- five members per autonomous region
- one member per national area.

These regional categories simply reflected the different importance given to particular national groups.

Figure 1.3 The structure of the USSR post-1936.

The Supreme Soviet met twice every year. Delegates were given the opportunity to find out about government policies, debate their implications and give them a stamp of approval. Additionally, republics were given the right to administer their own education systems, and the power to break away from the Soviet Union.

The role of the Communist Party of the Soviet Union (CPSU)

Even so, the Communist Party still dominated the union and republican governments; dissent from the party line was never tolerated, and the new constitution was similar to that which had been in existence since 1918. This was made clear in Article 126 of the Stalin Constitution, which stated that the party was the 'nucleus of all the public and state organisations of the working people'.

Further additions to the USSR

Estonia, Latvia, Lithuania and Moldova were joined to the USSR from 1939 to 1940. However, the next important change to the constitution of the USSR was in 1977. This introduced elements of liberalism; for example, the previous aim of creating an integrated Soviet nation was omitted, suggesting that demands by individual republics to secede would be carefully listened to. Thus, even with de-Stalinisation, the organisation and structure of central government remained virtually the same during the period up to 1964.

Summary diagram: Developments in central administration

The tsars
- Autocratic – officials and organs of government were answerable to the tsars
- Hierarchical
- Many organs – the Council of Ministers, the Imperial Council of State, the Committee of Ministers, the Senate
- Reform – a nod to democracy with the introduction of the *Duma*
- Local government – the *mir*, the *Zemstva*, the *Duma*
- Judiciary – liberalisation but with 'checks', for example land captains

CHANGE

The Provisional Government
- Democratic rather than autocratic replaced tsarism but unelected (the 'old guard')
- Hierarchical but shared power with the Petrograd soviet – the Dual Authority
- Two organs (Provisional Government and the Petrograd soviet)
- Reform – early changes provided greater freedoms to the people
- Judiciary – liberalisation; political prisoners freed (although exiled or reimprisoned later). Key cause of downfall (overthrown by Bolsheviks)

CHANGE or CONTINUITY?

The communists
- Autocratic and dictatorial – all officials and organs of government were answerable to the 'leader' (Lenin, Stalin, Khrushchev)
- Hierarchical
- Many organs – All-Russian Congress of Soviets, the Central Executive Committee (Politburo, Orgburo, Ogburo), the Council of People's Commissars (*Sovnarkom*)
- Reform – a nod to democracy with the introduction of the Supreme Soviet (Soviet of the Union, Soviet of Nationalities)
- Local government – soviets abandoned; localities governed by party cells and hierarchy of local party officials
- Judiciary – dominated by 'revolutionary justice'

3 Changes in local government

▶ *How important were changes to local government in altering the nature and scope of autocratic rule in the period from 1855 to 1964?*

Before 1861, provinces were largely under the jurisdiction of noble landowners, and village issues were discussed by the *mir*. The local nobility acted as a bridge between central government and the outreaches of the empire. This changed with the **emancipation of the serfs**. The nobility ceased to play a political role, and the management of local affairs was left in the hands of local police constables appointed by the interior ministry. In 1864, Alexander II also introduced the *Zemstvo* (*Zemstva* in plural) or regional council. This was characterised by the following:

- An elected membership was voted in by a mixture of landowners, urban dwellers and peasants. Electors were selected mainly by property qualification.
- *Zemstva* were located only in areas considered to be part of Great Russia.

In 1870, an urban equivalent was introduced called the *Duma*. The entry qualification to this body was even tougher than for the *Zemstva*, and thus excluded the urban proletariat.

The Third Element

Before October 1917, the *Zemstva* and *Duma* flourished, providing important services in the fields of education, public health and transport. However, central government increasingly found *Zemstva* members irritating. By the end of the nineteenth century, the councils in some provinces were dominated by teachers, lawyers and doctors who demanded that central government should be remodelled on the lines of the *Zemstva* and *Duma*. This liberal voice was named the 'Third Element'. The other elements were those employed in the 'administration' (government) and those who 'represented the social estates' (nobility).

Both the *Zemstva* and *Duma* (being labelled bourgeois and counter-revolutionary) were abolished after 1917. Local government was then dominated by soviets. This situation remained until the end of the period.

Soviets

The first workers' council or soviet emerged in St Petersburg at the time of the October Manifesto. Its aim was to coordinate strikes and protect factory workers. Fairly quickly, SRs and SDs looked to gain representation on the executive

KEY TERMS

Mir A group of elders who were responsible for governing the behaviour of members of rural communities or villages.

Emancipation of the serfs An announcement in 1861 that peasants would be freed from being owned, like any other property, by wealthy landowners and the state.

committee, and influence how the council was run. In 1917, the council was officially referred to as the Petrograd Soviet of Workers' Deputies, and the Bolsheviks began to dominate the executive committee.

The power of the soviets

From March to October 1917, some historians have claimed that the Petrograd soviet controlled Russia. It dictated when, where and how strikes would occur. Essential services, especially those connected with transport, were largely in the hands of the soviet. Petrograd Soviet Order No. 1 placed ultimate authority over soldiers in the hands of the soviet.

Judicial changes

The judiciary was an important organ of government. However, despite some reforms, the Russian legal system remained archaic compared with that of the West. The main changes were as follows:

- 1864 legal reforms: the introduction of a jury system for criminal cases; the creation of a hierarchy of courts to cater for different types of case; better pay for judges (lessening the chances of corruption); public attendance at courts was allowed.
- 1877: following an assassination attempt on Alexander II's life, a new department of the Senate was set up to try political cases. The **Vera Zasulich case** and the eventual murder of the tsar in 1881 indicated that the new policies of the Senate had failed.
- 1881: Alexander III moved away from the 'liberal' approach to law and order that had been adopted by his father. The police were centralised under the minister for the interior, special courts were designed for political cases, and justices of the peace were replaced by land captains.
- 1917 onwards: the period of communist rule was dominated by the idea of 'revolutionary justice'. This was epitomised by the new criminal code of 1921 that legalised the use of terror to deter crime (that is, all anti-revolutionary behaviour). The whole judicial system rested on this principle to the end of the period in question.

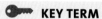 **KEY TERM**

Vera Zasulich case
Zasulich was a revolutionary who shot and wounded the governor of St Petersburg, General Trepov, in 1878. Trepov was a tyrant known for flogging political prisoners. Zasulich was put on trial but the jury found her not guilty as her actions were considered just. Some argued that this verdict showed that the 1864 legal reforms allowed revolutionary activity to flourish.

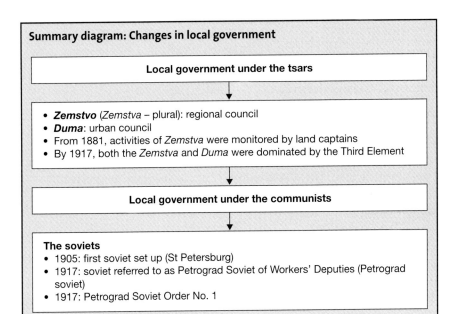

Summary diagram: Changes in local government

Local government under the tsars

- **Zemstvo** (*Zemstva* – plural): regional council
- **Duma**: urban council
- From 1881, activities of *Zemstva* were monitored by land captains
- By 1917, both the *Zemstva* and *Duma* were dominated by the Third Element

Local government under the communists

The soviets
- 1905: first soviet set up (St Petersburg)
- 1917: soviet referred to as Petrograd Soviet of Workers' Deputies (Petrograd soviet)
- 1917: Petrograd Soviet Order No. 1

 # Methods of repression and enforcement

▶ *What were the most effective methods used by the tsars and communists to control opposition?*

Repression means to control, restrain, prevent or inhibit the thoughts and actions of others. The use of repression by tsars and Bolsheviks presupposed that the thoughts and actions of others were so threatening that they needed challenging. 'Epidemics' of extreme repression are referred to as 'terror' and were especially evident during communist rule. The main tools of repression used by all rulers were:

- The secret police: to investigate, arrest, imprison, execute and exile 'opposition'.
- The army: to deal with riots and unruly mob behaviour (including strikes).
- Propaganda: to manipulate the ideals, values, beliefs and attitudes of the people.
- Censorship: to control access to information that might affect the ideals, values, beliefs and attitudes of the people.

These tools often coexisted, although there were times when one was more predominant than others. Sometimes repression was used to enforce policies, while at other times it existed to counter liberal reforms.

The secret police

The secret police worked beyond the 'law' and complemented the regular police force. Russian leaders had a long tradition of using groups to inflict violence on others to control their behaviour.

The Third Section of the Imperial Chancellery

This was a form of secret police inherited by Alexander II. In line with his reformist inclinations, Alexander II replaced the Third Section with the 'softer' Department of State Police (*Okhrana*) in 1880. However, the powers of this body were enhanced in the 1880s to counter the growth of political pressure groups and parties.

The *Okhrana*

The *Okhrana* lasted until February 1917, when it was disbanded by the Provisional Government as part of a more relaxed policy towards political dissidents. Until then, its role fluctuated according to circumstance. Alexander III utilised the *Okhrana* as a tool for spying on, arresting, imprisoning and/or exiling opposition. The relative stability of the 1890s led to the *Okhrana* taking a lower profile. *Okhrana* activity increased as the SRs and SDs took off, reaching a peak in 1905. Members of the *Okhrana* were used as **agents provocateurs** (as in the case of **Father Gapon**) and executioners.

From February until October 1917, the Provisional Government focused more on wartime security, and established the Counter Espionage Bureau of the Petrograd Military District. This was designed to weed out those who were undermining the war effort, including the Bolsheviks.

The *Cheka*

The *Cheka* (the All-Russian Extraordinary Commission for Combating Counter-Revolution and Sabotage) was established by the Bolsheviks in December 1917, and headed by a Polish communist, **Dzerzhinsky**. Their specific role involved dealing with counter-revolutionaries. By the summer of 1917, they had begun to clamp down on left-wing SRs, especially after members of this group were linked with an attempt to assassinate Lenin in August 1918.

The *Cheka* differed from previous variants of the secret police since they used terror to victimise people based on *who* they were, and not just because of their actions. Thus, Dzerzhinsky instructed *Cheka* members that:

> *Your first duty is to ask him to which class he belongs, what are his origins, his education, and his occupation. These questions should decide the fate of the prisoner.*

KEY TERMS

Okhrana The tsarist secret police (that replaced the Third Section) whose main job was to search for those who were determined to undermine the work of the government.

Agents provocateurs Those who tempt others to commit a criminal act so that they can then be charged.

KEY FIGURES

Father Gapon (1870–1906)

An Orthodox priest who led a Church-based union and later helped to organise a similar union for industrial workers. He led a march of St Petersburg workers on the Winter Palace in January 1905 to demand improved living and working conditions. The peaceful march was fired on by troops, and hundreds were injured or killed.

Felix Dzerzhinsky (1877–1926)

A Polish communist who came out of exile as a result of the February Revolution. He was appointed as head of the *Cheka* (1917–26) because of his ruthlessness, reliability and dedication to the cause.

Under the guidance of Trotsky and Dzerzhinsky, the *Cheka* formally implemented the **Red Terror**. Part of this involved enforcing War Communism (especially grain requisitioning), the '**Labour Code**', the elimination of *kulaks*, the administration of **labour camps** and the **militarisation of labour**.

After the Civil War, the *Cheka* was disbanded and replaced by the State Police Administration (GPU) in 1922. The latter was expanded in 1924 and renamed the United State Police Administration (OGPU). Although OGPU was not as brutal as the *Cheka*, it still inspired fear in the general populace.

The NKVD

To combat opposition to Stalin's personal dictatorship, the NKVD (the People's Commissariat for Internal Affairs) was formed in 1934. Headed by **Yagoda** (later **Yezhov**), the NKVD created a permanent form of terror. It was crucial to the imposition of purges, and was notable for gathering evidence against high-rank communists such as Bukharin, Kamenev, Zinoviev and Trotsky. The NKVD also helped to administer the *Gulags*; over 40 million people were sent to these prison camps during the Stalinist regime.

However, Stalin suspected the NKVD of conspiracy. In 1938, Yezhov was blamed for an anti-purge campaign. He was replaced by Beria, who proceeded to arrange the execution of Yezhov and his close allies. By the start of the Second World War, the NKVD itself had been purged of around 20,000 members.

The coming of the Ministry for State Security (MGB) and Ministry of Internal Affairs (MVD)

In 1943, the NKVD was replaced by the People's Commissariat for State Security (NKGB). This was subsequently replaced in 1946 by two bodies, the Ministry for State Security (MGB) and the Ministry of Internal Affairs (MVD). The MGB was responsible for ensuring that the general population was kept in line. The MVD was really another version of the NKVD. In 1953, these organisations were merged to form a large version of the MVD. Control of this body remained in the hands of Beria. However, soon after gaining control of the Party Central Committee, Khrushchev ordered Beria's arrest and trial. In December, he was executed.

The reorganisation of the MVD

Part of the de-Stalinisation process involved reshaping the security services. In March 1954, the MVD was reorganised into two departments. One was a refined version of the MVD, which retained the same title and was responsible for dealing with 'ordinary' criminal acts and civil disorder. The other was called the Committee for State Security (KGB), which was to focus on the internal and external security of the USSR, a task particularly important due to the Cold War.

The MVD and the KGB were placed under the direct administration of the party rather than an individual, and it became much easier to monitor security

measures. The new structure, coupled with the genuine desire to move away from the severe repression of the Stalinist era, had a noticeable impact on Russian society: the number of political arrests plummeted; the use of *Gulags* largely disappeared; and torture of dissidents appeared to be a thing of the past. By 1960, it is estimated that there were only about 11,000 counter-revolutionaries in captivity, a far cry from the 1930s and 1940s.

The army

At the start of the period, the army numbered around 1,400,000 men, most of whom were peasant conscripts. The officers were drawn from the nobility. At any point in time, the army could be used to deal with internal law and order issues, as well as to engage in wars.

The Crimean War (1853–6) revealed a number of deficiencies in military provision. The dismal military performance, coupled with the Emancipation Edict in 1861, led to important military reforms (see pages 134–5).

Russification under Alexander III led to the army having an enhanced role as a peace-keeping force and regulator of regional frontiers. Sometimes the army's use of excessive force – such as on Bloody Sunday, 1905 – caused significant outrage.

The army, strikes and the formation of the MRC

From 1905 to 1917, the army was used to dismantle strikes, protests and riots. In particular, the social unrest of February 1917 was dealt with forcefully by the army. However, troops had already displayed a propensity to desert and join protesters. It is estimated that about 150,000 members of the Petrograd Garrison supported revolution at that time. Lenin and Trotsky subsequently encouraged soldiers, especially from Petrograd, to form the Military Revolutionary Committee (MRC), which was to become the **vanguard** of the revolution.

During the October Revolution, the MRC and the **Red Guard** seized power from Kerensky. They quickly commandeered transport, public buildings, utilities and the **Winter Palace**. This appeared to involve minimal strategic planning; Trotsky observed that if a few hundred soldiers had remained loyal to the Provisional Government, the revolution could have been averted.

Once the Bolsheviks took control, they deployed the military to consolidate power. Troops were used to deal with flash strikes by civil servants and financial workers. The issue of how to end Russia's involvement in the First World War was tackled by replacing General Dukhonin with General Krylenko.

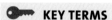

KEY TERMS

Russification A policy aimed at transforming the different peoples of the Russian Empire into 'pure' Rus (the supposedly original inhabitants of Russia).

Vanguard In this context, a leading group of people whose mission was to lay the base for a proletarian takeover of the governance of Russia.

Red Guard A general term to denote armed supporters of the Bolsheviks, especially in the second half of 1917.

Winter Palace Official residence of the tsars in St Petersburg.

The importance of the Red Army

Under the guidance of Trotsky, the Red Army was instrumental in enabling the Bolsheviks to win the Civil War. At the start of the war, the Red Army hardly existed, but by the end it consisted of over 5 million conscripts. In comparison, the White opposition could only muster about 500,000 troops. The army was also used to impose, along with the *Cheka*, War Communism (see pages 84–5). Despite creating a more disciplined army, Trotsky faced problems of desertion and rebellion. The most notable example was in February 1921 when sailors mutinied at **Kronstadt**. Trotsky ordered 50,000 troops to recapture the island; this was achieved with 10,000 Red Army casualties. The rebels who were captured were executed or exiled to the Arctic.

Stalin's use of the army

The use of the military to help implement economic policy was furthered by Stalin. The Red Army was again required to requisition grain, this time as part of collectivisation. It also helped to administer the purges, and played a role in the **Great Terror**. Ironically, the military leadership was consistently perceived as a threat by Stalin. He therefore removed a number of key military figures in the **Great Purge** of 1936–8, including the great Civil War hero Marshal Tukhachevski. By the end of the purge, over 40 per cent of the top echelon of the military had disappeared. This seemed illogical given rising international tensions following the Nazi seizure of power (1933) and Hitler's expansionist foreign policy.

The army in the Second World War

Russia's involvement in the Second World War resulted in enormous military casualties. There were some examples of desertion, but Stalin ordered Russian troops to fight 'to the last drop of blood', a policy responsible for the successful defence of Stalingrad and Moscow.

The army after the Second World War

From 1945 to 1953, military leaders were treated with suspicion despite their heroics during the war. Marshal Zhukov (chief of staff during the Second World War), for example, was removed from the Party Central Committee and exiled from Moscow. Additionally, the role of the armed forces began to change. Although they were still concerned with internal security, illustrated by their role in resolving the Doctors' Plot (see page 195), by the time Khrushchev came to power, they were far more focused on resolving international conflicts. With *détente*, an easing of tensions occurred, which in turn led to a reduction in the size of the army from 3.6 million to about 2.4 million. Nevertheless, flashpoints such as the shooting down of a US spy plane over Russian airspace in 1960 and the Cuban Missile Crisis of 1962 illustrated that Russia required a significant military presence.

KEY TERMS

Kronstadt A Baltic naval base.

Great Terror The period from 1936 to 1938 when the terrorisation of the Russian people reached a peak.

Great Purge The period from 1936 to 1938 when thousands of people were arrested, convicted and executed for committing 'counter-revolutionary' crimes.

Détente A relaxation in tensions between states during the period of the Cold War, although it is usually applied to the period from 1963 to the late 1970s.

Censorship

Censorship under Alexander II and Alexander III

Under Alexander II, Russia experienced *glasnost* (openness) for the first time. In 1865, censorship was relaxed, although the government retained the right to withdraw publications of a 'dangerous orientation'. Government departments also published newspapers (*Ruskii*) that provided information on official items. The result was an increase in the circulation of newspapers, periodicals and books, as illustrated by the statistics below:

- 1855: 140 periodicals (60 official)
- 1855: 1020 books published
- 1864: 1836 books published
- 1872: the first Russian translation of volume 1 of Marx's *Das Kapital* was published
- 1894: 89 newspapers
- 1894: 10,691 books published (roughly the combined total published in the USA and Britain).

The reactionary rule of Alexander III (1881–94) resulted in a clampdown on publications. Officials censored written material before it was published, and closed down certain newspapers, journals and educational institutions.

Censorship under Nicholas II

Nicholas II reverted to the *glasnost* of Alexander II. A considerable expansion of the press took place in 1894, and the number of different periodicals in circulation increased three-fold from 1900 to 1914. Prepublication censorship once more disappeared, although publishers could still be fined or closed down for circulating subversive material. During this time, newspapers aimed at the proletariat emerged. These included the '*Kopek* newspaper' (the penny paper) which, within two years of its appearance, reached a circulation of 25,000. Political matters discussed in the *Duma* also began to be reported in print, although the details were occasionally omitted or changed.

Censorship during the First World War

Russian people, especially troops, were subject to censorship during the First World War. Troops at the front gained most of their 'news' (including the fall of the Romanovs) from foreign broadcasts. When the Bolsheviks seized power, one of the first measures was to abolish press freedom in order to suppress 'counter-revolutionaries'. In 1921, the Agitation and Propaganda Department (Agitprop) was founded with the aim of promoting an idealised picture of Russian life. Schools, cinemas, the radio and libraries were all under surveillance to prevent the dissemination of counter-revolutionary material. Writers who supported the new regime flourished, while others such as

Zemyatin, who predicted a totalitarian state, were labelled subversive and victimised.

Censorship under Stalin

Under Stalin, censorship was increased. By 1932, all literary groups were closed down and anyone wanting to write had to join the Union of Soviet Writers (USW). During the first congress of the group in 1934, it was announced that members had to produce material under the banner of **'socialist realism'**. This involved writing to depict the struggle of ordinary people to overcome oppression. Any work had to be approved by the party. Some writers, such as Pasternak, changed their beliefs to fit in with the wishes of the USW. Others rebelled and were arrested, sent into exile (to labour camps) or executed.

The Second World War and the New Soviet Man

A high degree of censorship continued throughout and after the Second World War. Stalin was especially concerned to doctor information about the rest of the world. Radio airways were distorted, news was fictionalised and restrictions were put on all of the arts to prevent bourgeois behaviour. Writers were still valued highly as the 'engineer of men's souls' (Stalin) but only if they focused on glorifying Russia's achievements and promoted the concept of the **New Soviet Man**.

Censorship under Khrushchev

Under Khrushchev, censorship was eased. Books and libraries proliferated so that by the late 1950s nearly 65,000 books were being published per year, twice the number that came out in the mid-1920s. By 1959, there were 135,000 libraries containing around 8000 million books, a ten-fold increase on the numbers for 1913. Newspapers also flourished, with a total readership of nearly 60 million by the early 1960s.

Propaganda

The use of propaganda was closely linked to censorship. Although the tsarist regime promoted the Romanovs through pamphleteering, portraits, photographs and staged events – particularly after 1905 – the real masters of propaganda were the communists.

The use of slogans

The Bolsheviks were adept at using slogans to communicate their message to the population, such as 'Peace, Bread and Land' and 'All Power to the Soviets'. Just like the tsarists, they also used pamphlets, tracts, newspapers, photographs, portraits, posters and statues.

KEY TERMS

Socialist realism
The 'official' way of representing, through writing and the visual arts, the heroic efforts of workers and peasants to ensure the success of communism.

New Soviet Man The ideal Soviet citizen: hard working, law abiding, moral and supportive of the Communist Party.

A propaganda poster photographed in 1967 of Lenin, showing the words 'Lenin lived, Lenin is living, Lenin will live'.

The cult of personality

Lenin and Stalin promoted a cult of personality in which they were to be worshipped as heroes. Examples of the cult of personality include the following:

- the imagery of Lenin, which continued to be displayed after his death
- the embalming and display of Lenin's body in the mausoleum in Red Square
- the renaming of Petrograd as Leningrad (1924)
- the renaming of Tsaritsyn as Stalingrad (1923)
- the slogan 'Stalin is the Lenin of Today' (1924)
- various posters, photographs and statues depicting Stalin as a man of the people (usually dressed as a peasant).

Newspapers

Under the communists, the main newspapers, *Pravda* and *Izvestiya*, were primarily propaganda tools. Stalin used them to good effect to promote the achievements of the Five-Year Plans.

'Moscow by Stalin'. The text at the bottom of this poster from *c*.1940–50s reads: 'Under the leadership of the Bolshevik Party, under the guidance of the Leninist Central Committee and the sacred leader of the proletariat Comrade Stalin – onward to the heights of joy and happiness of mankind.'

Groups

Special youth organisations were established (the Pioneers and Komsomol) to protect the young from the 'degeneracy of bourgeois culture'. Komsomol members were encouraged to tell tales on those who criticised their leaders. Membership increased five-fold from 1929 to 1941.

The arts

The arts were manipulated to present a popular culture that emphasised the role of the 'little man' and traditional values. Any trends that veered from the norm, such as jazz music, were banned.

The Stakhanovite movement

Propaganda was used in the workplace to raise productivity. The best example of this was the creation of the **Stakhanovite movement**.

Leisure

Leisure pursuits were also targeted to promote communist ideals, and the Dynamo and Spartak Moscow football teams were used to show the rest of Europe how successfully Russian people could perform under communist rule.

The use of film and the cinema to promote communism

The film industry began in 1907, and by the time of the October Revolution of 1917, there were over 1000 cinemas. By the late 1920s, Stalin was using the cinema to promote collectivisation and his Five-Year Plans. Under the guidance of the Council of People's Commissars, Soviet cinema was immersed in 'socialist realism', although greater creative freedom was allowed after Khrushchev's de-Stalinisation speech. In 1959, 145 films were made, and the number of cinemas had increased to nearly 59,000.

 **KEY TERM**

Stakhanovite movement
Based on the extraordinary efforts of the Donbas miner Alexei Stakhanov, who produced way above the normal quantity of coal per man-shift. He was turned into a 'model' worker for others to copy. Those who did were given special rewards such as red carpets and holidays in Moscow.

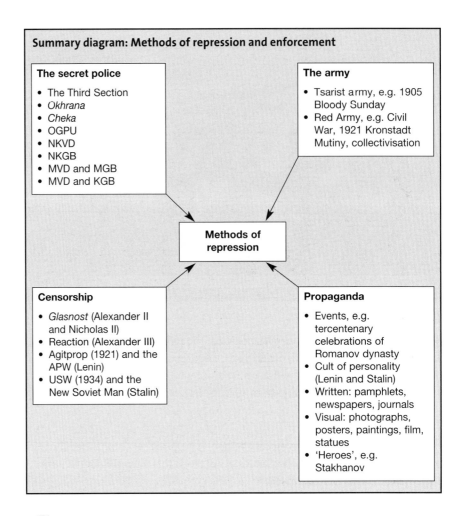

Summary diagram: Methods of repression and enforcement

The secret police
- The Third Section
- *Okhrana*
- *Cheka*
- OGPU
- NKVD
- NKGB
- MVD and MGB
- MVD and KGB

The army
- Tsarist army, e.g. 1905 Bloody Sunday
- Red Army, e.g. Civil War, 1921 Kronstadt Mutiny, collectivisation

Methods of repression

Censorship
- *Glasnost* (Alexander II and Nicholas II)
- Reaction (Alexander III)
- Agitprop (1921) and the APW (Lenin)
- USW (1934) and the New Soviet Man (Stalin)

Propaganda
- Events, e.g. tercentenary celebrations of Romanov dynasty
- Cult of personality (Lenin and Stalin)
- Written: pamphlets, newspapers, journals
- Visual: photographs, posters, paintings, film, statues
- 'Heroes', e.g. Stakhanov

5 The extent and impact of reform

▶ *How useful and appropriate were the reforms used by the tsars and communists as a tool to control opposition?*

The tsars and reform

All Russian rulers throughout the period used reforms as a means of controlling the behaviour of the population. The tsars tended to implement political, economic and social policies to appease opposition. Alexander II hoped that by freeing the serfs they would be happier and less likely to riot. Nicholas II introduced the *Duma* to quieten those who clamoured for constitutional reforms. The Provisional Government also passed liberal reforms such as the dismantling of the *Okhrana* which they hoped would create more stability. This approach did not seem to work, as the more freedoms the Russian people were given, the more they demanded.

The communists and reform

In contrast, the communists used reforms to deal with opponents in a more direct fashion. War Communism (see pages 84–5), collectivisation (see pages 92–5) and the Five-Year Plans (see pages 87–8) were all combined with repressive measures to ensure that they were successfully implemented. There was little scope to question the efficacy of these reforms. It was made clear that collectivisation, for example, involved making tremendous sacrifices that were for the good of the motherland. Anyone who disagreed was exiled or executed.

Summary diagram: The extent and impact of reform

The tsars and reform	The communists and reform
• Reforms used indirectly to appease the population and control opposition • Reforms often led to an increase in opposition	• Reforms used directly to control opposition • Reforms tended to crush opposition

---

6 The nature, extent and effectiveness of opposition

▶ *How far did the nature and extent of opposition change from 1855 to 1964?*

The opposition to regimes from political parties

Political parties were made legal in 1905, but were banned by the Bolsheviks in 1921. Before 1905, political groups did exist, although illegally, but were tolerated as long as their behaviour remained respectable.

The Populists (*Narodniks*)

The Populists consisted of Russian intellectuals who were given greater freedom to criticise tsarist rule following the reforms of Alexander II (see page 14). The chief proponents of the populist cause were Nikolai Chernyshevsky and Pyotr Lavrov. Both were influenced by the writings of Karl Marx (see profile on page 14), and used such ideas to formulate their own brand of popular socialism.

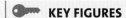
Chernyshevsky published *What is to be Done?* in 1863. Although it contained a simplistic message about how poor Russians could be released from their misery, it would have a profound impact on Lenin.

Lavrov took a more pragmatic approach by organising a 'Going to the People' campaign from 1873 to 1874. This involved approximately 4000 university students dispersing into the Russian countryside to educate the peasants politically. The movement became more organised when **Land and Liberty** was formed in 1876. However, the scheme failed, and there was disagreement over whether the group should employ direct action (including violence) or pursue a peaceful approach based on **Black Repartition**.

The People's Will

The People's Will was a terrorist group that emerged from the Land and Liberty movement. Formed in 1879, they turned to 'the propaganda of the deed' (violence) as a means to spark revolution. Their primary objective was to assassinate the tsar; four attempts were made on Alexander II's life before he was killed in 1881. In this sense, populist opposition was successful, although the assassination did not prompt a complete overthrow of tsarism.

The Socialist Revolutionaries (SRs)

The SRs emerged from the populist movement and continued to focus on improving the living conditions of the poorest people in society, including the growing urban proletariat. The Socialist Revolutionary Party was formed in 1901, and led by the intellectual Victor Chernov. By 1905, the group had split into the more radical left-wing SRs and the moderate right-wing SRs. The left employed direct action; from 1901 to 1905 they were responsible for about 2000 political killings, including **Grand Duke Sergei** and **Vyacheslav Plehve**. The right worked with other parties and groups, gathering support and momentum after the 1905 revolution (see pages 25–7). The right appealed to peasants, whereas the left focused on the plight of industrial workers. Despite the divisions, the SRs had the most support and were the biggest threat to tsarist rule before the October 1917 revolution.

The Social Democrats (SDs)

In 1898, the All-Russian Social Democratic Workers' Party was founded in Minsk. The group was influenced by an interpretation of Marx's work made by **George Plekhanov**, who emphasised the need to encourage **working-class consciousness**. However, since few workers had the time or inclination to engage with Marxist theory, some SD supporters focused on improving pay and reducing working hours. By 1905, there were signs of division between the Bolsheviks and the Mensheviks.

The Liberals

At the start of the period, liberal '**Westernisers**' (as opposed to **Slavophiles**) wanted Russia to be governed in a similar way to Western European democracies such as Britain. Liberal ideas were supported by the emergence of the *Zemstva* and the mid-1890s' revival of the concept of a *Zemstvo* union. In 1904, **Pyotr Struve** founded the Union of Liberation, which demanded greater freedoms and justice for all Russians. In particular, the union wanted fairer and more land distribution for peasants, a representative Constituent Assembly and improved conditions for industrial workers.

The Kadets and Octobrists

After the so-called revolution of 1905, the clamour for a constitutional monarchy gathered pace with the formation of the Constitutional Democrats (Kadets). Led by **Paul Milyukov**, this was the intellectual arm of the liberal movement, and went on to play a very important role as opposition within the first *Duma*. A more moderate liberal group also emerged at this time, called the Octobrists. These were individuals, such as **Alexander Guchkov** and **Mikhail Rodzianko**, who displayed loyalty to the tsar, but who wanted changes to the system of government. The two groups supported Nicholas II's October Manifesto (see page 27) and were therefore much maligned by more revolutionary organisations.

The success of opposition before 1917

Opposition to tsarism before February 1917 was divided between those who wanted change within the tsarist system and those who wanted to overthrow it. The major political changes promised by the October Manifesto were largely cancelled out by the Fundamental Laws of 1906, and the Romanov dynasty remained intact until Nicholas II found it impossible to cope with the effects of the First World War. The lack of effective opposition before 1917 was due partly to the control exerted by successive tsars, but also to the lack of unity within and between opposition groups.

Opposition to the Provisional Government

Despite a climate of collaboration, the Provisional Government faced a similar degree of opposition to that experienced by the tsars. The Bolsheviks came to dominate the opposition for a variety of reasons (see pages 30–1). However, by the end of September 1917, there was little to suggest that the Bolsheviks would attempt to seize power in the foreseeable future. Of more concern for the Provisional Government was the growing strength of workers' committees, especially in Petrograd. The vast majority of members of these committees were opposed to the interim government and were prepared to listen to what other groups, such as the Bolsheviks, had to offer. It was probably the groundswell of opposition from workers that paved the way for a Bolshevik coup, rather than the organisation and leadership of the party.

 **KEY TERMS**

Westernisers Those who wanted to modernise Russia in the same way as Western Europe.

Slavophiles Those who believed that Orthodox Slavs were superior to Western Europeans.

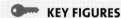 **KEY FIGURES**

Pyotr Struve (1870–1944)

Started his political career as a Legal Marxist (that is, one who preached an acceptable form of Marxism in the eyes of the authorities). He later changed to become a Kadet and then a White during the Civil War.

Paul Milyukov (1859–1943)

A historian and leader of the Kadets. He was also foreign minister in 1917.

Alexander Guchkov (1862–1936)

Leader of the Octobrist Party. He was also war minister in 1917.

Mikhail Rodzianko (1859–1924)

A prominent Octobrist Party member and president of the third and fourth *Dumas*.

Elections to the Constituent Assembly

Although the Bolsheviks had started to claim *de facto* rule, they failed to win a majority in elections to the Constituent Assembly. The results clearly showed that the degree of 'opposition' to them was substantial (see Table 1.1).

Table 1.1 Results of the election for the Constituent Assembly

Party	Votes	Seats
SRs	17,490,000	370
Bolsheviks	9,844,000	175
National minority groups	8,257,000	99
Left SRs (pro-Bolshevik)	2,861,000	40
Kadets	1,986,000	17
Mensheviks	1,248,000	16
Total	41,686,000	717

Lenin believed that the Bolsheviks would not be able to achieve and consolidate power through future elections to the assembly, and therefore chose to use military force to end it. The official justification for such action was that the elections had been rigged, and that, 'The Russian soviets place the interests of the toiling masses far above the interests of treacherous compromise disguised in a new garb.'

Opposition to the Bolsheviks was still rife, and concerns were expressed within the party over the methods adopted by Lenin. The reaction against Lenin was further strengthened by his desire to take Russia out of the First World War and strike a peace deal with Germany. The left SRs saw Lenin as a traitor to the revolution and a German collaborator.

The impact of the Civil War

Some historians believe that Lenin welcomed the Civil War since it provided an opportunity to destroy opposition. Indeed, the groups that made up the White armies (see page 151) were essentially political opponents from the Constituent Assembly. However, the existence of **Green armies** suggests that the nature of the war was not simply about party politics, but also concerned conflicts about nationalities and regions.

After the Red Army victory, Lenin presented a paper 'On Party Unity' in 1921; this laid the base for making all other parties illegal, and banned factionalism within the Bolshevik Party. From 1921 to 1964 (and beyond), Russia remained a one-party state.

The opposition to regimes from individuals and cliques

Both the tsarist and communist ruling elites experienced opposition from within. The tsars favoured removing opponents and **dissidents** from their post; those who suffered this punishment tended to remain loyal to the autocracy. For example, Sergei Witte, the finance minister from 1892 to 1903, was unexpectedly demoted to chairman of ministers. This did not dissuade him from accepting the more important role of prime minister from 1905 to 1906.

'Inside' opposition during the rule of Lenin

With the communists, opposition from inside the party varied according to circumstance and who was leader. During Lenin's stewardship, there were a number of occasions when internal disagreement threatened to derail the revolutionary movement:

- After the overthrow of the Provisional Government in 1917, a number of prominent Bolsheviks, including **Kamenev**, **Zinoviev** and **Rykov**, called for a coalition to be formed with other socialist groups. Although some left-wing SRs were allowed to join ranks, Lenin bullied his Bolshevik colleagues into rejecting an alliance with opposing political groups.
- The signing of the Treaty of Brest-Litovsk was opposed by the left, especially Trotsky. Lenin countered his opponents by claiming that the war would soon be over.
- The adoption of War Communism (see pages 84–5) during the Civil War was considered harsh by some party members. Lenin conceded to pressure for change and introduced his NEP (see pages 85–6). This heightened tensions and widened divisions. Right Bolsheviks favoured this temporary concession towards capitalism, while left Bolsheviks saw it as a betrayal of revolutionary principles.

The lead-up to the power struggle

Lenin's failing health before 1924 started a power struggle. There were three key developments before Lenin's death in January 1924:

- A clique called the Triumvirate (*Troika*) was instigated within the Politburo, consisting of Zinoviev, Kamenev and Stalin. Its purpose was to combat the growing influence of Trotsky, whom Lenin seemed to favour as a successor.
- In December 1922, Lenin provided his Political Testament, a document which criticised the personal attributes and achievements of many leading Bolsheviks. Stalin received heavy criticism for how he ran *Rabkrin* and his role in the 1921 **'Georgian affair'**.
- By January 1924, Stalin had worked himself into a position of power by holding various political posts, including that of general secretary (appointed in April 1922). As the historian Chris Ward (1999) has indicated, by the time Lenin's health started to deteriorate, Stalin was:

KEY TERMS

Dissidents Those who disagreed with the aims and procedures of the government.

Rabkrin The Workers' and Peasants' Inspectorate, a highly bureaucratic and overstaffed organisation.

'Georgian affair' The mishandling of Georgian nationalism by Ordjonikidze, the commissar for national affairs in Georgia. His actions were defended by Stalin.

KEY FIGURES

Lev Kamenev (1883–1936)

Leading member of the Politburo from 1919 to 1925.

Grigory Zinoviev (1883–1936)

Rose to prominence as chairman of the Petrograd soviet (1917) and later became chairman of Comintern (1919–26).

Alexey Rykov (1881–1938)

Best known for serving as prime minister from 1924 to 1930.

… the only leader who was simultaneously a member of the Politburo, Orgburo, Secretariat and Central Committee. In addition, he could look back on almost seven years' experience of military commissions and jobs in the state's embryonic administrative apparatus.

This partly explains why Stalin took over the mantle from Lenin with relative ease.

The power struggle

After Lenin's death, a certain amount of manoeuvring for power occurred, which highlighted the factions that still existed within the party. Leading Bolsheviks disagreed over three key issues:

- First, there was much dispute between left and right Bolsheviks over whether there should be a continuation of the NEP.
- Second, many demanded that a more openly democratic form of government should be adopted.
- Finally, the link between ideology and the future of communism caused much consternation. The left, under the guidance of Trotsky, continued to press for a Permanent Revolution (see page 19), while the right emphasised the need for socialism in one country.

Stalin displayed skill in manipulating debates and individuals to consolidate his position, thereby paving the way for a personal dictatorship.

Stalin's split with Zinoviev and Kamenev

The *Troika* successfully discredited Trotsky, who was replaced as commissar for war in January 1925. However, Kamenev and Zinoviev became concerned with Stalin's plan for dealing with peasants and his foreign policy. They attacked Stalin but with little success; both were removed as secretaries of their local party. The Politburo was simultaneously expanded (from six to eight members) and reinforced with Stalinists.

The United Opposition group

Trotsky, Kamenev and Zinoviev responded by forming the United Opposition group. Their opposition to the NEP and demands for more 'free speech' were treated with contempt. All were excluded from the Politburo. In 1927, Trotsky was expelled from the party, and after continuing to provoke trouble was exiled to Kazakhstan. In January 1929, he was expelled from the USSR altogether.

The proposals for collectivisation

Stalin's proposals for collectivisation (see pages 92–5), including renewed grain requisitioning, were opposed by those on the right, who thought it resembled aspects of War Communism. Bukharin was particularly vocal in expressing his concerns and, as a result of joining forces with Kamenev, was branded a **factionalist**.

 **KEY TERM**

Factionalist One who went about pursuing his or her own interests to the detriment of party unity.

The removal of Bukharin

In 1929, Bukharin was ousted from his positions as president of **Comintern**, editor of *Pravda* and member of the Politburo. Tomsky and Rykov also suffered demotions. Stalin simply gained the agreement of a core of loyal party members in order to remove 'critics' from positions of power. This was similar to how the tsars dealt with 'inside' opposition. Thus, with both the left and the right removed from key jobs, Stalin was free to dominate proceedings. Both collectivisation and a series of Five-Year Plans (see pages 87–8 and 92–5) were implemented with a great deal of speed.

Stalin's dominant position did not end criticism, but 1929 probably marks the point when it is difficult to distinguish between serious and imaginary challenges to Stalin's authority.

The purges

Throughout the 1930s, there was a change of policy: critics ceased to be removed from key political posts, and were instead removed from the party altogether. According to the historian J.N. Westwood (2002), purging involved:

> … thorough cleansing, and was used quite naturally to describe the periodic weeding out from party membership of those characters deemed unfit. From this small beginning the word came to describe a monstrous process of arbitrary arrests, fake trials, mass executions, and forced labour camps, which the weak and unlucky could not survive.

The purges of the 1930s were characterised by the following:

- Party members who failed to implement collectivisation adequately, or who disagreed with Stalin's attempt to '**liquidate the *kulaks* as a class**', lost their party card, reducing total membership by about a tenth.
- During the mid-1930s, the party shed a further third of its members who were seen to be resisting the pace of industrialisation and collectivisation.
- From the mid-1930s, some prominent Politburo members were exiled or executed after being called **oppositionists**. By 1939, Kirov, Kossior, Ordhonikze, Kuibyshev and Rudzuki were all dead.
- By the beginning of the Second World War, Stalin's paranoia over those he believed to be challenging his authority had receded.

Any internal opposition to Stalin was eliminated and not just displaced. In this sense, internal opposition was more limited in scope and achievement during the Stalinist era than at any other time in the period 1855–1964. During the rule of Khrushchev, however, de-Stalinisation resulted in an end to purging and greater tolerance of political criticism.

KEY TERMS

Comintern The Communist International body was established in March 1918 with the aim of spreading communism overseas.

Liquidate the *kulaks* as a class Stalin's policy to eliminate wealthier peasants (*kulaks*) as part of the class war in the countryside. *Kulaks* were considered to be bourgeois.

Oppositionists Those who opposed the communist revolution.

The opposition to regimes from peasants

Role of peasants

Although the majority of peasants remained largely ignorant of and apathetic towards political change, a significant number were politically active. Their level of commitment varied according to where they were located and their status in rural society. Older, more educated peasants tended to be more involved than others. Peasants often acted independently against changes considered detrimental to their well-being, and seldom showed an allegiance to political parties.

Peasant unrest

Given that peasants constituted 70–80 per cent of the population of Russia at any point in time, large-scale peasant uprisings were taken seriously. Peasant riots and protests were sometimes followed by significant reforms, although a disturbance was just as likely to be dealt with by force. Riots occurred mainly because of land distribution and access to food. Peasant opposition, ranging from mass demonstration to full-scale rioting, was prevalent from the time of Alexander II all the way through to Khrushchev.

The impact of the 1861 Emancipation Edict on peasant attitudes

The 1861 Emancipation Edict (see page 90) unleashed a number of disturbances involving thousands of peasants. This unrest quietened until the 1890s, when further outbursts of revolt were quelled with the help of land captains. Peasant rebellions reached a new level during the period 1900–7, prompted by unsatisfactory attempts to deal with issues relating to **redemption payments**, land distribution and rising prices. Peasants became more inventive and politically intelligent in the methods they used to demand improvements. Rural folk sometimes appropriated 'private' and state land (especially forest and grazing pasture), refused to pay taxes, robbed warehouses and stores, physically attacked landowners and resorted to **incendiary**.

The Black Earth region revolts

The revolts of 1906–7, especially in the **Black Earth regions**, were initially put down with a great deal of force. However, Stolypin subsequently carried out land reforms to appease peasant grievances. This indicates that peasants were successful in employing direct action on a wider scale.

From 1908 to 1914, Stolypin's reforms seemed to pacify peasant leaders, but the upheaval of the First World War ignited another phase of peasant revolt. From 1916, peasants protested at high food prices, and also the pressure of rising demand for food from urban dwellers. This was exacerbated by the lack of technology and materials (especially fertilisers) needed to improve productivity. Peasants were an integral part of the revolutionary events of 1917, launching attacks on landowners, destroying public utilities in provincial towns and

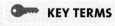

KEY TERMS

Redemption payments
The repayment of loans that had to be taken out to purchase land that was redistributed after 1861.

Incendiary Setting fire to rural property, usually farm buildings and hayricks.

Black Earth regions
The area from the south-western borderlands into Asiatic Russia.

engaging in **peasant vigilantism**. The peasantry was more organised than before, often with the aid of army deserters and educated peasants who formed peasant soviets.

The impact of the Civil War on peasant attitudes

Peasants rioted during the Civil War in an attempt to better their position. A number of quasi-independent peasant armies were established, led by heroes such as **Chapayev**, that sympathised with the Bolsheviks. But peasants could also be found supporting the White armies, and there was mounting resentment from peasants against grain requisitioning, which was an integral part of the Bolsheviks' War Communism (see pages 84–5). In response, the NEP (see pages 85–6) was introduced and used to appease peasants in a similar way to the 1861 Emancipation Edict and Stolypin's Land Reforms.

Collectivisation and peasant unrest

Stalin's collectivisation and dekulakisation programme ignited peasant unrest. Thousands of peasants died as a result of the different phases of collectivisation; there was opposition to the scale and speed of the reform, and the loss of the *mir* as an organising institution (dismantled in 1930). At the height of collectivisation, significant numbers of peasants refused to cooperate and showed outright dissent by slaughtering large numbers of cattle and horses.

Khrushchev and stability in the countryside

During the Khrushchev era, there was little rural unrest. However, Khrushchev's agricultural policies were not especially successful and by the end of his rule Russia once again faced food shortages (see page 96).

The opposition to regimes from workers

The nature of workers

The term 'worker' is usually used to denote a person employed in any industry found in an urban setting. It can also be used to refer to those employed in industries located away from the main cities (for example, miners). There were fewer workers than peasants, although the distinction between the two groups became blurred after the end of the Civil War when increasing numbers of peasants were transformed into the urban proletariat.

The treatment of workers by tsars and communists

As the pace of industrialisation quickened, especially during and after Witte's 'Great Spurt', workers became an increasingly valuable asset to tsarist and Bolshevik regimes. Although industrial employment offered more regular hours and better pay than work on the land, conditions were still poor. For example, there was no factory inspectorate until 1882, and a ten-hour working day for workers was not the norm until 1914. Under the communists, working

KEY TERM

Peasant vigilantism Rural people taking the matter of law and order into their own hands.

KEY FIGURE

Vasily Chapayev (1887–1919)

A celebrated Russian soldier and Red Army commander during the Civil War. He was 'the best known of the pro-Bolsheviks, being subsequently portrayed as a simple man capable of inspiring unruly and illiterate soldiers to heights of endurance and heroism' (J.N. Westwood, 2002). He drowned in a river while attempting to escape from the Whites.

conditions were not much better, although workers were allowed legal representation through trade unions. However, the entire period is littered with instances of workers protesting against employers and rulers about low wages, long working hours and poor working conditions.

Workers and politics

It is debatable whether worker protest can be interpreted as political opposition or economic grievance. However, both Lenin and Stalin believed that a true political revolution in Russia could only come as a result of workers becoming conscious of the iniquities of the 'system' that governed their behaviour. The formation, growth and role of soviets in the final revolution of 1917 add weight to the argument that workers played an important part in changing the nature of government in Russia.

Tactics used by workers

Workers used riots, and – in contrast to peasants – strikes, to achieve their aims. Strikes before the 1880s tended to be localised and small-scale affairs, but thereafter grew in size and degree of threat. The strike in 1885 at the Morozov dye works, for example, involved over 8000 workers. Although strike activity was frequently banned – for example, after the sympathy strikes following Bloody Sunday (January 1905) – or dealt with using extreme force – as happened to the Lena Goldfield miners in 1912 – workers continued to employ direct action up to and during the First World War. The most famous strike during the war period started on 23 February 1917 at the **Putilov works** in St Petersburg.

The Civil War as a turning point for workers

Many workers died in the fighting, which resulted in a shift of peasants from agricultural to industrial work. This created a factory workforce in the 1920s, considered by one historian to be '… ill educated, ill disciplined, and not particularly interested in the party'. This development, coupled with the emergence of the NEP, helps to explain why workers seemed fairly docile throughout the 1920s and 1930s. The authorities quickly dealt with any agitation, and Stalin's purges ruthlessly removed disruptive trade union officials. In general, workers accepted the Five-Year Plans, and Stalin purposefully used this economic policy partly as a way of controlling worker behaviour. Interestingly, by the 1940s there was a rise in the number of worker suicides associated with the pressures of failing to meet production targets.

The impact of the Second World War on workers

During the Second World War, and in contrast to 1914–17, there were no strikes, although there were early examples of a lack of support for the conflict. Industrial relations were stable under Khrushchev, although there were riots by

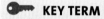

KEY TERM

Putilov works The biggest private factory in Russia by the start of the twentieth century. It specialised in iron production and became very important during the First World War in providing artillery.

workers over a perceived fall in living standards. In 1962, for example, workers at Novocherhassk protested against food shortages and rising food prices. As a result, the authorities killed twenty workers, and a number of ringleaders were later executed.

The impact of worker opposition

Worker opposition was effective in the sense that:

- The average working day was reduced from 11½ hours in 1897 to seven hours in the 1960s.
- Official inspection and administration of working conditions was established.
- A change in the political system in 1917 promised a dictatorship of the proletariat that would lead to full worker control of the country.

However, full worker control of the means of production, distribution and exchange never occurred and workers experienced living standards that fell below their own expectations. Workers were also continuously repressed using both the law and the full force of the police and armed forces.

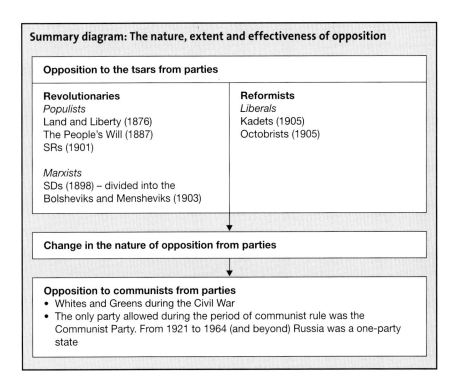

Summary diagram: The nature, extent and effectiveness of opposition

Opposition to the tsars from parties

Revolutionaries	Reformists
Populists	*Liberals*
Land and Liberty (1876)	Kadets (1905)
The People's Will (1887)	Octobrists (1905)
SRs (1901)	
Marxists	
SDs (1898) – divided into the	
Bolsheviks and Mensheviks (1903)	

Change in the nature of opposition from parties

Opposition to communists from parties
- Whites and Greens during the Civil War
- The only party allowed during the period of communist rule was the Communist Party. From 1921 to 1964 (and beyond) Russia was a one-party state

7 Attitude of Russian leaders to political change

▶ *How different was the attitude of the tsars towards political change compared with that of the communists?*

All the tsars showed a desire to maintain autocracy. Some attempts were made to introduce elements of democracy. Alexander II introduced the *Zemstva* and Nicholas II the national *Duma* but in both instances the changes were made alongside efforts to maintain tsarist rule. The *Zemstva* proved to be unrepresentative of the population as a whole and the *Duma* had its powers limited by the Fundamental Law of 1906.

The Provisional Government had a more positive attitude towards political change by aiming to set up a Constituent Assembly. The principles on which the achievement of this aim depended also led to political change of a more liberal nature such as the release of political prisoners and the formation of an alliance with the Petrograd soviet.

The communists initially wanted revolutionary political change; as a result, the tsar was forced to abdicate, the Provisional Government was constantly challenged and the Constituent Assembly disbanded. Once the October revolution was over, the communists were more interested in consolidating power using the political system they had created. Although constitutions were issued that appeared to give greater autonomy to certain regional groups in the Soviet Union, under Stalin power became more centralised. Stalin seemed intent on introducing totalitarianism using tools of extreme repression to do so. Khrushchev showed a greater willingness to embrace political change by de-Stalinising Russia and shifting authority to the party.

Summary diagram: Attitude of Russian leaders to political change

Attitude of the tsars
- To maintain autocracy (all tsars)
- To introduce some elements of liberal democracy (especially Alexander II and Nicholas II)

↓

Attitude of Provisional Government
- To base government on liberal principles
- To move towards a Constituent Assembly

↓

Attitude of communists
- To overthrow the Provisional Government (revolution) (Lenin)
- To consolidate communism (Lenin and Stalin)
- To centralise authority (Stalin)
- To move away from centralised authority (Khrushchev)

---

8 The extent of political change

▶ *To what extent did the political ideologies and structures of government change in Russia from 1855 to 1964?*

Under the tsars the ideology and structure of government largely stayed the same. Leaders made some changes but they were always subservient to the need to maintain autocracy. All of the tsars used a mixture of reform and repression to govern and to keep opposition under control. Thus, to label Alexander II the 'Liberator' and Alexander III the 'Reactionary' is misleading.

The Provisional Government's principles that guided the establishment of the Constituent Assembly contributed to its downfall. For example, releasing political prisoners allowed opposition groups to gather momentum. Also, the Constituent Assembly was short lived and was replaced in dramatic fashion by a Bolshevik dictatorship.

Political change under Lenin and Stalin mainly came about through the constitutions of 1924 and 1936. These extended the range of influence over a number of republics but also suggested that each member state would have a degree of autonomy. A more marked change occurred with de-Stalinisation and a move back to a form of democratic centralism.

Summary diagram: The extent of political change

Tsars	Continuity	Change
All	Ruled as autocrats; used repression and reform	
Alexander II Alexander III Nicholas II		The Liberator? The Reactionary? A liberator and reactionary?

Provisional Government	Continuity	Change
	Appointed from the fourth *Duma*; the 'old guard'	Adopted liberal principles; succeeded in establishing a Constituent Assembly

Communists	Continuity	Change
All	Ruled as types of autocrat (or authoritarians); used repression and reform	
Lenin		Introduced Marxism–Leninism; moved towards 'dictatorship of the proletariat'
Stalin		Introduced Marxism–Leninism–Stalinism; moved towards totalitarianism
Khrushchev		Introduced de-Stalinisation; moved towards democratic centralism

Chapter summary

In the sense that autocracy means a government headed by a ruler with unlimited power, there was little change in the way Russia was run between 1855 and 1964. Some may argue that the dictatorship established under Lenin was different from the tsarist autocracy in that the use of force to impose the will of the leadership was greater and more persistent. There was another twist to the story when Stalin came to power; his highly personalised approach to rule coupled with the 'Terror' resulted in an obedience from the people that was symptomatic of totalitarianism. Khrushchev felt that the legacy of Stalin was detrimental to the standing of Russia in the world and instigated further political change through the policy of de-Stalinisation.

Opposition was either 'real' or 'perceived' and came from inside and outside ruling elites. The extent of opposition can partly be measured by reference to numbers affiliating to opposition groups, although large numbers did not necessarily constitute more significant and effective opposition. Note that statistics for the amount of opposition are difficult to obtain and interpret.

The effectiveness of opposition can be viewed with respect to whether those who opposed rulers achieved their specific aims. It also needs to be considered from the perspective of rulers; the effectiveness of the tools used to control opposition is an equally important measurement of the overall impact of opposition.

 ## Refresher questions

Use these questions to remind yourself of the key material covered in this chapter.

1 To what extent did the tsars adhere to the principles of 'Orthodoxy, Autocracy and Nationality'?

2 How important was Marxism in influencing communist leaders?

3 How accurate is the term 'totalitarianism' when describing the rule of Stalin?

4 To what extent was de-Stalinisation a turning point in the governance of Russia?

5 Why did the *Dumas* have limited success?

6 How far did the structures of government change from 1855 to 1964?

7 How pivotal was the First World War in determining the course of Russian politics and government?

8 Why did opposition to the tsars grow after 1866?

9 How and why did the Bolsheviks come to dominate opposition to the tsars?

10 To what extent did the nature of opposition change under the communists?

11 Why were some national minorities more successful than others in opposing tsarist and communist rule?

12 To what extent was the use of the secret police the most effective tool in controlling opposition from 1855 to 1964?

13 How effectively did the tsars use censorship, compared with the communists, to control opposition in the period from 1855 to 1964?

14 How useful and appropriate were the reforms used by the tsars and communists as a tool to control opposition?

In-depth studies and debates

The examination requires you to study three topics in depth and for this unit they are:

- Alexander II's domestic reforms
- The Provisional Government
- Khrushchev in power 1956–64.

This section will go into more detail about the nature of government during the periods concerned. Some of the key debates about how Russia was governed will be introduced so that you will have enough depth of knowledge to be able to evaluate passages that are set on any of the depth study topics.

Key debate 1: how 'liberal' was Russian government from 1855 to 1881?

The main area of debate with respect to the rule of Alexander II is the extent to which the reforms he carried out genuinely granted liberty (freedom) to the peoples of Russia. Traditionally, he was viewed as the 'Tsar Liberator', mainly as a result of the Emancipation Edict of 1861 and its consequences. There are some historians, such as J.N. Westwood (2002), who have been happy to perpetuate the view that Alexander II intentionally carried out reforms that granted Russians greater freedoms so that they could live better lives. Hence, Westwood believes that:

> With the possible exceptions of Khrushchev and Gorbachev, no Russian ruler brought so much relief to so many of his people as did Alexander II, autocratic and conservative though he was.

Others, though, have emphasised the limitations of the reforms to argue that the tsar was concerned only with making some concessions to win support.

Despite his being labelled the 'Tsar Liberator', there is some consensus among historians that Alexander II never wavered from being an autocrat. Although, in 1862, from an assembly of 'liberal' nobility of Tver province, there was a questioning of the unrepresentative nature of central government, the tsar made only one change. The Personal Chancellery of his Imperial Majesty was abolished in 1861 and replaced with a Council of Ministers. This is often viewed as a relatively minor change but it did at least give the impression that Alexander wanted to show that he was willing to debate proposed policies before implementing them.

More contentious are the reforms made to local government. The significance of the *Zemstva* (see page 37) is debated for the following reasons:

- Some historians have claimed that the once the emancipation of the serfs occurred then local government had to change. The tsar was forced to introduce an element of democracy at local level but then seemed to regret this immediately. Liberal members of the *Zemstva* started to question the 'administrative monopoly of officialdom' and were critical of a regime that they perceived to be unresponsive to their demands.

- Both the district and provincial *Zemstva* were dominated by the nobility. The extent to which democracy was introduced is questionable. Also, the creation of the *Zemstva* appeared to divert the attention of the reformist nobility away from wanting changes to central government.
- Writers who appear sympathetic towards Russian tsarism have emphasised the successes of the *Zemstva*. For example, they did much 'good work' in the fields of education, public health and local economies. The original *Zemstva* were seen as so effective that, from 1870 onwards, the model was copied and applied to towns and cities.

There is no doubt that opposition to Alexander did increase but whether this meant that his assassination was then a certainty is open to debate. The historian Tom Kemp (1985) has argued that:

> *The efforts of Tsarism to survive, and reform in order to conserve, inevitably increased the numbers of the educated and potentially critical.*

The historian Orlando Figes (2014) also believes that opposition to Alexander II occurred logically as a result of his reforms. He claims that:

- The creation of *Zemstva* resulted in the emergence of the Populist movement.
- When the Populists failed, in the 'mad summer' of 1874, to gain support from peasants some of them turned to 'revolutionary terror'. This splinter group (the People's Will) turned to 'assassinating government officials in the hope that, if they weakened the autocracy, the peasantry would join them in revolt'.
- Four attempts were made to assassinate the tsar. It was only a matter of time before one succeeded (1 March 1881).

Not all agree with this deterministic, sequential approach. The historian J.N. Westwood has suggested that the threat of opposition from revolutionaries ebbed and flowed in the face of repression used by the tsar. For example, in 1877, the 'Trial of the 50' resulted in the long-term imprisonment of key Populists. Also, the historian Geoffrey Hosking (2002) has questioned whether the Populists were unsuccessful. He believes that 'going to the people' resulted in significant number of peasant groups being encouraged to 'share some of the radicals' ideas, for example about egalitarianism in landholding ...'. Thus, it was not necessarily inevitable that the tsar's liberal reforms plus the failures of the Populists would lead to Alexander II's assassination.

Key debate 2: to what extent was the Provisional Government doomed to fail from the start?

The origins of the Provisional Government can be dated to 1915. In that year, two-thirds of the *Duma* (mostly moderates) collaborated to form the Progressive Bloc. The aim was to create unity among different party members so that an agreed plan to manage Russia's war effort could be implemented. Nicholas II saw this as an affront to his authority and in August 1915 he ordered the *Dumas* to be suspended. The result was increased discontent with the tsar from across the political spectrum. In February 1917, a series of strikes and demonstrations led to the fourth *Duma* dissolving itself. By the end of the month, the Winter Palace and other government buildings had been taken over by revolutionaries. Chaos ensued until a Temporary Committee, created from the leading figures in the last *Dumas*, and a Provisional Executive of the Soviet of Workers' Deputies cooperated to formulate a programme for order to be restored.

On 1 March, the tsar agreed to hand over authority to the Temporary Committee and on 2 March he abdicated. The new Provisional Government, as it was labelled, was immediately revealed to the Russian peoples.

The formation and tenure of the Provisional Government have caused much debate among historians. The main bone of contention is the extent to which the government failed. Some believe that the Provisional Government was doomed from the start but did not help itself by making poor decisions. Others argue that the new government was successful in achieving its main aim, which was the preparation for elections to a new Constituent Assembly. It was not so much the failings of the Provisional Government that led to the October Revolution of 1917 but the determination of the Bolsheviks to seize power.

For those who view the Provisional Government as an abject failure, much is made of the initial composition of its Cabinet (see Table 1.2).

Table 1.2 Members of the Cabinet of the Provisional Government, March 1917

Name	Position	Background
Prince G.E. Lvov	Prime minister and interior minister	From one of the most respected noble families. Wealthy landowner. Ex-chairman of the Union of *Zemstva* and leader of the Progressive Bloc
P.N. Miliukov	Foreign minister	A member of the intelligentsia and founder of the Kadets (1905). A well-known critic of the tsar
A.I. Guchkov	Minister for war and navy	A wealthy industrialist and founder of the Octobrists (1905). Well known for his work as chairman of the War Industry Committee (1915). Respectful of tsarism but a critic of Nicholas II
V.N. Lvov	Procurator of the Holy Synod	From a noble family and staunch supporter of the Octobrists. Quite conservative in his views
A.A. Maniulov	Education minister	A member of the intelligentsia and the Kadet Party
A.F. Kerensky	Justice minister	A member of the intelligentsia and the Socialist Revolutionaries. Well known for his oratory skill when dealing with legal issues
M.I. Iereschenko	Minister of finance	A wealthy businessman and vice-chairman of the Central War Committee. He enjoyed watching ballet
A.I. Shingarev	Agriculture minister	A doctor and member of the Kadet Party
N.V. Nekrasov	Transport minister	Ex-vice-president of the *Dumas* and member of the Kadet Party

The historians J.N. Westwood (2002) and Ian Thatcher (2015) have claimed that the Provisional Government was initially 'popularly accepted'. Its members were, in the main, liberal minded and some, such as Milyukov and Guchkov, were well-known political figures. Others, though, were more obscure characters. The majority were masons, although the extent to which this may have caused consternation among the general public at the time is debatable. Of more significance is the fact that the new government lacked legitimacy as it was an unelected body made up from members of the Progressive Bloc. This view is strengthened by the response of a member of a crowd that listened to Milyukov's announcement of the composition of the Provisional Government; 'Who appointed you?' was shouted out. Milyukov rather lamely responded by stating it was 'the Revolution itself'. In general, as the historian Michael Lynch (2015) has pointed out, the Provisional Government was simply 'the old *duma* in a new form'.

Some historians have argued that the era of the Provisional Government was the only time that the Russian Empire was united. Others have pointed out that it was unlikely that the new government would have been able to sustain unity. It faced the following challenges from opponents, although most of the latter's grievances had mounted over a long period:

- From the outset, authority was shared with the Petrograd soviet, who opposed most of the Provisional Government's proposals. The Provisional Government had little option but to coalesce with the soviet given the degree of popular support the latter had from workers, peasants, soldiers and sailors. In particular, the two groups disagreed over Russia's involvement in the war. The Provisional Government wanted to push on for 'a decisive victory' while the Petrograd soviet demanded 'peace without annexations or indemnities', and also '**revolutionary defencism**'. The Provisional Government's stance was understandable; some success had been achieved on the Eastern Front in preventing a total German victory with the minimum of diversionary help from Russia's allies on the Western Front. The war had also captured the imagination of the populace; although some called for peace this would have to be seen as honourable (that is, as the soviet pointed out, 'without annexations or indemnities'). Thus, there is an argument that the Provisional Government had its hands tied with respect to continuing with the war but this policy was likely to undermine its stability.
- The first government established a set of eight principles by which it would rule (see page 120). These were classically liberal and included decrees on political amnesty and full freedom of speech. However, this allowed the proliferation of protest groups such as the Bolsheviks.
- The peasant land issue dragged on (see pages 90–2). Due to the nature of the problem, the Provisional Government argued that only an elected assembly could deal with it. This irritated peasant groups who wanted more immediate action to be taken.

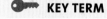 **KEY TERM**

Revolutionary defencism
Defence and protection of everything achieved by the revolution of March 1917.

An attempt to unite the Provisional Government and Petrograd soviet was made in May 1917 when a coalition government was formed. This was led by Prince Lvov, who invited six members of the Petrograd soviet to join. However, national elections to a Constituent Assembly were postponed, the land issue was ignored, workers' committees were clamped down on, and involvement in the war continued. All of this dampened support for the Provisional Government and caused rising militancy within the Petrograd soviet.

The historian Ian Thatcher has suggested that opposition in the form of Kornilov was the turning point in the fortunes of the Provisional Government. In August 1917, the military commander, Kornilov, marched with his troops to Petrograd with the intention of forcefully closing down the soviet. Kerensky seemed to believe that Kornilov, having defeated the soviet, would then move on to take over the Provisional Government and impose a military-style dictatorship. Kerensky, therefore, agreed to the Bolsheviks being given arms to defend Petrograd. In the end, a bloody conflict was averted. Railway workers refused to transport Kornilov's army. Kornilov also received advance warning of how quickly the Bolsheviks had mobilised their defences and decided that the proposed takeover had a good chance of ending in disaster. He therefore abandoned his plan and was arrested.

Thatcher has argued that the Kornilov affair was significant for a number of reasons:

- The Bolsheviks were viewed as heroes for organising the protection of Petrograd. They (the soviet) were also 'armed' by the Provisional Government, a recipe for disaster.
- It was evident that the Provisional Government was susceptible to being challenged by the military and, therefore, others who might want to use force to seize power.
- Kerensky was shown to be a weak leader compared with Lenin.
- After the affair, the Bolsheviks quickly gained more support so that by early September they had majorities in both the Petrograd and Moscow soviets. By the end of October, they had ousted the Provisional Government and taken control of Petrograd.

Overall, the Provisional Government struggled to deal with its opponents but this was probably due more to circumstance than to its incompetence.

Key debate 3: how far did de-Stalinisation represent a genuine break from the past?

From the 1920s until Khrushchev became prime minister in 1958, Russian communists on the whole believed that the Communist Party existed to develop ideology and to oversee the government. Quite simply, the role of the Soviet government was to supervise the running of Russia. Under Stalin, the party and government lost any freedoms they had and were answerable directly to him. The government became an organ which put into operation Stalin's policies.

Khrushchev wanted to move away from the highly centralised and personalised mode of government established by Stalin. To do this, he created a government that was more accountable to him but also to the party.

However, the historian Martin McCauley (1995) has proposed that Khrushchev only '… changed aspects of the [political] system and not the system itself'. Thus, he is seen to be successful in:

- making the Communist Party more accountable to the people
- reforming bureaucracy so it appeared less corrupt and more effective in dealing with the wants and needs of the population.

But McCauley believes that tinkering with the system and redirecting power to the party had a limited impact on presenting Russia, to the rest of the world, as a country that was moving away from the Stalinist years. This is mainly seen as a result of Khrushchev's adherence to the centralised planning of the economy and reluctance to embrace an economic system at least partly based on market forces. His critics seemed to detect a contradiction between his political and economic policies.

McCauley's interpretation seems rather harsh given the context that Khrushchev was working in and the underlying assumption made about the value of a more market-based economy. The Stalinist regime had built up a great deal of mistrust in the West about Soviet intentions during the early years of the Cold War. Through de-Stalinisation, Khrushchev could be viewed as having done his best to make relations with the West more cordial. Also, it is debatable whether a market-based or capitalist economy was and is the right way for any country to improve living standards.

Khrushchev experienced a degree of opposition from peasants and workers. Some have argued that during the Khrushchev era, there was very little rural unrest. Westwood has pointed out that 'for the first time since Peter the Great there was a genuine interchange between the tsar and people'. This was due to the fact that Khrushchev 'spent much of his time in the countryside, conferring with party secretaries, cajoling farm chairmen, and making promises to peasants in the kind of earthy language they could understand'. Despite this, Khrushchev's agricultural policies, especially the Virgin Land campaign, were not especially appealing to the Russian people; they soon started to express their discontent. When this happened, Khrushchev was not afraid to resort to force to deal with the unrest.

Another area of debate over opposition to Khrushchev concerns his eventual downfall. This is commonly attributed to:

- the failure of Khrushchev's agricultural policy
- loss of prestige over the Cuban Missile Crisis
- deterioration in relations with China

- Khrushchev's decentralisation of the government (which appeared to threaten the positions of key members of the bureaucracy)
- defence cuts, which annoyed the military.

The historian Norman Lowe (2005) has suggested that this is a rather simplistic way of looking at why the Russian leader was eventually 'persuaded' to step down. He believes the reasons were of a more personal nature:

> *Perhaps his colleagues were tired of his extrovert personality (once, in a heated moment at the United Nations, he took off his shoe and hammered the table with it) and felt he was taking too much on himself. Khrushchev had become increasingly aggressive and arrogant, and at times seemed to have developed the 'cult of personality' almost as much as Stalin.*

However, some historians such as Dmitri Volkogonov (1998), a critic of all Soviet leaders, believe that Khrushchev, through de-Stalinisation, 'achieved virtually the impossible' as 'in a fundamental way [he] also changed society'. It was probably these core changes made by Khrushchev that worried his contemporaries the most. It is likely that they viewed them as a predecessor to even more radical reforms and the deconstruction of the communist system in Russia.

Study skills: thematic essay question

How to plan the essay

The title of the unit, 'Thematic Study', makes it clear that the essay section should be approached thematically rather than chronologically, particularly if you want to reach the higher mark range. In answering essay questions, you are required to make connections, comparisons and links between different elements of the period and aspects of the topic. In the opening paragraph you should try to establish a hypothesis based on the question; this should be tested in the main body of the essay before reaching an overall judgement. This is much easier to do if you approach the essay through a thematic structure. In your answer you will need to cover the whole period, and answers should look to establish patterns of change and continuity and similarity and difference.

Given the large amount of material that you will have to handle, it is very important that you spend time carefully unpacking the question and planning your answer. As the essay should adopt a thematic structure, it makes sense if the plan follows the same format; it should not be chronological, going through the period of each ruler, or just a list of dates.

You will need to establish the themes you will consider, for example:

'War was the main reason why the opponents of the tsars from 1855 to 1917 were more successful than those who opposed the communist regime from 1917 to 1964.' How far do you agree?

In this essay you would need to consider a number of reasons and weigh up their relative importance against that of war in influencing the success of opposition. The plan will establish the themes you will consider, but will also provide you with an outline of the argument, or thesis, you will follow.

Consider the example essay plan below:

War: Russia's lack of relative success during the Russo-Japanese War and the First World War seemed to spur on opposition; the Russian people thought they suffered hardships which were unnecessary; Nicholas II was blamed and discontent was easy to harness by opposition leaders. The communists used war (the Civil War, the Second World War and the Cold War) to combat opposition.

Economic change: the adverse impact of (slow) industrialisation on living and working conditions gave workers the incentive to rebel; industrialisation and urbanisation also resulted in the politicisation of workers and a rise in working-class consciousness. This led to demands for social and political change.

Social change: some social reforms were seen not to go far enough or did not have the positive impact expected (for example, the Emancipation Edict of 1861). Others, especially in the field of education, resulted in an expansion of the intelligentsia (leaders of opposition groups).

Political change: the tsars were autocrats but enacted some liberal policies which were exploited by opposition groups; the communists moved towards totalitarian rule (especially under Stalin) and were mostly illiberal. Thus, success of opposition depended as much on how it was dealt with as the conditions which influenced its growth.

Conclusion: clearly war had an important influence on the extent and success of opposition throughout the period although the impact it had varied from the tsars to the communists. More significant was economic change as this created a greater consciousness among the Russian peoples for the need for reform. It was economic concerns that subsequently led to demands for social and political change.

The plan does not simply list the reasons, but offers a comment about their importance, and the conclusion offers a clear line of argument which has been supported in the previous paragraphs. Planning an answer will help you to focus on the actual question and marshal the large amount of knowledge you have, in this case about the influences on opposition. It should prevent you writing all you know about the influences and stop you going through the period ruler by ruler. With this approach you are more likely to make comparisons across the whole period, resulting in a good deal of synthesis.

How to write the opening paragraph

Having planned your answer, you are in a position to write the crucial opening paragraph, in which you should set out your line of argument – establish your thesis – and briefly refer to the issues you are going to cover in the main body of the essay. This will help you to remain focused on the actual question. In establishing your thesis, it might be helpful to consider the following questions:

- What was the situation at the start of the period?
- What was the situation at the end of the period?
- Were there any parts of the period where there was considerable change or does the pattern remain the same throughout the period?

These questions will help you to remain focused on the key elements being tested in this unit: continuity and change.

The following is an example of a good opening paragraph to the question:

‘War was the main reason why the opponents of the tsars from 1855 to 1917 were more successful than those who opposed the communist regime from 1917 to 1964.’ How far do you agree?

Response

The opponents to the tsars were primarily more successful as the circumstances they found themselves in, especially during wars, were more conducive to concessions being made by rulers. With newly found freedoms opposition groups flourished. The Bolsheviks and workers, in particular, exploited adverse conditions created by the First World War to challenge and overthrow the tsar, the Provisional Government and the Constituent Assembly. The adverse effects of industrialisation were exploited in a similar way to enable promises to be made for a brighter future for all Russians. Once the population supported the notion of revolution the communists then proved to be very skilful and ruthless in ensuring that anyone who veered from the revolutionary path was severely dealt with. The Stalinist era saw the emergence of totalitarian rule and zero tolerance of any kind of dissent. During the rule of Khrushchev there was more tolerance of dissidents in an attempt to win back support from the West but there was still little threat to the communist regime. Thus, the success of opposition was dependent not just on conditions conducive to economic, social and political change created by war but on how those in authority chose to deal with such change.

Analysis of response

- The opening offers a clear view about the role of war as a cause and the period during which it was relatively important.
- It outlines some of the other factors that will be considered and offers a view as to their relative importance.
- It reaches a judgement as to the most important cause – it is this line of argument that should be carried through the rest of the essay.

The focus of this section has been on planning and writing a good opening paragraph. Use the information in this chapter to plan answers and write the opening paragraph to the questions below.

Essay questions

1 How far was there more change than continuity in the way Russia was ruled in the period from 1855 to 1964?
2 To what extent was Alexander III the most autocratic ruler of Russia in the period from 1855 to 1964?
3 Assess the view that the causes of opposition under the tsars were different from those under the communists in the period from 1855 to 1954.

Study skills: depth study interpretations question

How to plan the essay

The specification identifies the three topics from which the interpretations question will be drawn. In answering this question, you have to assess and evaluate the arguments in the passages by applying your own knowledge of the events to reach a supported judgement as to which is the stronger interpretation.

The question will require you to assess the strengths and limitations of the two interpretations of an issue related to one of the specified depth studies. You should be able to place the interpretation within the context of the wider historical debate on the key topic. However, you will not be required to know the names of individual historians associated with the debate or to have studied the specific books of any historians, and it may even be counterproductive to be aware of particular historians' views, as this may lead to your simply describing their view, rather than analysing the given interpretation.

How should the question be approached?

Consider the question and the two passages below on the performance of the Provisional Government. In answering the question, it might be helpful for you to think of using a four-paragraph structure:

- In the first paragraph explain the interpretations in the two passages and place them in the wider debate about the performance of the Provisional Government.
- In the second paragraph use your own knowledge of the performance of the Provisional Government to assess the validity of the view expressed in Interpretation A. What knowledge do you have of the Provisional Government that either supports or challenges the view of Passage A?

- Repeat the second point, but for Interpretation B – what knowledge do you have of the Provisional Government that either supports or challenges the view of Passage B?
- In the final paragraph, reach a supported and balanced judgement as to which passage you think is more convincing as an explanation of the successes and failures of the Provisional Government.

Evaluate the interpretations in both of the passages and explain which you think is more convincing as an explanation of the successes and failures of the Provisional Government. [30]

PASSAGE A

With successive reshuffles that gave moderate socialists more influence, the Provisional Government lasted more than seven months. This in itself was quite an achievement, for it had little power and faced enormous problems. The Soviet's Order No. 1 threatened to deprive the government of an effective army. The old police, by general consent, had been disbanded, but the militia which was to replace them never became an effective force. The Soviet, because it controlled the workers' organizations, could deny vital services if it so chose; thus the measures taken by the Provisional Government needed the acquiescence of the Soviet leaders if they were to be effective. The Provisional Government, co-opted from the members of a Dumas elected on a narrow franchise and consisting of gentlemen favouring a western-style parliamentary democracy, could hardly claim to be a popular government, even though it was popularly accepted for the time being.

(J.N. Westwood, Endurance and Endeavour: Russian History 1812–2001, *Oxford University Press, 2002, p. 224.)*

PASSAGE B

Although it had ruled Russia for over 300 years, the Romanov dynasty collapsed in just a few days. Its passing was mourned by few of its former subjects. There was no serious attempt to reinstate Nicholas II, not even by Nicholas himself! The whole country seemed to breathe a sigh of belief, and looked forward to a better future they believed Russia's new government would bring. There was, in the words of the historian Christopher Read, 'a nationwide honeymoon. For the only time in its history, the Russian Empire was united'. Kerensky, the sole socialist member of the new Provisional Government, wrote in his memoirs of the new atmosphere of hope in Russia. Despite the good intentions of Kerensky and his colleagues, it proved difficult to create a new order which satisfied all Russians. The new Provisional Government had to face those same problems, exacerbated by Russia's involvement in the war, that the tsarist government had failed to solve, as well as to meet the eager expectations of 160 million people. In fact the Provisional Government proved quite unable to deliver what was expected. It was increasingly seen as a product of the old regime and as unrepresentative of the Russian people. Perhaps it would have been impossible for any government to succeed in the circumstances it inherited. The government lasted only a few weeks before being replaced by another, and then another. The 'honeymoon' was soon over and its authority gradually slipped away.

(Peter Oxley, Russia 1855–1919: From Tsars to Commissars, *Oxford University Press, 2001, p. 91.)*

Using this model, a developed plan to the same question might look something like this:

1 The two passages agree that although the Provisional Government eventually collapsed it did have some success. Passage A stresses the problems faced by the government from the outset and makes the point that in the face of such challenges it did well to survive for as long as it did. Passage B emphasises the fact that the Provisional Government was successful in creating an atmosphere of hope especially given the difficulties it faced in dealing with the war and associated economic problems

2 Passage A notes that even though the Provisional Government was initially welcomed its popularity quickly waned when it was realised that it was essentially the old Duma in disguise. There is evidence to support Passage A: the composition of the Provisional Government was made up mainly of liberals (such as Guchkov) and conservatives (such as Prince Lvov), individuals who were unlikely to be in touch with the needs of the population

3 Passage B focuses on the context within which the Provisional Government was operating and the fact that it failed to deal with the challenges it faced. However, a challenge to Passage B is that it largely ignores the establishment of the Constituent Assembly which had been the main aim of the government.

4 Both passages acknowledge that the composition of the Provisional Government and the circumstances it found itself operating in were major reasons for why it struggled from the start. However, Passage A highlights the important role of the Soviets in diminishing the authority of the government whereas Passage B fails to mention this. On this basis, Passage A seems the more convincing interpretation.

How to write the opening paragraph

Now look at this possible opening paragraph to the question above.

Response

The two passages have much in common. They both stress that the make-up of the Provisional Government and the challenges it faced made it difficult for it to get off to a good start. Although there is some acknowledgement of a degree of success for the government, both Passages A and B make nothing of the fact that the Constituent Assembly was instituted in a relatively short period of time. Passage A is quite convincing as an interpretation about why the Provisional Government struggled. There is much evidence to support the argument that the strength of the Petrograd soviet made it almost impossible for the Provisional Government to achieve anything that did not meet the approval of workers. Although Passage B is quite persuasive in arguing that the context made it difficult for the government to succeed, it gives little credit to the strength of leadership and administration of workers' organisations.

Analysis of response

- A sound observation is made about how both passages stress the challenges faced by the Provisional Government.
- There is also comment about how both show similarity in omission of a key development (the establishment of the Constituent Assembly).
- The response highlights that Passage A stresses the strength of workers' organisations (via the soviets); much recent research supports this view.

CHAPTER 2

The impact of dictatorial regimes on the economy and society

This chapter analyses the effects of the tsarist and communist regimes on the Russian economy and society. The main focus is on the pace and extent of change. It also considers the relationship between policies and economic and social change. Were reforms put into place to improve working and living conditions or did government policies lead to deterioration in the quality of life for the Russian people? This chapter tackles these issues under the following headings:

★ The extent of and reasons for economic change

★ The extent of and reasons for social change

★ Changes to living and working conditions of rural and urban people

★ Limitations on personal, religious and political freedoms

It also considers the debates surrounding the three in-depth topics:

★ To what extent did reforms made by Alexander II improve the status of Russian peasants?

★ Why is the Provisional Government often viewed as one that was reluctant to carry out reforms?

★ To what extent were the economic and social reforms made by Khrushchev a failure?

Key dates

1861	Emancipation Edict		1917	Decree on Land; introduction of State Capitalism; formation of the Supreme Economic Council (SEC)
1864	School boards and *Zemstva* were appointed to run elementary schools		1917–21	War Communism
1882	Factory inspectorate established		1921	New Economic Policy and Gosplan established; famine
1883	Peasant Land Bank was set up		1927–8	Famine
1891	Imposition of the Medele'ev tariff; famine		1928–32	First Five-Year Plan
			1929	Start of mass collectivisation and dekulakisation
1892–3	Witte's 'Great Spurt'			
1897	Rouble placed on the gold standard; first census		1932–4	Famine
			1954	Virgin Land campaign

The extent of and reasons for economic change

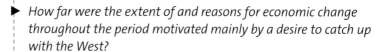

▶ *How far were the extent of and reasons for economic change throughout the period motivated mainly by a desire to catch up with the West?*

Industrialisation

Industrialisation is the term given to the manufacture of goods in workshops and factories. Throughout the period from 1855 to 1964, Russian leaders were keen to accelerate the industrialising process, although there was a consistent emphasis on heavy (iron, steel, coal and engineering) as opposed to light industry. This was connected to the main motive for industrialising, which was to 'catch up with the West'; the great Western powers, especially Britain, France and Germany (especially after 1871) had seemingly based their economic progress on the development of the iron and coal industries. Russian leaders sought to emulate the industrial revolutions that had occurred in these countries as they believed that this was the obvious way to increase and maintain world power status. However, the methods used to achieve this varied from leader to leader according to the circumstances they found themselves in.

Russian industrialisation proceeded through different phases due to differences in political leadership but also because of a changing world context. However, a common thread that affected development was the relationship with agricultural activity and the peculiar nature of Russian society. This needs to be borne in mind when analysing and evaluating the following stages of growth.

Alexander II and the proto-management of the economy

Before Alexander II (1855–81), there had been a reluctance to engage in industrialisation as this was associated with the rise of an urban proletariat, which, in other countries, had displayed a propensity to revolt. However, Alexander II recognised that the threat of peasant unrest was just as great and that this could be dealt with to an extent by moving rural workers off the land and into industry. Factories warranted a '**new work discipline**', from which evolved a way of controlling the activities of the bulk of the population.

The rule of Alexander II marked a more committed move towards state involvement in industry with the appointment of **Mikhail Reutern** as minister of finance (1862–78). He adopted a sensible approach that revolved around continued railway construction, the attraction of foreign technical expertise and the employment of foreign investment capital. As a result, modernisation and expansion occurred within the 'staples' (iron, coal, textiles) as well as the newer industries (such as oil). For example, Ludwig Loop from Manchester helped to

KEY TERM

New work discipline
Factory owners introduced strict rules and regulations that were required for employees to work safely and efficiently with machines. This was especially important for recruits from the countryside who were used to working according to 'nature's clock'.

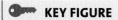

KEY FIGURE

Mikhail Reutern (1820–90)

Reutern was born in Poreche, Smolensk. After helping to implement the Emancipation Edict of 1861, Reutern went on to become minister of finance (1862–78). He was best known for introducing a unified state budget. He resigned in 1878 having struggled to get to grips with the financial implications of the Russo-Turkish war (1877–8).

develop the Russian textile industry and the Nobel brothers were responsible for the growth of the modern oil industry around Baku in the Caucasus.

Equally impressive was the work of the Welshman J.J. Hughes, who transformed iron and steel production at Ekaterinoslav. He was employed in 1871 by the Russian government as an expert in the manufacture of armour plate. By 1884, his New Russian Coal, Iron and Railmaking Company was the largest producer of pig iron in the whole of the empire. By the start of the twentieth century, Hughes and his associates were also responsible for about half of the steel production of Russia. This was accompanied by social investment; Hughes constructed a new town, Yuzovo, replete with English schools, public houses and, by 1904, 32,000 Welsh Russians! This was a clear demonstration of the value of employing foreign technical expertise to move Russia forwards and was a trend that continued throughout the period.

Railway construction

The use of foreign expertise was not entirely new and this was well illustrated in the field of railway construction. The first railway in Russia was completed in 1837 during the reign of Nicholas I and was the work of Gerstner, an Austrian. This was followed by the more ambitious St Petersburg to Moscow line, which opened in 1851. The project was stimulated by the success of the Manchester to Liverpool railway, although the final design and construction were mainly influenced by the American engineer George Washington Whistler. It was built to a very high technical standard and illustrated that where there was a will there was also a way for Russia to keep up with its Western counterparts.

Reutern built on this foundation so that there was a seven-fold increase in the amount of railway track opened, from 2194 miles in 1862 to 13,979 miles in 1878 (see Table 2.1, which places these figures in a wider context on page 80). Through the capacity of railways to '**break bulk**' at speed, this expansion gave a significant boost to the industrial sector. It was undoubtedly a major reason for the doubling of industrial output and an average annual growth rate of six per cent during Reutern's term of office. In fact, Clive Trebilcock (1982) has claimed that this was 'the country's first respectable performance in manufacturing' and so impressive that it allowed Russia to cushion itself against the European economic depression from 1873 to 1882.

Railway construction further illustrated the importance of attracting foreign investment capital. Reutern secured foreign monies and investment through a variety of novel approaches including the issuing of **government bonds**, **taxation exemptions** and **monopoly concessions**. Some of the money that went straight to the Russian government was used to protect railway projects against failure. Wherever possible, construction was placed in the hands of private contractors (as was the norm in the West) and, to secure their services, the government made guarantees to bail out projects if they encountered financial difficulties. This inevitably resulted in a certain amount of corruption

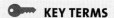

KEY TERMS

Break bulk The carriage of low-value, high-density goods in large quantities. That is, heavy, bulky goods such as coal and iron ore.

Government bonds A way of investing in the government by buying bonds (loan certificates) and cashing them in at a later date with interest.

Taxation exemptions Being allowed to pay lower tax in return for lending money to the government.

Monopoly concessions Being given the right to be the only seller of a particular product.

Russian workers in the nineteenth century working on the Trans-Siberian Railway.

Table 2.1 Growth of Russian railways from 1866 to 1956

Year	Mileage of track	Freight traffic (millions of tons)
1866	2,194	3
1878	13,979	Statistics unavailable
1883	14,700	24
1891	17,264	Statistics unavailable
1901	31,125	Statistics unavailable
1903	36,400	76
1913	43,900	158
1956	74,600	1371

 **KEY FIGURE**

Nikolay Bunge (1823–95)

Before becoming minister of finance, Bunge had worked as professor of economics at Kiev University. He also had experience of local administration and was considered to hold liberal political views.

(for example, financial help was given to certain companies when it was not really needed) as well as an expensive transport system. Due to the very high costs of construction and operation, about 94 per cent of railway lines were in private hands by 1880.

According to Trebilcock (1982), Reutern created the 'first (proto-) state managed exercise in industrial advance' but, as with other economic ministers, his efforts were cut short by the coming of war (Russo-Turkish War 1877–8). Nevertheless, he paved the way for others to follow, especially Sergei Witte.

Reforms after the death of Alexander II

After Reutern's demise and the assassination of Alexander II in 1881, further economic reforms were enacted by the new finance minister, **Nikolay Bunge**

(1882–6). These included fiscal amendments (the abolition of Salt Tax in 1881, and in 1886 the Poll Tax, based on the number of people in a household), the creation in 1883 of a **Peasant Land Bank** and a move towards greater state ownership of the railways. The latter started a process that eventually led to 69 per cent of the system being under public control by 1911. This more liberal approach did not last long as Alexander III blamed Bunge for a dramatic fall in the value of the rouble in the mid-1880s and replaced him with **Ivan Vyshnegradskii** (1887–92). This man was more of a hardliner but managed to balance the government budget while also making a surplus of income. He achieved this through more efficient utilisation of income from taxes, railways, crown properties, the state bank and treasury. More significant was the revenue raised through the **Medele'ev tariff of 1891** and income gained by exporting large amounts of grain even when there was the prospect of a domestic shortage and starvation. The 1891 famine was seen partly as a result of Vyshnegradskii's policies, and despite his other achievements, he was forced to give way to Count Witte (1893–1903).

The 'Great Spurt'

The appointment of Witte marked a distinct break from the past. Previous ministers had attempted to stimulate Russian industrialisation but in relative terms their achievements were modest. By 1893, Russian economic activity still revolved predominantly around agricultural production. Witte was the first one to show total commitment to industrialisation in an attempt both to compete with other industrialised nations and to improve Russian military capability. This was to be achieved mainly at the expense of agriculture (part of the so-called 'substitution' effect, with more investment being made in industry than agriculture), which caused suspicion and consternation among sections of the Russian elite. Witte claimed that 'all thinking Russia was against me', which emphasises how radical he thought his approach was. The main strands of his plan were as follows:

- Witte went back to the idea of taking out foreign loans, raising taxes and interest rates to boost available capital for investment in industry.
- Witte also resurrected Reutern's idea of encouraging foreign experts to come to Russia.
- A major development was the placement, in 1897, of the rouble on the **gold standard**. The idea behind this was to give potential investors confidence in the value of the Russian currency.
- Witte insisted that most investment went on heavy industry and the railways, as this was what had made Britain, France and Germany great economic powers and had already reaped some dividends for Russia.
- Further industrialisation was to be planned and managed mainly by the state, with a move away from private enterprise.

KEY TERMS

Peasant Land Bank A bank especially set up by the government to allow peasants to borrow money at relatively cheap rates to allow the purchase of land.

Medele'ev tariff of 1891 Named after Dimitry Medele'ev, who put together a 700-page book of tariffs (taxes) that should be applied to all imports of goods.

Gold standard The fixing of a country's currency to a specific quantity (and therefore value) of gold.

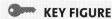

KEY FIGURE

Ivan Vyshnegradskii (1831–95)

The son of a priest. He was educated at a church seminary before becoming a professor at the St Petersburg Technological Institute. Before entering the Ministry of Finance he gained useful experience of the private business sector by acting as director of the South-Western Railway Company.

The effect of this was a so-called 'Great Spurt' in economic and industrial activity, which resulted in the following:

- Coal production doubled and that of iron and steel increased seven-fold.
- A stimulus was provided to the development of more specialist and 'new' technologies in the oil and chemical industries.
- The total amount of railway track opened rose from 17,264 miles in 1891 to 31,125 miles in 1901. Much of this was facilitated by the stupendous growth in capital from abroad, which increased on average by 120 per cent every year from 1893 to 1898.
- Income earned from industry shot up from 42 million roubles in 1893 to 161 million roubles by 1897.

There was also an indication that Russia had at last started to catch up with other industrialised nations; by 1900, for example, France had been ousted into fourth place in world iron production. All of this, according to Trebilcock (1982), led to an annual average rate of increase in industrial production of 7.5 per cent, 'far exceeding Russian achievement for any comparable period before 1914 and establishing one of the most impressive performances in late nineteenth-century Europe'.

Criticisms of Witte's policies

However, some historians have argued that Witte's achievements have been exaggerated. First, Witte focused on the development of heavy industry and neglected other parts of the industrial sector such as engineering and textiles. This was short-sighted, as to an extent the demand for metals (and hence coal) came from other industries such as cotton textiles. Second, the reliance on foreign capital has been criticised as being dangerous as loans could be recalled at short notice and reliance on foreign technological expertise stunted the emergence of home-grown talent. Third, although the railway system expanded considerably it was still very costly and not as impressive as that which existed in other parts of Europe. By 1914, for instance, Russia had eleven times fewer miles of track than Germany. Most railway investment was made in the Trans-Siberian line started in 1892 (but never fully completed). Although this greatly aided the industrial and agricultural expansion of Siberia, it was rushed and poorly constructed. Finally, Witte paid scant attention to agriculture, which caused rural discontent and distrust from other members of the government. This was one of the key reasons for his downfall in 1903.

Some believe that Witte's industrial programme was a dress rehearsal for Stalin's industrialisation of the 1930s. There are similarities but there was no 'natural' progression from one to the other. The First World War and the Russian revolutions ensured further twists in the move to greater industrialisation.

The First World War and industrialisation

In August 1903, Witte was dismissed from his post. Nicholas II had developed an **expansionist foreign policy**, which Witte opposed mainly on the grounds of cost. This also coincided with a dip in the economy. However, Witte's fall in favour was short lived. After a disastrous war against Japan (1904–5) and the social unrest of 1905, Witte was appointed prime minister. Pyotr Stolypin was put in place as minister of finance and their joint efforts resulted in a revival of the economy. From 1909 to 1913, industrial output increased on average by seven per cent a year and **gross national product (GNP)** by 3.5 per cent a year.

Some historians have reflected on this economic performance after 1905 and argued, counter-factually, that without the First World War Russia would have caught up rapidly with the West. Other evidence suggests this would not have been the case. By 1913, the overall production levels in particular industries still lagged considerably behind those of competitors. For example, Russian coal production at the start of the war was ten per cent of that produced by Britain and **GNP per capita** was only twenty per cent of that found in Britain. Although production had increased in many industries, productivity had not. The factories that were in operation employed vast amounts of labour to compensate for a lack of investment in modern technology and equipment. Despite this, the vast numbers of industrial workers were employed in small-scale, handicraft-based enterprise; this was not the sign of a developing economy. Many of the gains that appeared to be made on behalf of the Russian people were masked by a substantial increase in the size of the population. Given the lack of attention paid to agriculture, the chances of further periods of starvation were high.

The fact that the Russian economy fell apart during the First World War adds further weight to the argument that Witte's reforms had only a short-term positive effect. Despite having the largest stock of gold reserves in Europe in 1914, this was still not enough to pay for the armaments required to fight a successful war. Industry struggled to meet the demands of the armed forces and the railway system was inefficient. More money was borrowed from abroad, taxes were increased and the gold standard was abandoned. This led to rampant inflation. The price of fuel and food quadrupled in the first two years of the conflict and wages failed to keep up. The First World War was yet another disastrous war for Russia but this time with far more dramatic consequences. By the end of 1917, the Romanov dynasty had ended and was replaced by Bolshevik rule; this marked a major turning point in the way the Russian economy was to be managed.

War Communism and the New Economic Policy (NEP)

By November 1917, Lenin had started to deal with the exigencies of war by introducing State Capitalism. This involved the state taking complete control of the economy until it could be 'safely' handed over to the proletariat. This was not

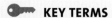

KEY TERMS

Expansionist foreign policy Foreign policy that involved the acquisition of territory from other countries (or sometimes expanding influence over such territory).

Gross national product (GNP) The total value of all the goods and services produced in a country.

GNP per capita Gross national product per head of the population. This is often used as a measure of living standards.

part of some grand plan; it was simply a reaction to the crisis situation that the Bolsheviks found themselves in. Nevertheless, it still fitted with (or was made to fit) Bolshevik ideology. State Capitalism was introduced by way of the following:

- November 1917 Decree on Land. This involved the division of private landholdings that were then handed over to peasants.
- November 1918 Decree on Workers' Control. Workers' Committees were given 'extra' powers to run factories.
- December 1917 Formation of the Supreme Economic Council (SEC). The SEC was formed to manage key industries that were **nationalised** by the Bolsheviks. This did not prevent 'local' nationalisation occurring via soviets (workers' councils). The nationalisation process was therefore tightened by two further decrees: one in the summer of 1918 and the other in the spring of 1919. These resulted in the nationalisation of all enterprises employing more than ten workers and without compensation. The effect was to create over 30,000 nationalised economic entities by 1920, ranging from windmills to huge steel plants. The SEC soon struggled to cope with the management of this (and was soon made subservient to the more powerful Council of Labour and Defence, personally chaired by Lenin).

Lenin obviously believed that centralised control of this nature was essential if Russia was to survive the effects of war. However, there was much opposition to it both within and outside the party, which was further fuelled by the signing of the Treaty of Brest-Litovsk in March 1918. Russia struck a peace deal with Germany but only after agreeing to hand over valuable territory (see page 32). For Lenin, this was an essential move as it shortened a conflict that was likely to end in total ruination of the economy. He also knew that it was likely to hasten the move towards civil war and the creation of further economic problems.

The Civil War (1917–21) pretty much nullified any positive impact that State Capitalism may have had. Industrial output in a number of sectors fell dramatically. For example, the production of coal fell from 29 million tons in 1913 to 8.9 million tons in 1921. Inflation had got so out of hand that the rouble by October 1920 was worth only one per cent of its value in 1917. This resulted in the virtual abandonment of the currency so that, for example, 90 per cent of all wages paid to workers by the start of 1921 were '**in kind**'. Some services such as tram rides were free as it was impossible to pay for them. Such a drastic situation clearly required a change of approach.

War Communism

During the Civil War, Lenin used State Capitalism alongside grain requisitioning to create what was labelled War Communism. The key features of War Communism were as follows:

- Nationalisation (state control) of larger enterprises and a state monopoly of markets for goods and services. The nationalisation of industry and state

KEY TERMS

Nationalisation The state control of industry and commerce by taking ownership of the means of production, distribution and exchange of goods and services.

In kind Payment other than by using money, such as the exchange of goods and services.

monopoly of markets caused unrest as it meant that individuals lost the freedom to produce and sell goods at a time, price and place that suited them. They lost all ownership and hence control over the means of production, distribution and exchange.

- Partial militarisation of labour. The militarisation of labour was also disliked as people were forced to work solely to meet the needs of the war.
- Forced requisitioning (taking) of agricultural produce. Grain requisitioning was the most hated policy as it involved taking away surpluses of food and grain, which meant a disincentive to grow more than was actually needed by an individual household. Often, the majority of food would be taken from a household to feed the army and urban workers. The overall result was starvation in rural areas.

By 1921, workers, peasants and party members were clamouring for something 'new' to resolve the hardships caused by both the First World War and the Civil War. It is debatable as to how far Lenin viewed War Communism as a short-term emergency measure but he was quick to change tack and replaced it with his New Economic Policy (NEP).

New Economic Policy (NEP)

The key features of the NEP were as follows:

- Denationalisation of small-scale enterprise and a return to private ownership. This was to allow small workshops to flourish to produce consumer items such as clothes and shoes.
- The continuation of state control of heavy industry but with the use of trusts. These organisations were to pay strict attention to accounting procedures and were responsible for the purchase of raw materials and equipment and the payment of wages.
- Rejuvenation of trade through the removal of restrictions on the private sales of goods and services. Shops flourished, rationing was ended and a new, revalued rouble was introduced.
- A return to the encouragement of foreign trade, investment and the import of foreign expertise.
- An end to grain requisitioning and a return to peasants being allowed to sell surpluses in local markets.

The short-term impact was impressive. Industrial output increased rapidly and this was reflected in the greater amount of food and consumer goods found in shops and markets (see Table 2.2, page 86). This was linked to the emergence of a new breed of entrepreneur, the **Nepman**. By 1923, Nepmen were responsible for over 60 per cent of retail trade but they had already started to annoy people with their underhand wheeling and dealing. Another cause for concern by that time was the emergence of what Trotsky called the 'scissors crisis'. The supply of food increased at a rate that far exceeded domestic demand, resulting in a swift fall in prices. In comparison, the supply of manufactured goods increased

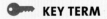 **KEY TERM**

Nepman The 'new' type of businessman that emerged as a result of the NEP.

Table 2.2 Russian agricultural and industrial production 1921–6

Output	1921	1922	1923	1924	1925	1926
Grain harvest (millions of tonnes)	37.6	50.3	56.6	51.4	72.5	76.8
Sown area (millions of hectares)	90.3	77.7	91.7	98.1	104.3	110.3
Industrial (factory) production (millions of roubles at 1926–7 value)	2,004	2,619	4,005	4,660	7,739	11,083
Coal (millions of tonnes)	8.9	9.5	13.7	16.1	18.1	27.6
Electricity (million of kilowatt-hours)	1,945	775	1,146	1,562	2,925	3,508
Pig iron (thousands of tonnes)	116	188	309	755	1,535	2,441
Steel (thousands of tonnes)	183	392	709	1,140	2,135	3,141
Cotton fabrics (millions of metres)	105	349	691	963	1,688	2,286
Rail freight carried (millions of tonnes)	39.4	39.9	58.0	67.5	83.4	–*

*Data not available.

at a much slower pace, which left prices relatively high. Peasants were therefore reluctant to sell surpluses at low prices but the frustration was that industrialists needed them to do this so that they could afford to buy their products. As the historian J.N. Westwood (2002) has pointed out, this was 'less serious than it seemed at the time' as it was relatively short lived. The Bolshevik government quickly found a way of resolving the problem.

As with War Communism, the NEP was promoted by the Politburo as 'a temporary deviation, a tactical retreat'. Despite this, debate raged over the extent to which the NEP was a betrayal of the October Revolution and communist ideals. This was partially resolved with a demand for political unity after the fright of the 1921 Kronstadt rising (see page 43). With the death of Lenin, though, in 1924, and the ensuing power struggle, the divisions within government widened and centred on the effectiveness of the NEP. Those in favour of continuation were known as the Rightists (right opposition) and those who opposed were called the Leftists (left opposition). During this time Stalin remained fairly ambivalent about the NEP but as the longer term effects of it were felt he became a major critic. This coincided with him taking leadership in 1929, and it was not long before he abandoned the NEP and created the Great Turn.

Stalin, Khrushchev and the Five-Year Plans

There were two general aims that underpinned Stalinist economic policy. One was to launch a war against Russia's tsarist past. Stalin believed that Russia had failed to keep up with the West due to the incompetence of the tsarist regimes but more generally because the tsars were enemies of the workers. Only with a system that allowed more worker autonomy and that encouraged workers to believe that they were the key to economic success, would Russia become a major industrial force. The second aim was to prepare for potential conflict with Russia's capitalist enemies. The development of heavy industry was the key to expansion and modernisation of the armed forces, which was essential to the defence of Russia. These aims were also linked to the wish for **economic autarky**.

Stalin believed that the only way his aims could be achieved was by abandoning the NEP completely and replacing it with a policy that revolved around strict state control and centralised planning. Industrialisation was to be stimulated through the setting of production targets. These targets were to be achieved over a series of five-year periods. From 1929 to 1964, there were seven Five-Year Plans. Ironically, this policy involved very little strategic planning in the modern sense. Targets were set by the ruling elite and were often based on very flimsy research. Managers at local level were ordered to achieve them and were in constant fear of failing.

In theory, there was a structure to the target setting and planning process. It resembled the following:

- Initial targets were stipulated by key officials in the party. **Gosplan** (the State Planning Commission) was given the task of researching and calculating figures needed for target setting for individual industries.
- Targets and other appropriate information were then passed on to industrial commissariats to frame a plan of some sort for clearly defined areas of economic activity. Initially, there were four commissariats (heavy industry, which was the most important, light industry, timber and food). By the beginning of the third Five-Year Plan, there were twenty of these bodies.
- The 'plans' were then passed on to regional managers/directors to implement. In reality, the plans were little more than very detailed instructions about what had to be achieved. There was very little guidance on how targets were to be arrived at and on the availability of resources needed to support the planning process.

The first plan was officially introduced in spring 1929 at the Sixteenth Party Congress. As it was outlined then, it rather bizarrely covered the period from October 1928 to September 1933. In practice, the first plan, as with the second, did not run its full course and came to an end in December 1932. This was due to the government exaggerating achievement, claiming that the plans were so successful, in hindsight, that targets had been met well ahead of schedule. The

KEY TERMS

Economic autarky When a country can provide all of the resources it needs without having to trade.

Gosplan A group originally set up in 1921 to plan for industrialisation and economic growth.

reality was that workers had struggled to meet what were totally unrealistic targets, especially after Stalin audaciously decided to revise them upwards towards the end of each plan. Nevertheless, centralised planning was the main characteristic of industrialisation until the end of the period. A summary of what was achieved can be seen in Table 2.3.

Table 2.3 Achievements of the Five-Year Plans 1928–60

Product	1928	1940	1945	1960
Electricity (millions of kilowatt-hours)	5.0	48.3	43.3	292
Oil (millions of tonnes)	11.6	31.1	19.4	148
Coal (millions of tonnes)	35.5	166	150	510
Gas (millions of cubic metres)	0.3	3.4	3.4	47.2
Steel (millions of tonnes)	4.3	18.3	12.3	65.3
Tractors (thousands)	1.3	31.6	7.7	238
Plastics and synthetics (thousands of tonnes)	–	10.9	21.3	312
Clocks and watches (millions)	0.9	2.8	0.3	26
Cement (millions of tonnes)	1.8	5.7	1.8	46

The statistics in Table 2.3 need to be treated with some caution. They are based partly on 'official records' but also on adjustments made by historians to compensate for inaccuracy. Under the first two plans, managers quite obviously submitted false claims about production levels, as they feared the possible consequences of not achieving the targets that they were set. Fabrication of production levels backfired on the managers when Stalin became so impressed with achievement that he revised the targets. However, it is understandable why they did this given the climate of fear that had been manufactured. Nevertheless, the statistical 'evidence' suggests that each plan had a fair amount of success. Interestingly, the greatest achievement would appear to be during the post-war period. Much of this was down to ordinary Russian people working extraordinarily hard to rebuild their country, rather than to effective planning. Khrushchev's continuation of centralised planning resulted in further economic growth and more diversification in what was produced. But, his first plan was abandoned and his second correlated with a slowdown in the rate of growth, which makes Khrushchev's achievements less impressive than Stalin's.

All of the plans had strengths as well as limitations, as outlined in Table 2.4.

Agriculture

Agriculture remained an important industry in its own right throughout the period. The majority of the population continued to be employed in agricultural work despite moves to industrialise Russia. The tsars and the communists had two things in common when it came to agricultural policy making.

Table 2.4 Successes and limitations of the Five-Year Plans 1928–65

Plan	Successes	Limitations
First: 1928–32	There were significant increases in the output of heavy industry The engineering industry developed considerably, especially with respect to the production of machine tools and turbines New specialised industrial centres emerged, for example, Magnitogorsk in the Urals. Agriculture was stimulated as tractor works expanded	Consumer industries (those producing goods and services for direct consumption by the population) were neglected, causing discontent among certain sectors of society Small specialist workshops disappeared. A shortage of skilled workers was apparent. This was partly due to show trials and purges. Although production levels rose, targets were not met. There was quite a dramatic shortfall in some industries, such as chemicals
Second: 1933–7	The electricity industry took off and heavy industry built on the base laid by the first plan. Over 4500 new enterprises were started. Engineering became self-sufficient and no longer relied on imports of specialist equipment. Something resembling a genuine transport and communications network was put in place. The chemical industry made up for the lack of progress during the first plan. Certain metals were mined for the first time – tin, zinc and copper. Specialised training schemes for workers were implemented. Targets were scaled down and a more rational approach to planning was adopted. The commissariats were better organised and more effective	Consumer industries continued to decline although some flourished, for example, footwear, meat packaging and ice-cream. The oil industry was very slow to expand compared with Western counterparts
Third: 1938–41	Production and productivity in heavy industry continued to be impressive although regional variations became more apparent. There was a notable improvement in the quantity and quality of armaments produced	Russia's entry into the war (1941) led to a diversion of resources to fuel the war effort. There was a shortage of raw materials. There was generally a slowdown in the pace of progress. Some historians have attributed this to the purges as well as the war. By the end of the third Five-Year Plan there were many features of a lack of planning: shortages, bottlenecks and a lack of 'expert' workers
Fourth: 1946–50	This seemed to be linked to a rapid recovery of the economy. Pre-war production levels were reached within three years	The Russian people were placed under extreme pressure to help Russia get back on its feet
Fifth: 1951–5	This was a period of fairly rapid growth, especially with respect to agricultural equipment	Too many resources were devoted to 'projects' that had little positive economic benefit, for example, hydroelectric schemes
Sixth: 1956–60	There was a shift from the old staples, for example, textiles, to modern industries, for example, plastics and synthetics. Consumer goods became more prevalent	Over-optimistic targets were set, resulting in the plan being abandoned after two years
Seventh: 1961–5	There was substantial increase overall in production of a range of goods. More realistic targets were set	There were signs that the rate of growth in production had slowed down, especially when compared with rivals such as the USA

First, agriculture was always seen as subservient to the needs of industry. Thus, government policies focused on reforms that increased food production and productivity to provide sustenance for the expanding urban proletariat. Second, those who worked on the land were treated as second-class citizens. The poor treatment of peasants reflected the view that industry had to come first so that Russia could catch up and compete with the West.

Land ownership

The issue of peasant land ownership was one that all Russian rulers failed to deal with effectively. Under the tsars, land redistribution policies never met the rising expectations of the peasants. Under the communists, all land was appropriated and it was managed by the state. However, this simply fuelled resentment, especially as it was evident that the ruling elite and hangers-on kept aside a fair amount of land for personal use.

The emancipation of the serfs 1861

The Emancipation Edict of 1861 laid a platform for all further agricultural reform. Despite appearing to be a progressive measure that brought Russia in line with the West, it proved to be very controversial both at the time and since (see the Depth study on Alexander II, pages 118–19, for details of the debate). The fact that by 1917 peasant access to land, in terms of quality and quantity, was still a burning issue suggests that the reform of 1861 was not a great success.

Alexander III and agriculture

In 1891, during the reign of Alexander III, there was a disastrous famine. The tsar blamed this partly on poor farming techniques deployed by peasants. To encourage the spread of good practice a ministry of agriculture was established shortly after the famine. However, as the historian J.N. Westwood (2002) has pointed out, officials also claimed that rural troubles were due to the character of peasants. They were considered to be generally 'resentful, indolent, disrespectful, unruly and intoxicated'. The tsar's solution to this problem was to employ a special kind of local official, the land captain, to keep discipline in rural areas.

The Stolypin reform

Rural unrest peaked during the years 1905–7. Nicholas II responded by instructing Stolypin, appointed as prime minister in 1906, to revamp government policy over land distribution. Stolypin's aim was to use land redistribution to build and strengthen the class of more able, educated and 'best' peasants. The hope was that they would then act as a role model for other peasants to follow as well as act as a force against the *mir*. To this end, the Stolypin reform (or 'wager on the strong' as it was sometimes called) involved the following:

- Unused or poorly utilised land was made available to the Peasant Land Bank (established in 1883). Forward-looking peasants could then buy the land from the bank on favourable terms.
- Peasants who were still farming strips (small plots spread over two to three fields) due to the strength of the *mir* were given the right to **consolidate** their land into smallholdings (small farm units). Hereditary household plots were not affected by this and it was also stipulated that land could not be immediately sold on to non-peasants. These provisos were designed to ensure that the mainstay of the Russian rural economy became the small peasant farm run independently by peasants.

In reality, the plan backfired due to the following reasons:

- The process led to an expansion in the numbers joining the wealthier class of peasants who in theory would be more loyal to the tsar. However, they were not totally satisfied with the stipulations of the Stolypin reform as they believed that the best land was still inaccessible to peasants.
- By 1914, about 2 million peasants had left the village communes, leaving some regions very short of rural labour. The First World War accelerated this trend. Such an exodus added to the challenge of keeping supplies of food going to the growing urban population.

The Decree on Land

The Provisional Government did little to resolve land issues. During the July Days, peasants seized land by force. The Bolsheviks exploited this trend by promising 'Peace, Bread and Land'. By October 1917, the Bolsheviks had proclaimed that they were the party representing peasant and worker interests. Once they seized power they immediately issued their Decree on Land, which aimed to ensure that the majority of peasants were kept onside. However, this did not stop the communists treating the peasants as an underclass in the same way that the tsars had done. War Communism (see pages 84–5) was the prime example of the contempt shown for peasants, especially with the imposition of grain requisitioning.

War Communism and the *kulaks*

A major feature of War Communism was the forceful taking of grain from peasants who had supposedly hoarded surpluses. By this time, Lenin had identified three types of peasant: the poor, the middling and the *kulak*. The *kulak* were blamed for food shortages and were punished by having not only food but also seed corn and personal property confiscated. Committees of the village poor were set up with the sole aim of denouncing *kulaks* and, with the help of the *Cheka*, were used to 'unleash a class war'. In fact, although Lenin had changed his view about the importance of the peasants to the revolution, the latter were still viewed with disdain by the Bolsheviks. The consensus was that they were ignorant, backward and superstitious and worked against the interests

KEY TERM

Consolidation The joining together of resources. In this context, smallholdings were granted that were equivalent to the area of the strips farmed under the old way of farming.

of the proletariat. It was not surprising, therefore, that they became scapegoats for some of the economic problems experienced by the Bolsheviks in the years immediately following the revolution.

The NEP and the *kulaks*

When the NEP replaced War Communism, the attitude towards the *kulaks* changed. They started to be viewed as the 'more cultured and educated peasants'. Wealthier peasants seemed to grow in number and were more easily identifiable through official definition. In 1925, a *kulak* was a peasant who owned at least three cows (in 1928, the figure was increased to six). Despite being tolerated in general, *kulaks* were still treated more severely than other rural folk. Under the tsars, *kulaks* stood out and were disliked for being money-lenders. With the Bolsheviks it was never really clear as to who actually was a *kulak* as opposed to an ordinary peasant. However, Bolshevik leaders associated grain hoarding and therefore shortages with the *kulaks*. Needless to say, wealthier, more productive peasants were persecuted and blamed for the shortcomings of Bolshevik agricultural policy.

Kulaks suffered from higher taxes, were disenfranchised and their children were refused entry to state schools. But within the peasant class the *kulaks* were respected for being not being afraid to voice concerns about peasant working and living conditions. Here lies the real reason as to why the authorities were so intent on victimising the *kulaks*.

Collectivisation

Collectivisation refers to the process of bringing a number of small farm units together to form bigger farms. The idea was that peasants would then collaborate to produce as much food as possible to feed themselves and the growing urban proletariat. Farms would be managed so that land was utilised in the optimum way to ensure that nobody starved. This system was based on the belief that shortages were due mainly to surpluses being hoarded until they could be sold in markets at the highest possible prices. Such a practice was allowed under the NEP but Stalin came to view it as bourgeois and anti-revolutionary.

From the beginning, the Bolsheviks wanted to create collective farms but stalled as a result of resistance from peasants. Lenin urged a gradual approach to collectivisation to be taken, which would result in the creation of 'civilised cooperatives'. This was fine except that many considered it unacceptable during a food crisis. Thus, just before Stalin emerged as leader of Russia, only about three per cent of peasant farmers were working on a collective.

Mass collectivisation

The famine of 1927–8 prompted Stalin to push for mass collectivisation. He was more generally motivated by the wish to create 'socialism in the countryside'. In turn, this involved getting rid of the NEP, eradicating the so-called wealthier class of peasants (the *kulaks*) and marginalising 'rightists' who supported a more commercially based agricultural policy.

Dekulakisation

Under Stalin, collectivisation went hand in hand with dekulakisation. The treatment of *kulaks* during this period followed a similar pattern throughout Russia. Wealthier peasants were 'visited' by **Komsomols** and **plenipotentiaries**. *Kulak* houses would then be stripped bare in an attempt to locate hidden wealth. Clothing, food, fuel, furniture and other personal belongings were confiscated and sold or given away to other villagers. In anticipation, *kulaks* often sold their goods, slaughtered animals and even abandoned their homes to flee to the towns. If caught by the authorities, their fate depended on how they were categorised:

 **KEY TERMS**

Komsomols Members of the youth organisation known as the Young Communist League.

Plenipotentiaries Officials who had 'total' power at a local level.

- 'Fortunate' *kulaks* were those who were reallocated land often of a very poor quality. They were then given unrealistic food production targets, which they invariably failed to meet. The result was that they were deported to work camps in inhospitable places such as Siberia.
- Standard *kulaks* were simply robbed and sent straight to concentration camps, where they tended to die fairly quickly.
- Malicious, ideological or 'sub'-*kulaks* (*zlostnye*) were those who actively opposed collectivisation. They either were transported immediately, again to concentration camps, or were more likely to be shot.

It is estimated that from the beginning of 1928 to the end of 1930, between 1 million and 3 million *kulak* families (6–18 million people) were deported. On top of this, about 30,000 *kulaks* were shot. In this sense, Stalin achieved his aim to 'liquidate the *kulaks*' as a class. However, in many ways *kulaks* were a myth. The term was invented to provide an excuse to blame certain people for the failings of communist agricultural policies. Up to the end of the period there were always some peasant farmers who seemed to be more productive than others, simply because they were good at farming. To classify them as an elite group within the peasant class was very misleading.

Stalin's collectivisation policy got underway in November 1929. Together with dekulakisation, Stalinists saw this as a 'class war in the countryside' that was to be carried out quickly and systematically. Collectivisation was actually meant to be voluntary but, in reality, it usually occurred as follows:

- The principles of collectivisation were explained to villagers at special meetings organised by plenipotentiaries.

- A mixture of poorer peasants, Komsomols and politically aware workers were recruited to seek out wealthier peasants and denounce them as *kulaks*. This helped to create a sense of fear within a community, which subsequently made it much easier to encourage others to sign up to the collective programme. Other incentives were offered such as the prospect of working with a new tractor and combine harvester.
- The result was the formation of either **Kolkhozy** ('pure' collectives) or **Sovkhozy** (state collectives).

<table>
<tr><td>

KEY TERMS

Kolkhozy A farm owned and partly organised by the state but worked on by peasant farmers not directly employed by the state. Members could own a house, a small plot of land and a few animals.

Sovkhozy Farms owned by the state and worked on by state employees.

</td></tr>
</table>

By March 1930, Stalin claimed that 58 per cent of all households had been collectivised, which was a gross exaggeration. Nevertheless, 'mass collectivisation' had a dramatic effect, as witnessed by widespread opposition from peasants and local officials. Such resistance often took the form of direct action, as was the case at Bryansk-Oblast where peasants actually drove away a party of Komsomols who were insistent on commandeering the church bells. Resistance came in other forms such as migration. In Kazakhstan, collectivisation virtually destroyed the nomadic way of life. The peasants there reacted by moving out of the region into China. The population of Kazakhstan fell by 75 per cent within a few years.

Stalin blamed this kind of scenario on regional officials who, he argued, had become 'intoxicated with success'. By the end of March 1930, the pace of collectivisation slackened and Stalin coupled this with a proclamation allowing peasants to quit collectives they had recently signed up to. The inevitable mass exodus followed, only to be quickly clamped down on by renewed pressure to collectivise by the end of the year.

Renewed collectivisation

The move back towards intensive collectivisation resulted in about 50 per cent of all peasants once again being brought together in *Kolkhozy*. By the end of 1937, the figure had increased to 93 per cent. In contrast to the first wave of collectives, peasants were now allowed to keep small plots of land. Also, blocks of 40 farms were organised through motor-tractor stations (MTS). As the title suggests, these were originally organisations through which tractors and other heavy equipment could be loaned to peasants. An MTS would be responsible for distributing seed, collecting grain, establishing levels of payment for produce and deciding on what produce farmers could keep for their own consumption.

The famine of 1932–4 disrupted the development of collectivisation (see page 109). Partly as a result of this, a special charter was issued in 1935 to improve payments to farmers in the *Kolkhozy* and to give owners of small plots more legal security. Interestingly, the small plots proved more productive than the collective farms, especially when it came to supplying dairy goods.

By 1941, 98 per cent of all peasant households worked on collectives. Despite an improvement in conditions on collective farms, they were still disliked by peasants.

There were a number of reasons for resistance:

- The traditional way of organising farming was valued by peasants. The abolition of the *mir* in 1930 was considered a major blow to village autonomy.
- Collectives deprived peasants of the right to make a little extra income, which would keep them just above subsistence level. They also placed restrictions on the variety of crops that could be grown and other rural activities that had previously been tolerated and enjoyed.
- The 1932–4 famine suggested that many that collectives were likely to contribute to food shortages rather than help to relieve them. Many believed that as requisitioning (taking grain from peasants by force) was part of the collectivisation policy, the famine was largely 'man made'.

Khrushchev's agricultural policies

Khrushchev showed a great interest in agriculture and professed to be something of an expert on all aspects of farming. One area Khrushchev focused on for improvement was the organisation of agricultural production. More emphasis was placed on increasing production through state farms. This was partly at the expense of smaller collective farms, many of which were merged. Other measures included the change in the role of the Ministry of Agriculture from being involved in planning and implementing policy to that of an advisory body and the abolition of MTS. However, the historian Geoffrey Hosking (2002) is probably correct in stating that Khrushchev 'never fully got to grips with the authoritarian and bureaucratic structure of agricultural administration, which offered producers few incentives to improve either output or productivity'.

The question of providing more incentives was addressed through raising the prices for state procurements (amounts of food taken directly by the state from farmers), reducing the actual amounts to be procured, reducing taxes placed on peasants and increasing the provision of electricity to more isolated rural areas. Some success was achieved, although increases in the price of food angered urban dwellers. It was unfortunate that Khrushchev's main drive to increase the incentive to raise production preceded the disaster years of 1962 and 1963; bad weather resulted in a terrible harvest. Riots broke out in the countryside but more seriously in towns. The most notable incident was at the Budyenni Locomotive Works in Novocherkassk, where the KGB ended up killing 23 protesters.

Virgin Land campaign

From the start of his rule, Khrushchev displayed a keenness to increase quickly the amounts of cereals produced. To this end, in 1954, he introduced the Virgin Land campaign. The aim of this was to increase the amount of land to be cultivated. This was not new; Stolypin had introduced the idea but dekulakisation had put a halt to the process. The results were as follows:

- In 1950, 96 million acres of land were given over to the production of wheat. By 1964, this had increased to 165 million acres.
- Urban dwellers started to feel that their food requirements were at last being adequately met.
- However, the approach to using the 'virgin soil' was flawed. The land was overused with little attention paid to crop rotation. The effect was a reduction in soil fertility. Also, little was done to counter soil erosion, a result of the virgin soil regions being arid, close to the Central Asian desert and prone to wind storms. Generally, Khrushchev wanted his policies to be implemented speedily and, as a result, he cut corners. In the long term, productivity and production slowed, the first major indication of which came in 1963. The disastrous harvest of 1963 (due mainly to drought) saw grain production fall to 107 million tons compared with 140 million tons in the previous year. Many historians believe that the Virgin Land campaign was the main reason for Khrushchev's downfall in 1964.

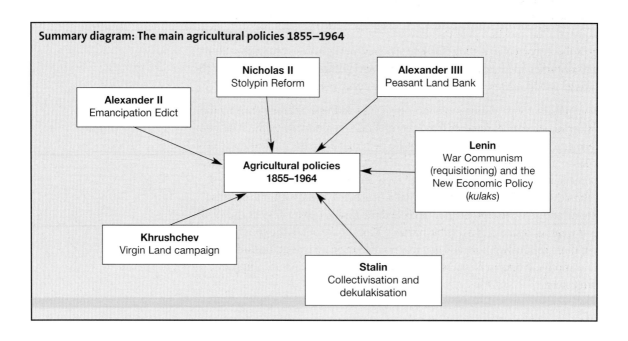

Summary diagram: The main agricultural policies 1855–1964

2 The extent of and reasons for social change

▶ *To what extent did the communists instigate more social change than the tsars?*

Population growth

The population of Russia grew significantly during the period in question. Much of this was due to a '**natural rate of growth**', although this was indirectly affected by the political, economic and social policies implemented by various regimes. Demographic change was also influenced more directly by measures designed to control birth rates and migration. The table below indicates how the population grew and includes separate figures for the urban population.

Table 2.5 The population of the Russian Empire and the USSR from 1858 to 1960

Year	Total (in millions)	Percentage in towns
1858	74	6
1870	86	11
1897	125	15
1913	166	18
1920	137	15
1926	147	18
1939	191	32
1950	178	39
1960	212	49

The first official **census** was not taken until 1897 and the figures before this time are, to some extent, '**guesstimates**'. Even the official census material needs to be handled with caution due to the inconsistent methods used to collect data. The statistics also need to be considered in light of the fact that the extent of the empire and Soviet Union changed significantly over the period.

With this in mind, a number of important trends can be observed:

- The biggest spurts in population growth occurred from 1870 to 1914 and during the inter-war period. In both cases, this was due more to an increase in birth rates than to a fall in death rates. Rising birth rates were stimulated by industrialisation (Witte's 'Great Spurt' and the Five-Year Plans); industrial work gave the prospect of more regular employment and, therefore, slightly higher levels of real income. Therefore, there was a tendency for people to marry earlier and have more children, as it was affordable. This trend was especially strong given that industrialisation also created public health

KEY TERMS

Natural rate of growth
The relationship between birth rates and death rates and how this affected population growth. If the birth rate increased and the death rate fell, the natural rate of growth would have been relatively high.

Census An official count of the number of people in the population.

Guesstimates Estimates of what happened but based on guesswork, usually as a result of flimsy or missing evidence.

problems that resulted in rising mortality rates. Other influences that caused death rates to rise included wars and Stalin's purges.

- Unsurprisingly, industrialisation stimulated urbanisation. Increasing numbers of people moved to the big cities, especially St Petersburg and Moscow, in search of work. This had serious implications with respect to living standards and, more specifically, the availability of housing.

A number of government policies had a direct impact on demographics. Most of these were introduced during the period of communist rule:

- The Emancipation Edict of 1861 gave freedom to peasants to marry anyone they wanted. However, **civil marriage** for peasants was not officially introduced until after the October Revolution of 1917. Ironically, this led to more families splitting up as 'official' divorce became an option. To counter this, Stalin provided various financial incentives to 'strengthen' the family unit. This was considered to be especially important during the Second World War, which demanded that the Russian people should maintain unity and a common purpose to defeat the enemy. Hence, in 1944 for example, the 'Distinctions to Mother Heroines' scheme was introduced whereby women who at any one time had ten or more children were given substantial money rewards.
- In 1926, abortion was legalised. This seemed to result in a fall in the birth rate, which prompted a revision of the law; abortion was only allowed if the life of the mother was thought to be threatened. Subsequently, the birth rate rose only to fall again after all restrictions on abortion were lifted in 1955.

In general, government policies on family planning were never clear or consistent except during times of crisis.

Changes in social structure

The structure of Russian society had a bearing on the policies of governments but equally ruling elites had an impact on the way social groups were organised. The hierarchical structure of Russian society was similar for the period up to the October 1917 Revolution, as shown in the box on page 99.

A number of features and developments are evident from the box:

- Russia was still a very rural-based society by the end of the nineteenth century. Over 80 per cent of the population was still dependent on agriculture. This meant that the Russian economy was still undeveloped and backwards; the other great European powers had a far greater proportion of their populations engaged in industrial activity.
- The distinction between traditional peasant and industrial worker was becoming blurred. Large numbers of peasants were moving towards cities and towns to take up employment in industry. An 'aristocracy of labour' among some peasant industrial workers emerged. These were individuals who developed special skills and offered their services as teams, or *artels*, as they were known.

KEY TERM

Civil marriage Legal marriage whereby civilians are allowed to choose their partners.

The structure of Russian society from 1855 to 1917

The tsar and the nobility (about two per cent of the population)

Aristocracy included families that could trace their roots back to the original founders of the Russian state. Male members used the title of prince or grand prince/duke if related directly to the tsar. The rest of the nobility was shaped by a table of ranks first introduced by Peter the Great, and which lasted until 1917:

- nobles of inherited title (barons, counts, and so on) – the lesser nobility
- nobles holding foreign titles
- nobles created by royal patent
- nobles gaining rank in the bureaucracy
- nobles who gained an officer's commission.

The clergy and the 'middle classes'

The 1897 census revealed a burgeoning 'middle class' made up of the following:

- Christian priests
- non-noble bureaucrats
- 'honoured citizens' – those given special titles based on their duties and commitment to the Russian Empire

- merchants
- petty commercial classes.

The lower classes

The lower classes consisted mainly of peasants (still amounting to about 80 per cent of the population by the time of the First World War). But peasants were not a homogeneous group and, to an extent, this was revealed in the census. The different categories were as follows:

- peasants in rural areas – isolated in very scattered communities
- peasants in towns
- Cossacks – peasants from south-east Russia renowned for their horse-riding skills and who were given certain privileges for serving in the cavalry under the tsar
- settlers
- foreigners
- others – there was little indication of what constituted 'others'.

- The rise of the middle classes was significant. Although small (numbering about 2 million in 1914) and divided (between the commercial and professional classes), this group presented an increasing threat to the monopoly of power enjoyed by the upper nobility and aristocracy.

The nobility was in relative decline, due to their extravagant spending and the rise of the middle classes. For decades, many of the nobility had lived beyond their means and had mortgaged property to pay off debts. When, in turn, repayments became difficult, many sold big chunks of land to peasants. Thus, in total, by the mid-1870s, the gentry owned about 200 million acres but this fell to about 140 million acres, with over 90 per cent of the reduction being accounted for by peasant purchases. Nevertheless, the hard-core nobility remained and it was that group that was most significant in ensuring that the tsar maintained autocratic rule.

Although the basic structure of society remained the same, there were enough subtle changes to suggest that the way Russia was governed would also have to alter.

The social structure under communism

Under the communists there was, by definition, no class-based society. In theory, society consisted of workers who would eventually govern without the help of a cadre (a group of key officials). The reality was different. Soviet communism was characterised by a hierarchical bureaucracy led by a small elite, which governed over the people. Even among workers there were status rankings. For example, some were considered technical experts and were often given privileges (as long as they continued to toe the party line). By the early 1930s, about 1.5 million workers had purportedly been promoted to managerial positions. Thus, there was more continuity than change in how society was organised under the tsars and the communists.

Education

Both the tsars and the communists attempted to expand the provision of education at all levels. Despite this, there were times when too much education, especially for the masses, was considered dangerous. Subsequently, there were periods when reform slowed down or where improvements were actually undone by a reversion to repression. Of particular note is the way in which some rulers used education to impose Russification (see Chapter 4 for details).

Throughout the period, schooling was available at elementary (primary) and secondary level, although free secondary schooling for all was only introduced during Khrushchev's time in power.

Elementary (primary) schools

Before 1864, provision of elementary schools was through wealthy, benevolent (kindly) individuals or the Church. Parents paid fees for their children to attend and the curriculum centred around the three 'Rs' (reading, writing and arithmetic) with some religious instruction. Pupil attendance was erratic and achievement poor, as witnessed by the relatively low literacy rates. Thus, by the mid-1860s, only seven per cent of army recruits (who were mainly peasants and therefore representative of the whole population) were considered literate. Prompted partly by the repercussions of the Emancipation Edict and also by the need to modernise, in 1864, Alexander II introduced a major education reform. He placed the responsibility for the administration and expansion of elementary education with school boards, which in turn were run by the *Zemstva* (see page 37). This had an immediate impact in that the number of available school places, especially in more isolated places, rose and the quality and variety of provision also improved. The only drawback was that the composition of the boards was dominated by the clergy, nobility and government officials, thus casting some concern over what kind of education would be provided and how accessible it would be to the very poor. Also, there was something of a dual system as the Church still provided schools.

In 1870, some of the authority of the *Zemstva* was taken away by the minister for education, **Dmitri Tolstoy**. By 1877, the ministry had almost total control over what the *Zemstva* could do. Central government officials had authority over the appointment of teachers, the length of the school day and year, and quality checks by way of a new schools' inspectorate.

Under Nicholas II, the first *Duma* announced a plan for 'universal primary education' to be achieved by 1922, although the First World War and the 1917 revolutions put a stop to the plan. Nevertheless, expansion in the number of schools and pupils attending continued. Table 2.6 gives a good indication of the progress made.

The *Zemstva* clearly did a good job in providing more schools and provided a solid platform for the Bolsheviks to build on. The first commissar for education, Lunacharsky, had absolute control of all educational institutions. These included Church schools, which in 1918, were handed over to local soviets to administer. Those responsible for schooling under Stalin carried out the aim of the first *Duma* by, in 1930, making attendance at primary school compulsory for all up to the age of twelve. As a result, another leap forward in the numbers attending occurred:

- 1929: 8 million pupils were attending primary schools
- 1930: 18 million pupils were attending primary schools.

Under the communists, the primary school curriculum continued to revolve around developing basic literacy and numeracy skills. 'Extra' subjects were linked to the concept of revolution, and the teaching of religious scriptures disappeared.

The expansion of provision was linked to a 'war on literacy' (the campaign to improve literacy levels) in general; it was quite usual for adults as well as young children to attend elementary schools with the aim of creating a more educated and capable workforce. The Stalinist system of primary education clearly suited the needs of the communists and remained in place until the end of the period.

Secondary schools

The history of Russian secondary schooling was dominated by the debate over whether the traditional gymnasia (grammar schools) should be replaced with institutions that provided a mixture of academic and vocational subjects. All of the tsars retained the gymnasia, but modifications were made to the curriculum and to admissions procedures. Alexander II introduced a 'new code' for secondary schools, which allowed for the continuation of traditional gymnasia provision alongside modern, 'real' gymnasia. The traditional gymnasia taught mainly Russian plus the classics (Latin and Greek) and games (physical education). In contrast, the 'real' gymnasia taught subjects such as modern languages, science and mathematics, all of which were considered by some conservatives to engender a 'spirit of revolution'.

 **KEY FIGURE**

Dmitri Tolstoy (1823–89)

Born into one of the most notable aristocratic families and was sent to be educated at the exclusive Tsarkoe Selo *lycée*. In 1856, he became the chief procurator of the Holy Synod before moving to the ministry of education (1865–80).

Table 2.6 The approximate number of primary schools in Russia 1880–1914

1880	1896	1914
23,000	79,000	81,000

As a result of these reforms, the number of pupils attending secondary schools doubled from 1855 to 1865. The middle classes seemed to benefit significantly from the increase in places. The conservatives, epitomised by Dmitri Tolstoy, reacted by campaigning for universities to only accept pupils who attended the classic gymnasia; that is, children of the nobility. In fact, Tolstoy manipulated the secondary school curriculum and university entrance examination system so that middle-class children were virtually excluded from progressing to tertiary education. Alexander III took the exclusion policy a step further by banning 'lower-class' children from attending secondary schools. Until the Bolsheviks came to power, secondary schooling remained the preserve of the elites in Russian society despite the inroads made by the middle classes.

The Bolsheviks scrapped the bourgeois gymnasia and replaced them with polytechnics. These schools placed heavy emphasis on skills development that would be directly related to a particular area of work. Not all party members agreed with this policy, and by the 1930s there was a return to a mixed provision of old-fashioned grammar schools and purely vocational-based institutions. However, the greatest emphasis was placed on the development of vocational education, especially when the Five-Year Plans were implemented. The figures showing the increase in secondary schools under Stalin therefore mainly reflect a growth in vocational education:

- 1931: 2.5 million pupils were attending secondary schools
- 1932: 6.9 million pupils were attending secondary schools.

Khrushchev reverted to secondary schools based on the polytechnic model. Other changes included the scrapping of all school fees (introduced by Stalin in 1939), the closing down of co-educational boarding schools, the creation of specialist academies and the spread of correspondence courses. Such progressive policies, though, were balanced by a number of restrictive measures including the rewriting of 'official' history books to reflect the disengagement from the Stalinist past.

Universities

Higher educational provision probably gave Russian leaders the most cause for concern. Universities were potentially the breeding grounds for opposition groups and it is of little surprise that students were clamped down on hard if they showed any sign of subversive activity. In 1861, for example, students from St Petersburg University were accused of sedition (anti-tsarist activity) and were punished by having a range of privileges withdrawn. Generally, though, leaders were keen to see universities grow and provide educated people who would enable Russia to enhance its world status.

A statute of 1863 reinstated a large degree of autonomy to universities. A special council for each of the existing eight universities governed the nature of teaching, publications by academics and student discipline. But, despite the statute, the Ministry of Education had the final say on what was to be taught and how it was to be taught.

Under Alexander III, university autonomy was chipped away at. For example, elections to the university councils were scrapped and replaced by an appointment system, and a more rigorous inspection process was introduced. Nevertheless, the universities continued to flourish. By the end of the nineteenth century, there were nine institutions catering for about 16,500 students.

The importance of Moscow University

Nearly a quarter of Russia's students were placed at the University of Moscow, which typified the university set-up. At Moscow, there were four departments:

- law
- medicine
- physics and mathematics
- history and philology.

Students attended lectures and submitted written papers to be discussed with tutors and/or other students. Women had very limited opportunity to attend, and poorer students found life very difficult as there was only limited financial help from tsarist governments. Students belonged to a variety of student societies and the student council. The focus of extracurricular activity was invariably current affairs or aspects of high culture. When meetings got out of hand and became linked to demonstrations, the authorities became very oppressive. Whips were used to disperse unruly student groups and arbitrary expulsions were commonplace. Repression of students reached new levels under Stolypin, with all non-academic meetings in all universities being made illegal.

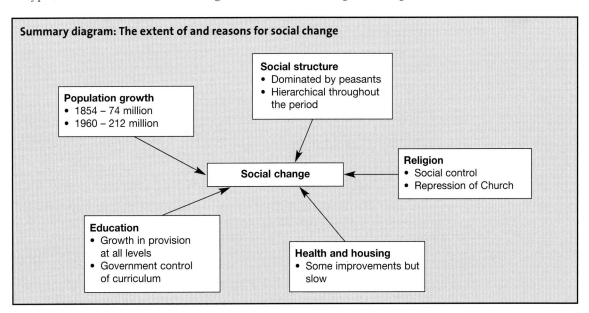

Summary diagram: The extent of and reasons for social change

Changes to living and working conditions of rural and urban people

▶ *To what extent were the living and working conditions of peasants and workers improved in the period from 1855 to 1964?*

Urban housing

By the end of the nineteenth century, about fifteen per cent of the Russian population lived in towns and cities, compared with 80 per cent in Britain and 40 per cent in the USA. Only nineteen cities had more than 100,000 inhabitants. St Petersburg (1.25 million) and Moscow (1 million) were by far the largest cities.

Much of the detailed information we have about urban living conditions comes from the census, although the first of these was not carried out until 1897. Urbanisation continued at a rapid rate after 1897. For example, by 1914 the populations of the two main cities and others, such as Riga and Kiev, almost doubled. The main result of rapid urbanisation was an increase in public health problems. Housing was generally erected quickly and on the cheap. By modern standards, buildings were of a poor quality with inadequate drainage, water supplies and sanitation. Demand for reasonable accommodation at affordable rents always outstripped supply. This led to overcrowding and the inevitable spread of diseases such as cholera. A spin-off of this, according to the historian Hans Rogger (1983), was that the 'brutishness of the working man's life tended to make him difficult and explosive'.

At the start of the First World War, in 1914, there were over 1000 towns containing about 2 million buildings. Over half of all housing was constructed from wood and therefore prone to fire damage (see the painting on page 105). Homes and streets were mostly lit by paraffin lamps; only 74 towns had access to electricity and 35 to gas. Around 200 had piped water and 38 a sewerage system. But even where facilities were fairly widespread, disease still multiplied. Cholera was especially rife in St Petersburg (about 100,000 deaths in 1910) even though its citizens experienced living conditions marginally better than elsewhere. Conditions in this city were further improved with the installation of a sewerage system in 1911, showing that politicians were willing to act when situations became really desperate. Also, cholera outbreaks always provoked a positive reaction to reform as the disease affected all classes in society.

Factories were nearly always located on the edge of cities. As transport links were slow to develop, it became necessary to provide special worker housing on site. Worker 'barracks' were hastily built and were invariably overcrowded and insanitary. Shift systems resulted in workers (and their families) sharing bunk

Fire in the Village, 1885, an oil painting by N.D. Dmitriev-Orenburgskii (1838–98).

beds. In small-scale enterprises, workers usually slept in the workshop. Skilled workers were better off as they could afford to rent private rooms, but on the whole factory workers experienced some of the worst living conditions found anywhere in Russia.

The Decree on Peace (see page 32), issued after the Bolsheviks seized power, partly focused on what the party intended to do about property, including housing. Dwellings in towns and cities were to be wrested from private owners and handed over to the proletariat. To ensure this was done fairly, the redistribution was placed in the hands of the soviets. Some improvement occurred as a result but this was short lived.

During Stalin's rule, housing conditions deteriorated. Overcrowding once more became the norm. In Moscow in the mid-1930s, for example, 25 per cent of the population was living in one room that was shared between two or more households. A further 25 per cent lived in communal dormitories. Furthermore, about five per cent lived in a bathroom, kitchen, corridor or hallway. The result was that living space had fallen from 8.5 m² in 1905 to 5.8 m² by 1935. The Stalinist policy was to allocate space rather than rooms to individuals and families. Even when some were lucky to get their own room in one of the new communist high-rise **tenements**, bathrooms and kitchens would be

 **KEY TERM**

Tenements Similar to blocks of flats.

shared. Outside observers were shocked and surprised at the low priority given to housing in a country being built on socialist principles. The communists responded to criticisms by stating that sacrifices had to be made in the short term to enable the Russian economy to expand. Generally, most social projects were put on hold so that attention could be focused on achieving the aims of the Five-Year Plans.

The Second World War resulted in swathes of Russia becoming depopulated and over 25 million Russians being made homeless. Stalin made some attempt to address the problem, but it was Khrushchev who launched a housing programme of huge proportions. Between 1955 and 1964, the housing stock doubled and the principles behind communal living were abandoned. One result was that the population were happy that at last some of their aspirations were met. A more worrying development was that some benefited more than others through the emergence of **housing cooperatives**. These benefited better off professionals who could afford to pay deposits on new cooperative housing (usually 15–30 per cent of the purchasing price) and make loan repayments at reasonable rates of interest. Finally, by the end of the period, the authorities sensed that living standards were improving as more people wanted to stay in the comfort of their homes rather than attend political meetings.

Rural housing

For the majority of the period, housing for the 'average' peasant remained the same. It consisted of a single-room wooden hut (*izba*) heated by an oven, which also served as a sleeping platform. Such accommodation was invariably overcrowded, especially given that animals were also housed in the hut. The nature of hut building varied from region to region but generally such accommodation was poor by modern standards. It was cold, damp and grubby and added to the misery of the peasants. However, it was at least cheap to construct and, once it was erected, peasant families had control over how the accommodation could be used.

Under Stalin, there was a change to this situation for some peasants with the construction of 'special' housing blocks located on the periphery of collective farms. Under Khrushchev, the plan was to take this idea further to construct self-contained 'agro-towns'. As with the tenements for urban workers, rural housing was built quickly and cheaply and was subsequently of a poor standard. They became very overcrowded and residents found themselves subject to the public health problems experienced in the towns and cities. Displaced *kulaks* suffered even worse conditions. When forced from their properties they were usually dumped in barracks or given tent accommodation in a field. Overall, little was done by any Russian leader during the period to aid improvements in rural housing.

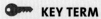

KEY TERM

Housing cooperatives
Organisations formed by employees who belonged to the same work enterprise or professional union. They were given first pickings over new state housing as long as they could meet government-set prices.

Food and famine

The staple food for all Russians throughout the period was grain, especially rye. Buckwheat was also popular, being used to make dumplings and pancakes. Cereals were often eaten with meat dishes, although in many areas there was a scarcity of animals. Fish was consumed in large quantities in regions that had a coastline or where there were bountiful lakes. More significant than the consumption of meat was that of vegetables. Potatoes, turnips, beetroot, cabbage, garlic and onions were grown and eaten all over Russia. Fruit was also produced, especially apples, pears and plums, and cherries were a speciality in the area of Vladimir (about 150 miles east of Moscow). People living close to woodlands had the added bonus of being able to gather mushrooms and berries. In terms of drink, ale, mead, tea and, of course, vodka were preferred. Overall, it would appear that the Russian diet was relatively rich and varied and that, given the emphasis placed on agriculture, there was little need for the Russian people to go short of food.

The reality was that the whole of the period was characterised by intermittent food shortages and full-blown famines. This was due to a number of reasons:

- a tendency towards monoculture (in this case, an overreliance on grain)
- the restrictive practices of the *mir*, for example, the insistence of the *mir* on the growing of certain crops
- severe weather conditions in particular years
- government policies (grain requisitioning and collectivisation; see pages 92–4 on the impact of collectivisation).

Even before 1855, food shortages had consistently caused governments concern. When Alexander II came to the throne he was worried that if shortages continued to occur there would be widespread social unrest. To this end, in 1864, he placed the *Zemstva* in charge of drawing up emergency measures to deal with famines. This still did not prevent people starving and dying from hunger in large numbers. There were a number of famines before the First World War but by far the most severe was that of 1891.

The famine of 1891

A major challenge for the *Zemstva* happened in 1891 when adverse weather resulted in half the provinces of Russia suffering from food shortages that were unprecedented. The provincial governments appeared to cope very well but the famine, made worse by outbreaks of cholera and typhus, still resulted in about 350,000 deaths. Some blamed central government for this. Vyshnergradsky, the finance minister, had raised the tax on consumer goods, which meant that the population had to pay more for everyday items. Peasants appeared to sell off any surpluses of grain they had stored to cope with the inflated prices. Therefore, the shortage of food due to poor harvests was exacerbated. Alexander III tried to counter criticisms by banning exports of grain, setting up a Special Committee on Famine Relief and funding emergency help from two 'extraordinary' lotteries. For most, this was too little too late and it provided an added incentive to join one of the revolutionary groups emerging at the time (see page 50).

Food supplies and the First World War

During the first three years of the First World War there were good harvests, although those in towns and cities did not necessarily reap the benefits; much grain was used to feed troops and there were also problems in getting foodstuffs into urbanised areas (see below). Bread queues of eight hours or longer became the norm (later leading to the view that the 'revolution started in the bread queue'). Some peasants hoarded grain and/or fed their animals (rather than slaughter them early, which critics argued needed to be done in times of crisis). An inadequate transport infrastructure, including a railway system largely being used by the military, also made accessing food difficult.

The Russian people hoped that with the fall of the tsar and the ending of the war there would be greater access to food. However, their hopes were dashed due to a continuation of problems linked to the availability of land and how it was farmed.

Food crisis of 1918

By 1918, another food crisis loomed. Peasants had continued to hoard and valuable agricultural land had been lost as a result of the Treaty of Brest-Litovsk (see pages 196–9). The Bolsheviks responded to this by introducing grain requisitioning. This was the practice of taking food and grain surpluses from some peasants and redistributing it among those who were in greatest need. Most of the redistributed foodstuff went to the towns and cities.

Kulaks were blamed for the shortages and subsequently persecuted. Peasants reacted angrily by resorting to violent protest, refusing to sign up to collectives and resisting the demand to create surplus supplies of grain. By 1920, the *Cheka* and the Red Army had been instructed to seize all food supplies for redistribution and not simply surpluses. More violent reaction occurred and by the end of 1921 the countryside was in a state of utter chaos. All of this coincided with another severe famine.

The famine of 1921

Although the Bolshevik policies towards the immediate post-war food crisis contributed to the famine, droughts followed by severe winters in 1920–1 also had a dramatic effect. Ukrainian food production fell by twenty per cent during this time. Due to an almost complete shutdown of the Russian railway system, which emanated from the Civil War, it was extremely difficult to transport produce over even moderately long distances. It was also virtually impossible for urban dwellers to travel to where there might have been food supplies. The end result was a death toll of over 5 million. The crisis was also characterised by rumours of bodysnatching and cannibalism. Like Alexander III before him, and Stalin at a later date, Lenin was partly blamed for the famine as he was slow in his response and reluctant to accept aid from the **American Relief Administration**. In fact, any kind of charitable aid was treated with suspicion and there were instances where members of relief agencies were arrested by the *Cheka* and exiled.

Stability in the countryside by the mid-1920s

By the mid-1920s, stability had been restored to the countryside. There were decent harvests in 1926 and 1927 but in 1928, food shortages reappeared. Much of this was due to the weather, although peasants had also reduced the amount of land sown. In addition, *kulaks* were blamed for hoarding grain. Requisitioning was once again resorted to by Russian officials. In 1928, treatment of wealthier peasants worsened with the introduction of the Urals–Siberian method. Under this scheme, villagers were encouraged to reveal grain hoarders and those who showed bourgeois tendencies in exchange for rewards.

The famine of 1932–4

A combination of the effects of the first phase of collectivisation and poor harvests due to terrible weather conditions led to the most disastrous famine of the whole period. Although the number of deaths resulting from starvation and disease was similar to that for the 1921 famine, many more suffered as a result of repression by the Stalinist regime:

- The death penalty was imposed for stealing grain (even though the grain might have legally belonged to the accused).
- Peasants who ate their own seed corn were shot along with those sent to guard it.
- Discussion of the grain crisis was banned; this was a necessity as Stalin publicly denied a food problem existed.
- Severe restrictions were also placed on those who wanted to move around to look for food.
- The reaction of some peasants did not seem to help. Animals were slaughtered in preference to handing them over to the authorities. A horse shortage ensued, which slowed down the ploughing of fields. Cattle often froze to death on collectives that lacked big enough barns to house them.

By 1935, matters seemed to improve and food production increased slowly. However, on the eve of the Second World War it was unlikely that total food output had reached pre-First World War levels. Generally, the diet of workers in particular seemed to worsen under the communists. By the late 1930s, for example, the consumption of meat and fish had fallen by 80 per cent.

KEY TERM

American Relief Administration A US relief mission to aid Europe, including Russia, after the First World War. The director of the organisation was Herbert Hoover, future US president.

The Second World War and food supplies

During the Second World War, the policy towards collectivisation was relaxed. With the removal of restrictions on the size of private plots of land, food production rose. However, this was short lived as another famine took place in 1947. The pattern of poor harvests and associated food shortages continued during the rule of Khrushchev. Despite the Virgin Land campaign (see page 96) and improvements to the **state pricing mechanism** for agricultural produce, food still had to be imported. Critics at the time and since believed that adherence to a policy of subsidised 'socialised agriculture' simply led to inefficiency and a situation whereby the demand for food in Russia always outstripped the ability of Russian farmers to meet it.

Rural work

In general, work on the land was dictated by 'nature's clock'. Specific tasks had to be completed at certain times of the year. The success of peasant farmers was determined more by the quality of soil, the weather and their innate ability to farm rather than by government policies.

Nevertheless, the emancipation of serfs, the appointment of land captains, grain requisitioning, collectivisation and the Virgin Land campaign all influenced the conditions under which peasants worked. Agricultural work obviously involves hard physical labour but at least before the Bolshevik takeover peasants were able to control the pace at which they worked and how much they produced. The only restrictions outside those provided by nature were those imposed by the *mir* (see page 37). For most peasants, the main aim was to produce as much as possible so that they could feed their families, pay off debts and save a little for bad years. It is quite incorrect to assume that the Russian agricultural system before communism was simply based on achieving subsistence levels. To achieve a surplus, peasants worked most days of the week from dawn to dusk and often under harsh climatic conditions. There was still time for festivities; holy days (holidays) often coincided with celebrations linked to particular seasons.

Under the communists the nature of rural work changed. How much was produced and the methods used were dictated by central government policy. Collectivisation resulted in the requirement that peasants worked cooperatively and to set targets, most of which were seldom achieved. Investment was made in new agricultural techniques and technology to boost productivity. The tractor was heralded as a major breakthrough, although it was utilised with mixed levels of success. Overall, peasants' work under communist rule was far more regulated, and individuals who did not toe the party line were liable to be punished severely (see pages 93–4).

KEY TERM

State pricing mechanism
The government policy of providing official prices for goods and services.

Urban work

Reasons for poor working conditions

Those who worked in towns and cities were employed in either the service industry or manufacturing. The worst conditions were present in factories, although most of these, along with other heavy industry (for example, mines, steel plants and engineering works), were located on the edge of conurbations. As there was no factory inspectorate until 1882, working conditions for many industrial workers, especially those employed in textiles, were dangerous and unhealthy. Even when inspectors were introduced, they were largely ineffectual as they were too few in number and had limited powers of enforcement. Thus, for example, despite factory legislation of 1882 banning the employment of children under the age of twelve, it was possible for employers to continue to use child labour as they were unlikely to be found out.

The New Work Discipline

In fact, the introduction in February 1920 of *Rabkrin* (the Workers' and Peasants' Inspectorate) under the communists was a backward step as this body became a talking shop rather than one that enforced industrial law. Hours were long by modern standards, pay was relatively low and the enforcement of the 'new work discipline' was done harshly.

The use of fines (often ten per cent of wages) as a punishment for petty wrongdoings was especially disliked by workers. Workers were also threatened by being 'purged', especially if they were considered to be anti-revolutionary. Officials sometimes claimed that certain workers were intent on disrupting production by damaging machinery ('wrecking') or purposely working slowly so as to prevent the implementation of the Five-Year Plans. Furthermore, women and children were treated more severely than men. It took some time for all of this to change.

Hours of work

By the end of the nineteenth century, laws were being introduced that governed the length of the working day. But hours still fluctuated across the period depending on who was ruling. It is worth noting that there were particular times when excessively long hours were accepted as necessary by all concerned, such as during periods of war. Table 2.7 summarises the trend in working hours. Note that some of the figures represent what happened directly after legislation was passed. Where 'the norm' is stated this means the average working day imposed by employers. Sometimes employers under the tsars found loopholes in the law and pushed workers to work longer than the statutory hours. Under the communists, working hours were strictly controlled by the state.

Table 2.7 Trends in working hours in Russia 1896–1958

Year	Hours	Comment
1896	11-hour working day (10 hours on Saturday). This was fixed by law	Workers were not obliged to work on Sundays. Small workshops were not covered
1914	9–10-hour working day was the norm	Statutory holidays had been introduced by this time
1917	8-hour working day was the norm. This was a result of a decree made by the Provisional Government	Bolsheviks quickly brought in laws to improve working conditions to illustrate that they were the workers' party
1932	10–12-hour working day was the norm	Stalin claimed the demands of the first Five-Year Plan meant workers had to endure a longer working day
1939	7-hour working day was the norm	Workers were rewarded for their efforts in implementing the Five-Year Plans
1940	8-hour working day was the norm	This was due to the war. Holidays were also disallowed
1958	7-hour working day was the norm	Khrushchev wanted to move away from the oppressive Stalinist years. The 7-hour day remained to the end of the period

Wages

By Western standards, industrial wages were low during the whole period, although it is difficult to provide details as accurate statistical evidence is lacking. Women received less than men on average even when they were employed in the same work. Low pay was partly offset by the introduction in 1903 (adapted in 1912) of a **workers' insurance system** and, under the communists, by **bonus schemes**. The latter were popularised through the Stakhanovite movement (see page 47) and some workers did very well out of them. From the beginning to the end of the first Five-Year Plan (1928–32), however, real wages fell by 50 per cent. They rose again after this time but it was not until 1954 that they started to reach the levels of the early 1920s. Wage differentials increased substantially under Stalin as a result of the piece-rate payments. Some workers were paid more than others simply because they produced more. The piece-rate system was meant to provide an incentive to workers to be more productive.

KEY TERMS

Workers' insurance system Insurance against being injured in the workplace. Other schemes, against ill-health, old age and unemployment, were also introduced through the 1924 and 1936 constitutions.

Bonus schemes Where extra payments were made to workers for exceeding individual production targets.

Summary diagram: Changes to living and working conditions of rural and urban people		
Conditions	**Tsars**	**Communists**
Rural housing	Wooden huts – idealised by folk literature but cold and damp	Remained the same but some move towards agro-towns
Urban housing	Relatively poor with respect to quantity and quality. Public health problems	Characterised by overcrowding but some improvement under Khrushchev
Rural work	Governed by 'nature's clock'; some improvements through reforms but control by *mir*	Governed by political regime through collectivisation (although less so under Khrushchev)
Urban work	Poor conditions (long hours, low pay, strict discipline) but some reforms aided improvement	Similar poor conditions but hours much lower by end of period. Workers prone to being purged under Stalin especially if considered to be 'wreckers' (saboteurs)

Limitations on personal, political and religious freedoms

▶ *To what extent were the limitations on personal, political and religious freedoms greater under the tsars than the communists?*

Civil rights refer to the rights that citizens have to the personal freedom to speak, think and act. This freedom is usually associated with the law, politics and religion. Details on the limitations on many of these rights, especially legal and political, have been covered in other sections of this book. This section will therefore focus mainly on religious freedom. As a generalisation, poorer Russians had far fewer rights than the wealthy throughout the period. However, under Stalin even members of the ruling elite were likely to lose their basic rights through being purged.

Personal freedoms

Both the tsars and communists were adept at controlling the personal freedoms of individuals by using the legal system, the police ('normal' and secret), the armed forces, propaganda and censorship. These have all been discussed in Chapter 1. Generally, the people were allowed to exercise their free will as long as it did not conflict with the interests of autocracy and totalitarian rule. When a more liberal climate was created it was often short lived or countered by a string of repressive measures.

Political freedoms

The basic political rights that supposedly existed in the democracies of the West were never apparent in Russia at any time during the period under consideration. On occasion, individuals were allowed to belong to political parties and trade unions and some were even allowed to vote (see Chapter 1). But the key point to be made is that such political rights were never universal or consistently granted. As with personal freedoms, whenever leaders felt their authority was being challenged by political activity from below, they reacted with repressive measures. The only exception was during the time of the Provisional Government, when a more tolerant approach was adopted towards grass-roots political activism.

Religious freedoms

Orthodox religion

Orthodox and non-Orthodox religion remained under state control across the period. The Orthodox Church was important to the tsars as it acted as a useful form of **social control**. Many of the clergy, such as the highly regarded Father John of Kronstadt, were happy to support autocracy even though they championed the plight of the poor. The Church actually relied on governments for money and the encouragement given to the people to attend services. Even when Pobedonostsev tightened control over the activities of senior clergy very few dissented. Under the communists, religion was considered the **'opium of the people'**. Immediately after the 1917 Revolution it appeared that the Church would be left to its own devices. But, in response to the Orthodox Church bringing back **patriarchy**, the Bolsheviks made the 'Decree on the Separation of the Church from the State and School from the Church'.

Restrictions on the Church

This placed severe restrictions on the activities of the Church, including the withdrawal of state subsidies and the prevention of religious groups from possessing property (including icons). During the Civil War many churches were closed and their property was confiscated. Anti-religious pressure groups designed to promote atheism were encouraged to form, most notably the League of the Militant Godless (1925). The only concession under Lenin was the appointment of a Church spokesperson. Stalin continued to close churches and many of the clergy suffered during the Great Terror (see page 55) of the late 1930s. According to the historian Walter G. Moss (2005), by 1938 there were only sixteen working Orthodox churches, compared with 224 in 1930, and the number of clergy had been reduced by 60 per cent.

Khrushchev also had little time for religion and believed that to speed up the full implementation of communism, religious prejudices had to be eradicated. To this end, the Twenty-second Party Congress of 1961 introduced a new 'moral code', which was essentially a substitute for the Bible.

KEY TERMS

Orthodox and non-Orthodox religion
Orthodox religion was the established and traditional beliefs of the Russian Orthodox Church, which had its roots in the Greek Orthodox Church. Non-Orthodox refers to any set of beliefs that differed from those of the Russian Orthodox Church.

Social control Control, usually by politicians, of the beliefs, attitudes and actions of members of society through the careful organisation and administration of particular institutions, for example, education, religion and the media.

'Opium of the people'
The view that religion was like a drug that took people's minds off worrying about economic and social problems. It was coined by Karl Marx in *Contribution to the Critique of Hegel's Philosophy of Right* (1843–4).

Patriarchy A male-dominated form of organisation and rule.

Non-Orthodox religion

The main beliefs that fell under the heading of non-Orthodox were those of the **Old Believers, Sectarians**, Catholics, Protestants, Jews, Muslims and Buddhists. Although there were times when there was a relaxed attitude towards these groups, most leaders either encouraged conversion to the Orthodox Church or resorted to restriction of practice. Thus, for example, a law of 1883 gave Old Believers the right to meet in their houses of prayer but banned any public promotion of their beliefs. Nicholas II modified this, in April 1905, and also allowed Orthodox believers to convert to other Christian denominations. But in 1910, the rights of the non-Orthodox were again restricted, with the increasingly popular Baptists being hardest hit. During the communist period most sects were forced to operate 'underground'.

Minority religious groups

Minority religious groups were targeted during the Second World War, as they were associated, usually incorrectly, with collaborating with the enemy. After the war, non-Orthodox believers suffered a similar fate to those of Orthodox leanings. An official anti-religious campaign launched in 1958 meant that religious activity of any kind was under scrutiny unless it was conducted in an 'official place'.

In conclusion, religion was never banned as such, but it was very difficult for believers of any kind to carry on their practice without being scrutinised by the authorities. Nevertheless, it was not until 1958 that religion was considered officially to be unscientific and therefore to the detriment of the well-being of the people.

KEY TERMS

Old Believers Those who believed in the most traditional form of the Russian Orthodox Church. They also thought that they were more Russian than other Russians.

Sectarians Anyone who belonged to a group that held extreme, and often unusual, religious views.

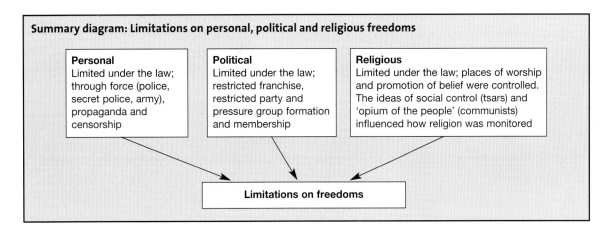

Summary diagram: Limitations on personal, political and religious freedoms

| **Personal** Limited under the law; through force (police, secret police, army), propaganda and censorship | **Political** Limited under the law; restricted franchise, restricted party and pressure group formation and membership | **Religious** Limited under the law; places of worship and promotion of belief were controlled. The ideas of social control (tsars) and 'opium of the people' (communists) influenced how religion was monitored |

Limitations on freedoms

Chapter summary

The regimes of the tsars and the communists had both positive and negative effects on the economy and society of the Russian Empire and the Soviet Union. A common theme that runs through the period was the wish by all leaders to industrialise to a level that was comparable to that of the West.

The 'Great Spurt', the New Economic Policy and the Five-Year Plans were all designed to boost heavy industry and increase the rate of economic growth. The rates of growth were not consistent and generally lagged behind Western economies. For the tsars, industrialisation was important in order to ensure that Russia retained its status as one of the Great Powers. Wars such as the Crimean War and the First World War demonstrated how far behind Russia was technologically. The communists were also concerned with world status, especially after the Second World War, and, as with the tsars, they were also aware of the need to prioritise heavy industry so that the military would be fully equipped to defend the homeland. What all dictatorial regimes seemed less concerned about was sharing some of the fruits of economic growth among the bulk of the population. Most of the available indicators point, at best, to a slowly rising standard of living for the masses over the whole period. Rapid urbanisation was characterised by a multitude of public health problems which most governments struggled to deal with or even chose to ignore.

The agricultural sector was always secondary to the needs of industry. Reforms occurred that were designed to increase production and productivity but only to ensure that workers were adequately fed. Famines were common and were often fuelled by requisitioning. Problems relating to land ownership were never tackled effectively.

Social policies also lacked consistency and oscillated from reforms that benefited many to repression that spread terror. Overall, there was real progress in the field of education with respect to the number of schools, the spread of universities, compulsory attendance, the rising school leaving age and the decrease in illiteracy. Acting as a check against this were restrictions placed on the curriculum, Russification and the use of schools, especially by the communists, as a form of social control. Help for families, the sick and the elderly was never systematically offered. Insurance schemes were very slow in being introduced and never seemed to cover more than the most basic needs. Religious groups were tolerated, especially under the tsars, but all leaders were keen to ensure that Orthodox and non-Orthodox Churches were made to obey the whims of government.

Changes in regimes undoubtedly altered the functioning of the economy and the impact this had on social change. However, the common aim to industrialise Russia and increase economic growth was largely achieved during the period. The downside to this was that living standards never seemed to reach levels that ordinary Russians found acceptable.

Refresher questions

Use these questions to remind yourself of the key
material covered in this chapter.

1 What were the aims of the tsars with respect to
industrialisation?

2 Why was railway construction so important under
the tsars?

3 Was the 'Great Spurt' a turning point in the
economic fortunes of Russia?

4 What impact did the First World War have on the
Russian economy and society?

5 What were the aims of the communists with
respect to industrialisation?

6 How were State Capitalism, War Communism
and the New Economic Policy connected?

7 How successful were the Five-Year Plans?

8 Why did peasant concerns over land continue
throughout most of the period?

9 What was Stolypin's role in reforming agriculture?

10 How far was collectivisation a failure?

11 What were Khrushchev's successes and failures
when it came to economic and social reforms?

12 What impact did population change have on the
Russian economy and society?

13 What were the major changes in education across
the period?

14 How far did the living and working conditions of
the Russian people improve across the period?

15 What civil rights did Russian peoples lose and gain
under the tsars and the communists?

In-depth studies and debates

Remember that the examination requires you to study three topics in depth and for this unit they are:

- Alexander II's domestic reforms
- The Provisional Government
- Khrushchev in power 1956–64.

This section will go into more detail about the reforms made during the periods concerned. Some of the key debates about the extent and success of reforms will be introduced so that you will have enough depth of knowledge to be able to evaluate passages that are set on any of the depth study topics.

Key debate 1: to what extent did reforms made by Alexander II improve the status of Russian peasants?

The main area of debate with respect to the rule of Alexander II is the extent to which the reforms he carried out genuinely granted liberty (freedom) to the peoples of Russia, especially peasants. Traditionally, he was viewed as the 'Tsar Liberator', mainly as a result of the Emancipation Edict of 1861 and its consequences. There are some historians, such as J.N. Westwood (2002), who have been happy to perpetuate the view that Alexander II intentionally carried out reforms that granted Russian peasants greater freedoms so that they could live better lives. Hence, Westwood believes that:

> *With the possible exceptions of Khrushchev and Gorbachev, no Russian ruler brought so much relief to so many of his people as did Alexander II, autocratic and conservative though he was.*

Others, though, have emphasised the limitations of the reforms to argue that the tsar was concerned only with making some concessions to win support.

The Emancipation Edict was the most important measure enacted by Alexander II as, from this, other economic, social and political changes became a necessity (see pages 64–5 for discussion of these changes). Before the edict, peasants were the property of landowners or the state and lived and worked under a system known as serfdom. Being a serf meant that you were under the total control of a noble or the state and had no access to land. Yet peasants claimed they had a 'natural' right to the land as they were the class in society that were constantly working the soil to feed the Russian population. Labour and military services were provided in return for food and shelter. Serfdom was really a form of slavery.

The conditions laid down by the edict were as follows:

- All privately owned serfs were freed. Those kept by the state were to be emancipated in 1866. Freedom entailed peasants being able to own property, run their own commercial enterprises and marry whoever they wished.

- Nobles had to hand over a proportion or allotment of land to peasants. This was measured and allocated by official surveyors.
- The state provided compensation to landowners which was often based on valuations way above the market level.
- Peasants had to help pay for the compensation through redemption payments (that is, repayments of loans that allowed peasants to make the compensation). These were to be paid over a 49-year period at six per cent interest. Legal rights to the land were only confirmed after the last payment was made. An alternative was for peasants to continue to work on the land of a noble for so many days in a year to compensate for their own land allocations.
- The administration of redemption payments was carried out by the village council of elders (the *mir*). This group also ensured that land could not be sold on before the final redemption payment had been made.

The reform taken at face value would justify Alexander II being given the title of 'Tsar Liberator'. It has been described as 'an enormous step forward': as well as giving peasants their freedom they also acquired their own parcel of land. But it has often been pointed out that there was considerable opposition to the statute from landowners even though the compensation clauses did much to allay their fears. The main reason for this was that the nobility had been struggling to maintain their large estates before emancipation. Many had taken out large loans to help cover day-to-day costs. The revenue from redemption payments tended to be diverted to repay debts. If this failed, estates were broken up and sold off. Thus, by 1905, the land owned by the nobility had been reduced by about 40 per cent.

Many peasants also reacted badly to the reform for the following reasons:

- Generally, peasants were allocated poorer quality land. They also received less, on average, than they had been farming before emancipation.
- Many peasants struggled to earn enough from the land to meet redemption payments. Financial difficulties were made worse by the necessity to pay rural poll taxes.
- Peasants were not totally free in so far as they had to answer to the *mir*. Decisions about what was to be produced and how crops were to be cultivated still had to be made by the village elders. It was also the responsibility of the *mir* to ensure that the principle of **subsistence farming** was adhered to. As a result, the more able peasant farmers had no incentive to produce surpluses and were reluctant to invest to improve the land.

Thus, it would seem that the freedoms given to peasants were rather limited and this remained the case throughout Alexander II's reign.

 **KEY TERM**

Subsistence farming
Ensuring that just enough was produced to keep members of a community fed over a given period.

Key debate 2: why is the Provisional Government often viewed as one that was reluctant to carry out reforms?

The Provisional Government paid little if any attention to economic and social reform. Its main aim was to enable reform of the political system through the setting up of a Constituent Assembly; by the start of January 1918 this had been achieved.

Despite the fact that the Provisional Government achieved its main aim, historians, such as Martin McCauley (1995), have claimed that it could have carried out economic and social reforms that would have helped it to maintain power. This would then have given the temporary regime the chance to prepare more thoroughly for elections to the new assembly. McCauley claims that 'the greatest feature of the government was inactivity'. His view is that the Provisional Government attempted the following but this was not enough to appease workers and peasants:

- Political prisoners were released.
- Secret courts were ended.
- Freedom of the press was instigated.

The major issues of worker demands for an eight-hour day and peasant demands for more land were largely ignored. Also, the government's policy of continuation in the war resulted in food shortages, inflation, and demonstrations by workers, soldiers and sailors. By not being more reforming, the Provisional Government is considered to have led to rejection by 'the vast majority of the army and population'. Hence, by the time the Constituent Assembly was put in place there was much grass-roots scepticism about whether it would succeed.

The counter-argument to this is that the early changes made by the Provisional Government were intended not as reforms but as principles which would aid major political change. The lack of an economic and social programme of reform was understandable given the war situation, one which had been inherited from the previous regime. McCauley's claim that there was a lack of urgency about the government seems unfair given the scope of internal and external challenges it faced (see pages 65–8)

Key debate 3: to what extent were the economic and social reforms made by Khrushchev a failure?

A fairly common view is that Khrushchev attempted to make some quite innovative and radical changes but was largely unsuccessful due to a lack of cooperation from senior Communist Party officials and bureaucrats. Some historians though, such as Donald Filtzler (1993), have suggested that Khrushchev's schemes were poorly thought out; it was this that caused a change in the initial level of support he had for his ideas.

Filtzler has argued that Khrushchev's reforms were often seen as 'hare-brained' (poorly thought out) for the following reasons:

- Reforms such as the Virgin Land programme were well intended but were badly planned; initially grain production increased substantially but this tailed off due to the poor quality of land used and a lack of fertilisers.
- The highly bureaucratic Soviet 'system' was too cumbersome to allow for reforms to be implemented quickly enough.
- Khrushchev failed to realise that some Communist Party members may have felt threatened by the changes he made.
- The reforms were not as radical as they needed to be to cope with the challenges left by the Stalinist regime (such as the 'backwardness' of industry and agriculture).

This view has been challenged by historians such as Norman Lowe (2005), who have emphasised that Khrushchev's reforms were a considerable achievement given the context in which he was working. Stalin had left agriculture in a perilous state and Russian industry had mainly been geared up to meet the demands of war (the Second World War and the Cold War). Khrushchev recognised this and did his best to address these problems. Thus, Lowe has argued that:

- It was only in 1963 that a significant fall in grain production was witnessed and that was mainly down to poor weather; the weaknesses of the Virgin Land scheme have therefore probably been exaggerated.
- Khrushchev made quite a radical change to the industrial infrastructure (in a relatively short period) by focusing on the establishment of light industries (those that produced consumer products). This seemed to raise living standards; for example, from 1955 to 1966, the number of washing machines per thousand of the population increased from 1 to 77.
- The Russian leader had to prioritise, to an extent, political problems. Furthermore, such problems were dealt with effectively through, for example, the ending of Stalinist *Gulags* and the placing of the NKVD under the control of the party and the state.

Therefore, McCauley's view that Khrushchev's reforms made him a 'courageous failure' seems rather simplistic. Given the challenges he faced, Khrushchev did much to improve the lives of Russian peoples in a short period of time.

Study skills: thematic essay question

How to develop analysis and write a paragraph that shows synthesis

The skills are the same as those you have developed for essay writing in units 1 and 2. However, in this unit there is a significant emphasis on *synthesis* across the whole period. We have already stressed that the title of the unit, Thematic Study, makes it clear that the essay section should be approached thematically rather than chronologically, particularly if you want to reach the higher mark range. In answering essay questions, you are required to make connections, comparisons and links between different elements of the period and aspects of the topic; this is that crucial element of synthesis – the comparison between different parts of the period – to show similarities and differences between events or people. It is not enough to simply list examples from across the period in each paragraph, you must make direct comparisons between them. You do not need to make comparisons across the whole period in every paragraph, but the whole period will need to be covered in the essay.

As with essays in units 1 and 2, you should aim to write analytically. This is perhaps the hardest, but most important skill you need to develop. An analytical approach can be helped by ensuring that the opening sentence of each paragraph introduces an idea, which directly answers the question and is not just a piece of factual information. In a very strong answer it should be possible to simply read the opening sentences of all the paragraphs and know what argument is being put forward.

'The pace and extent of industrialisation were just as great under the tsars as under the communists from 1855 to 1964'. How far do you agree?

Possible opening sentences for an answer in response to this question could be as follows:

- Relatively speaking, the attempts by Reutern and Witte to industrialise Russia were on a similar scale to those attempted by the communist rulers.
- The construction of the Russian railway system, acting as an adjunct to industry and as an industry in itself, gathered most momentum under the tsars.
- Compared with the tsars and Stalin, Lenin's attempt to increase the pace and extent of industrialisation was limited; this was due mainly to the impact of the First World War and the Civil War.
- Stalin's Five-Year Plans to industrialise Russia were introduced at a pace that was unmatched by any attempts made by the tsars to Westernise the Russian economy.
- Under Khrushchev, policies towards industrialisation were simply an extension of those adopted by Stalin who, in turn, built on the foundation laid by Witte.

You would then go on to discuss both sides of the argument raised by the opening sentence, using relevant knowledge about the issue to support each side of the argument. The final sentence of the paragraph would reach a judgement on the role played by the tsars and communists in the development of the aspect of industrialisation under discussion. This approach would ensure that the final sentence of each paragraph links back to the actual question you are answering.

If you can do this for each paragraph you will have a series of mini-essays, which discuss a factor and reach a conclusion or judgement about the importance of that factor or issue.

Developing synthesis

Some of the opening sentences have already hinted at comparisons between different periods, but this comparison would need to be developed and more of the period covered if an answer was to reach the highest level. The two paragraphs below illustrate what is a weak approach and does not really illustrate synthesis, and a strong approach, which shows a high level of synthesis.

Response A

An important aspect of industrialisation for the tsars and communists was the construction of railways. Railway construction had started before 1855. The first Russian railway was finished in 1837 during the reign of Nicholas I. This was added to in 1851 when the St Petersburg to Moscow line was opened. Railway construction moved forward during the reign of Alexander II. Under the guidance of Reutern the amount of railway track opened increased seven-fold. When Alexander III replaced his father as tsar he decided to further improve the railway system so that by 1891 over 17,000 miles of track existed (compared with about 14,000 miles in 1878). Under Nicholas II, Witte carried railway construction to new heights, with 31,125 miles of track being available by 1901. However, Witte seemed to neglect finishing the Trans-Siberian Railway so this was a bit of a backward step. The communists also continued with railway building. They were keen to use the railways to transport grain and industrial products during times of war. This then stimulated the iron, steel and coal industries in particular. By the end of the period over 74,600 miles of railway track existed.

Response B

The construction of the Russian railway system, acting as an adjunct to industry, gathered momentum under the tsars. In 1866, there were 2194 miles of track, which increased to nearly 44,000 miles by the time of the abdication of Nicholas II. Under Alexander II, Alexander III and Nicholas II, the railway system grew mainly to 'break bulk' for agriculture and industry, thus allowing more (heavy) goods to be transported more quickly and at up to half the cost of using alternative methods of transport. Railway extension also meant that raw materials could be brought to industries more effectively. Thus, under Reutern, for example, the expansion of railways was said to have been responsible for an annual growth rate in industrial output of six per cent. Lenin, Stalin and Khrushchev continued to pay attention to the utility of railways, which resulted in a considerable expansion of track made available. By 1956, 74,600 miles existed carrying over 1371 million tons of industrial and agricultural products. Such an increase undoubtedly served to meet the demands of the Five-Year Plans and collectivisation. However, there was a major difference between different regimes with respect to how railways were used. Alexander II and Alexander III had less need to use the railway for the purposes of communication and the transport of different types of passengers. This changed with the impact of Russification (up to the end of the period) and wars. The former led to greater demands for independence by national minorities and hence the need for a transport system that would enable politicians and the military to quickly get to hotspots of protest in the empire. Similarly with war, especially the two world wars, Lenin and Stalin found a need to move soldiers efficiently to the fronts of fighting. Thus, although the continued expansion of railway building across the whole period was undoubtedly linked to the demands of industry and agriculture, the railways took on a new significance, especially under the communists, due to the need for the transportation of passengers.

Analysis of responses

Response B is the stronger answer and displays high-level synthesis:

- Response A is a mixture of description and explanation about how (and to what extent) railway construction in Russia expanded; there is no link or comparison between the periods of tsarist rule in terms of the significance of railway building. Also, the attempt to show the extent of change and/or continuity between the tsars and communists is rather weak.
- There is sound detail in Response A, and there is some argument and analysis about the importance of each period.
- There is no judgement in Response A as to which period was the most significant.
- Response B compares the similarities and differences in how railways were used by the various rulers.
- Response B shows synthesis across most of the period, with examples from the 1860s through to the 1950s.
- There is just as much detail in Response B, but it is used to support the argument; 'own knowledge' is made to work and is not simply imparted knowledge.

You should now try and write paragraphs similar to Response B for the other themes that were considered in the opening sentences.

You can also try writing paragraphs for essays from the list below. In order to ensure that you have demonstrated synthesis across the period, you should highlight the examples of synthesis and make a checklist to ensure that your paragraphs cover all of the period from 1855 to 1964.

Essay questions

1 'The pace and extent of industrialisation were just as great under the tsars as under the communists from 1855 to 1964.' How far do you agree?

2 To what extent did Russian leaders make changes to agricultural policies only to serve the needs of industry from 1855 to 1964?

3 To what extent were peasants continuously treated with contempt and inhumanity during the period from 1855 to 1964?

4 Assess the reasons for fluctuations in living standards of urban dwellers during the period from 1855 to 1964.

5 'There was never any prospect of Russian people gaining full civil rights during the period from 1855 to 1964.' How far do you agree?

Evaluation and the historical interpretation in-depth question

In the first chapter we considered how to structure and plan an answer to the in-depth interpretation question. This chapter will look at how to evaluate, or apply your own knowledge, to one of the interpretations to judge its strengths and weaknesses. In the first paragraph you will have explained the two interpretations and placed them in the context of the wider historical debate about the issue.

Read the two interpretations below about the extent to which the policies of Alexander II improved the lives of the Russian people.

Evaluate the interpretations in both of the passages and explain which you think is the more convincing as an explanation of how the policies of Alexander II impacted on the lives of the Russian people.

PASSAGE A

The main events of his [Alexander II's] reign were, first and very foremost the freeing of the serfs; then, and partly in connection with this reform, real changes in local government, justice, education and the army. As so often happens, reform and relaxation were followed by protests, manifested notably by a revolutionary movement. The 'Tsar Emancipator' also had to cope with two burdens that had afflicted his father; cholera and the Poles. These trials led to reaction, and there was a partial return to tactics of repression. However, just before his assassination and having, as he thought, succeeded in calming the Empire, Alexander was considering a new series of reforms to relieve political pressures. Throughout the reign there was steady economic progress, expansion in Central Asia, some attempt to overcome the financial consequences of the Crimean War and a continuation of railway-building. In foreign affairs there was a rather unnecessary war against Turkey but Alexander was able to avoid other large-scale conflicts.

(J.N. Westwood, Endurance and Endeavour: Russian History 1812–2001, *Oxford University Press, 2002, p. 66.)*

PASSAGE B

In view of Alexander II's character – he was rather indolent and indecisive and despite public displays of emotion and kindheartedness capable of maintaining a severe police regime with all its attendant cruelties – it is surprising that it was especially his reign that became associated with the period of great reforms in Russian history. To the extent that in an autocracy good deeds are credited to the autocrat personally, he earned the title 'Tsar Liberator'. Nevertheless, his personal contribution to reforms was less positive than his more admiring biographers would have us believe. In many ways his influence impeded the practical realization of reforms that had become law. He was indecisive and throughout his reign alternated between reforming impulses and reaction. As his advisers he selected both true reformers such as Dimitri Milyutin [see pages 134–5] and extreme conservatives, men such as Dimitri Tolstoy, and kept both in office simultaneously. It was only with reluctance that Alexander took up the root cause of Russia's social ills, the problem of the serfs. Once a programme of emancipation had been devised, the other practical reforms of his reign followed from that.

The 'great reforms' of the 1860s did not liberate the Russian people. The process was so gradual, and the contrast between aspirations, the laws of the state and the realities of the situation were so stark, that the degree of discontent was raised more by the hope of reform than satisfied by their application.

(J. Grenville, Europe Reshaped, Blackwell, 1999, pp. 262–3.)

In evaluating the strengths and weaknesses of Passage A, consider the following response.

Response

According to the interpretation, Alexander II's reforms had both a positive and negative impact on the lives of Russians. Peasants, in particular, were given more freedoms, especially as a result of the Emancipation Edict of 1861. This had the knock-on effect of pushing the tsar to make positive changes in local government, the judicial system, education and the army. In general, the Russian people benefited from greater freedoms and opportunities provided by the reforms. However, the interpretation also highlights that Alexander II's policies backfired to an extent as by granting more liberties he gave the opportunity for the people to protest. It is indeed apparent that not long after the Emancipation Edict was issued, peasants complained that the distribution of land was unfair and that redemption payments were likely to make retaining land very difficult. Also, after the protests and assassination attempts, the tsar made the decision to resort to repression, which detracts from the reputation he formed as 'Tsar Liberator'. Overall, the interpretation gives a favourable assessment of Alexander II's policies; when compared with those of Nicholas I and the 'reaction' of Alexander III, Alexander II's achievements do seem to have marked a turning point in the lives of Russian people. However, throughout his reign, the tsar imposed his policies as an autocrat and the interpretation does not stress this enough.

Comment

- The response does start to evaluate the view of the interpretation about the impact of Alexander II's policies on the Russian people.
- Evidence from the interpretation is used to support the claim that it is a valid view.
- Detailed own knowledge is then applied to reinforce and support the evidence in the interpretation.
- A precise example of reform (Emancipation Edict) is used to support the claim.
- There is further evaluation referencing Alexander II's propensity to use repression when required.
- The evaluation finishes with balanced comment about how the interpretation stresses the positive side of the tsar's policies.

Activity

- Use information from this chapter to evaluate Passage B.

It might be helpful to consider the following questions to help you to structure your answer:

- What is the view of Passage B about the extent to which the policies of Alexander II improved the lives of the Russian people?
- What evidence is there in the interpretation to support your view?
- What knowledge do you have that supports this view?
- What knowledge do you have that challenges this view?

Check your work and highlight the evaluative words that you have used.

CHAPTER 3

The impact of war and revolution and the development of the Russian Empire and the USSR

This chapter focuses on how wars affected the development of the Russian Empire and the USSR throughout the period. To understand the consequences of wars, it is helpful to understand how they came about and unfolded. However, examination questions on this issue will always centre on the impact of wars on the development of the Russian Empire and the USSR. Where wars prompted economic and social change, this often had a knock-on effect for governments. Wars always disrupted patterns of economic growth, which meant that politicians then had to devise strategies for economic recovery. Thus, it is important to consider how wars had an impact on the economy and society and not just directly on politics and government.

Russians were involved in eight different wars from 1855 to 1964. The chapter covers these chronologically as follows:

★ The Crimean War 1853–6

★ The Russo-Turkish War 1877–8

★ The Russo-Japanese War 1904–5

★ The First World War 1914–18

★ The Russian Revolution 1917

★ The Russian Civil War 1917–21

★ The Second World War 1939–45

★ The Cold War 1947–64

It also considers the debates surrounding the three in-depth topics:

★ How far were Alexander II's reforms due to the Crimean War?

★ How far was the First World War responsible for the downfall of the Provisional Government?

★ How effectively did Khrushchev deal with the challenges posed by the Cold War?

1 The Crimean War 1853–6

▶ *What were the consequences of the Crimean War for the development of Russian government?*

The Crimean War was fought between Russia and the **Ottoman Turks**, with the latter supported by France and Britain. As with all the wars during the period, an understanding of the origins of the conflict helps to explain how it impinged on the development of government. The first section on origins provides background information and looks at events in the 1820s. Although this book covers the period from 1855 to 1964, it is relevant, with the Crimean War, to consider events that precede the start of the war. It would otherwise be very difficult to make any judgement about the relative importance of the war. Remember, though, that the OCR specification requires students to focus on the *effects* of wars on government, society, nationalities and the economy.

Long-term origins

Russia, along with the other **Great Powers**, was concerned to resolve the **Eastern question** in a way that best preserved its economic and political interests. A number of events illustrated how worried Russian tsars were over the crumbling Ottoman Empire (see Figure 3.1, page 130):

- In 1827, Russia, along with Britain and France, decided to support an agreement with Turkey to allow the Greeks to govern themselves (Greece had been part of the Ottoman Empire). The **sultan** of Turkey was reluctant to stick to the agreement, which resulted in the Battle of Navarino Bay. Russian, British and French naval squadrons combined to defeat the sultan's naval fleet. After this, Tsar Nicholas I reached an agreement with the sultan (under the Akkermann Convention) that allowed Russian merchant shipping easier access through the **Straits** and the Turkish seas. Two months later, the sultan reneged on the agreement and a full-blown war between Russia and Turkey ensued. After major Russian victories in the Balkans and Caucasus, the Treaty of Adrianople was signed. The Treaty of Adrianople (1829) stipulated that:

- The sultan had to honour the Akkermann agreements.
- Territory in the Caucasus and mouth of the Danube on the Black Sea was ceded to Russia.
- The Danubian **principalities** of Moldavia and Wallachia (both occupied by Russia during the war) were to be recognised as temporary Russian **protectorates**.

The war against Turkey had bothered Nicholas I as he believed that it contradicted the concept of **legitimism** that underpinned his foreign policy. Partly to make up for this, in 1833 he decided to help the Ottomans in a struggle against Egyptian rebels led by Mehmet Ali. Russian efforts were rewarded through the Treaty of Unkiar Skelesi.

KEY TERMS

Ottoman Turks Those who were part of the dynasty originally founded by Osman (c.1300) which governed the Turkish Empire until 1922.

Great Powers Britain, France, Russia, Germany (Prussia before 1871) and Austria-Hungary before 1914.

Eastern question The issues that arose over the decline of the Turkish Ottoman Empire.

Sultan Muslim head of the Ottoman Empire.

Straits The stretch of sea from the Dardanelles into the Bosphorus.

Principalities Territories ruled over by a member of a royal family, usually a prince.

Protectorates States that were temporarily protected by another, usually more powerful state.

Legitimism The policy based on the idea that what was being done was right and just in the eyes of the majority.

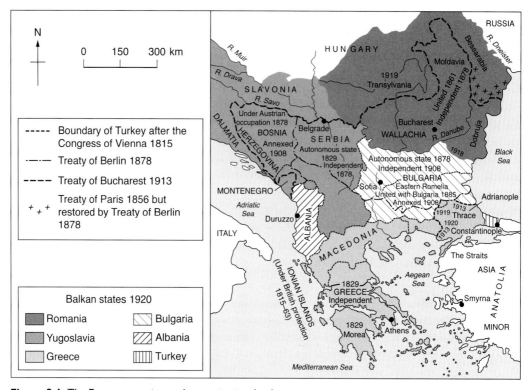

Figure 3.1 The Eastern question and countries involved.

The Treaty of Unkiar Skelesi (1833):

- Resulted in Turkey agreeing to close the Straits, during time of conflict, to foreign warships.
- It was also implied (although not clearly stated) that Russian warships would be allowed to enter the Bosphorus and, thus, the heart of the Ottoman Empire.
- The historian Walter G. Moss (2003) believes that this was the first attempt by Russia to 'transform the Turkish core area into a Russian protectorate'.
- In return, Russia agreed to support Turkey if it was attacked by another of the world powers.

A further revolt by Mehmet Ali culminated in the signing of the Straits Convention (1841). This, partly as a result of pressure from the other Great Powers, weakened Russia's arrangements with the Turks:

- All of the major European powers conceded that Turkey should ban all foreign warships from entering the Straits during periods of international tension.
- To clarify the confusion over the 1833 agreement, Russian warships were banned from the Dardanelles and the Bosphorus.

Although this aggrieved Nicholas I, he knew that Russia was not really in a position to go to war with any of the other European powers. He therefore proceeded to use diplomacy to ensure that Russia's interests in the East were preserved.

Short-term origins

By the middle of the nineteenth century, a dispute between Russia and France arose over Orthodox Christian and Catholic rights and duties in the Holy Lands, which were part of the Ottoman Empire. Arguments over this issue escalated and sparked the beginning of the Crimean War:

- Before the squabble erupted, Russia had persuaded the sultan to allow special privileges to be granted to Orthodox Christians in the Holy Lands. This was considered fair as Orthodox Christians represented a majority in the region and contributed much to the local economy.
- This arrangement was challenged, in 1851, by Charles Louis Napoleon (Napoleon III), the first president of the French Republic and Emperor of France from 1852 to 1870. He stated that, according to a rather obscure treaty of 1740, the French had a moral obligation to be the sole protectors of Christians in the Holy Lands. This sudden renewal of claim was made as a result of the French leader's desire to win back support from prominent members of the French Catholic Church.
- Late in 1852, the sultan agreed that Catholics should be consulted over the restoration of the **Holy Sepulchre** in Jerusalem and were to be given access to Bethlehem's Church of the Nativity.
- Nicholas I was understandably annoyed by the French intervention and sent Prince A.S. Menshikov to Constantinople to obtain confirmation of Russia's 'superior' rights in the Holy Land. The Turks were very worried by Menshikov's claims about the numbers of Christians and amount of territory that needed to be controlled by Russia and therefore refused his demands.
- In July 1853, Nicholas retaliated by sending troops into the principalities of Moldavia and Wallachia. Requests from the Turks, British and French were made for Nicholas to backtrack but he refused. Turkey then declared war on Russia (October 1853) and the British and French sent fleets to the Dardanelles, formally declaring war on Russia in March 1854. Nicholas then changed his mind and withdrew forces from the principalities, in August 1854, in an attempt to appease his European rivals. His actions came too late and by October the Siege of Sevastopol (the main port in the Crimea) had begun.

 **KEY TERM**

Holy Sepulchre The cave outside Jerusalem in which the body of Christ is believed to have lain between his burial and Resurrection.

The origins of the war show the tsar's concern to preserve Russia's status as one of the Great Powers. It was important for Nicholas to stand up to the British and French so that the Russian people maintained faith in the Romanovs and, hence, in autocracy. However, the background to the war also showed that Nicholas had many reservations about taking on the other powers; he was not confident that Russia had the right economic and social infrastructure to win a major conflict. The implication was that the Russian government would have to make some radical changes if Russia was to maintain its standing in the world.

The impact of the war

The poor showing of the Russian military during the war coupled with the stipulations of the Treaty of Paris led to public discussion about the future of the Russian Empire. A significant number of Russians, especially those known as Slavophiles, questioned how great Russia really was. Many argued that Russia's status as a great world power had been severely damaged.

Casualties

According to the historian Alan Farmer (2001), 'the Crimean War involved far heavier casualties than any other European war fought between 1815 and 1914.

The course of the Crimean War: main events

- November 1853: the Russians destroyed the Turkish fleet at Sinope. The sinking of part of the Turkish fleet was a response to a major Turkish attack on Russian forces positioned in Wallachia. Over 4000 Turks were killed and the incident sparked intense protest from Britain and France.

- January 1854: both the British and French navies were positioned in the Black Sea by this date. However, British politicians, despite public pressure, were still intent on averting a full-blown war.

- February 1854: Britain and France sent Russia an ultimatum to withdraw from the principalities, which was ignored. The British and French now felt obliged to commit to war.

- March 1854: British and French declared war on Russia and gave support to the Turks.

- August 1854: under pressure from the threat that Austria might join the war on the side of the British and French, Russia decided to pull out of the principalities. Austria proceeded to make peace proposals (the 'Four Points'), but these were not accepted by the tsar until November 1854. By that time, Britain showed a willingness to prolong the war to impose further damage on Russia and force the tsar to make greater concessions over access to the Black Sea.

- September 1854: Britain and France invaded the Crimea. However, they were slow to attack the key Crimean port of Sevastopol. This allowed

Russian forces to regroup within the port, which inevitably led to a siege. The Battle of Alma was the first major confrontation of the Crimean campaign. It was noteworthy due to the fact that the Russians lost 6000 troops and were using outmoded weaponry (Russian guns were captured that dated back to 1799). Other notable battles occurred at Inkerman and Balaclava but they failed to achieve a breakthrough for any of the forces concerned.

- February 1855: Nicholas I died of pneumonia. He was replaced by his son, Alexander II.

- October 1854 to September 1855: the Siege of Sevastopol. This was a long, drawn-out affair mainly due to adverse winter weather conditions, the fortifications of Sevastopol and the resilience of the Russian defenders. However, by August 1856, the Russians were suffering from 2000 to 3000 casualties daily. After a series of severe artillery bombardments in the late summer of 1856, the Russians eventually surrendered. The strategic importance of the port meant that surrender was a major setback for the Russians.

- September 1855 to January 1856: the war petered out during this period. Austria renewed threats to join the war and Russia eventually agreed to peace talks based on the original 'Four Points' plan (see above).

- March 1856: Treaty of Paris was agreed.

Between 650,000 and 750,000 are thought to have died. Britain lost 22,000, France 90,000, Russia 450,000 and Turkey about 150,000. Only one in five lost their lives in battle: most died of disease.'

The Treaty of Paris, March 1856

This resulted in the following:

- The duty to protect Christian subjects in the Ottoman Empire was handed over to the other European powers.
- Russia gave up its claim to act as the protector of the principalities.
- Russia had to agree to hand a substantial chunk of Bessarabia (part of the south-west Russian empire) to Moldavia.
- Most importantly, Russia was prohibited from maintaining a fleet in the Black Sea and had to remove all naval fortifications along the Black Sea coastline. Given the logistical importance of this to Russia, such a measure was humiliating.

The treaty obviously highlighted the weak position Russia found itself in. As the historian Geoffrey Hosking (2002) has argued, 'at a stroke Russia ceased to be a leading guarantor of the *status quo* and became a revisionist power, dedicated to regaining sovereign power over its own coastline'. Ironically, the seemingly harsh terms of the treaty illustrated how fearful the other European powers were of the **Great Russian Bear** and that the military weaknesses revealed in the war might easily be remedied.

 **KEY TERM**

Great Russian Bear
A term used by the West to describe the perceived military threat posed by Russia.

The war had an indirect impact on the development of Russian government in that it appeared to act as a catalyst for a number of significant economic, social and political reforms. A more direct impact came in the changes to the way in which localities' national minorities were governed, although this was linked to the major social reform of Alexander II's reign, the emancipation of the serfs.

The emancipation of the serfs

The Crimean War supposedly revealed Russia, in comparison to the other combatants, to be backward and underdeveloped. This was especially true when it came to transport, communications and the use of technology in general. Industrialisation had taken root in Russia, but it was progressing at a much slower rate than in Britain and France. For many Slavophiles and Westernisers, the root cause of this stagnation was the continued existence of serfdom. The Slavophile Samarin claimed that:

> *We are defeated not by the external forces of the Western alliance, but by our own internal weaknesses … stagnation of thought, depression of productive forces, the rift between government and people, disunity between the social classes, and the enslavement of one of them to another … prevent the government from deploying all the means available to it … and mobilising the strength of the nation.*

This was a sentiment that Alexander II sympathised with and it encouraged him to 'reform from above'.

Whether the tsar would have abolished serfdom regardless of the war is open to conjecture, but it is worth noting that Nicholas I had considered the idea but rejected it as it would have led to 'an even more ruinous evil' (that is, the loss of authority and land by the nobility). Also, it was some time after the war that the edict was actually made, suggesting that other considerations had to be made before the reform could be enacted (see profile on page 14). As serfdom had underpinned the way in which Russian society was structured, organised and administered, it was natural that its abolition would lead to some changes in the way Russia was to be governed.

Reform of local government

The emancipation of the serfs resulted in a reduced political role for the nobility at local level (see page 37). The creation of the *Zemstva* filled the gap but was also significant in that members of local government now had to be elected. Although this element of democracy was watered down by the fact that there were property qualifications attached to voting, it gave some indication that tsars might be prepared to lessen their autocratic grip. In the longer run though, when the *Zemstva* started to flex their muscles (see page 37), the tsarist regime returned to repression to quieten them.

Reform of the military

If Russia was to maintain its world status, it was crucial that a modernisation of the military occurred. At the start of the war, the Russian army consisted of about 1 million men made up mostly from peasants. To instil order, harsh discipline was enforced, including the notorious 'running of the gauntlet', a punishment which involved running through a tunnel of soldiers who would beat the miscreant with wooden clubs.

Accommodation was poor, which had the knock-on effect of diseases spreading; it is estimated that from 1833 to 1855, about 1 million soldiers died through ill-health. Coupled with the lack of decent clothing and equipment (including weapons), this meant that the morale of Russian troops was low. Leo Tolstoy summed up the situation towards the end of the war when he said that 'we have no army, we have a horde of slaves cowed by discipline, ordered about by thieves and slave traders'. It was no wonder, therefore, that many figures in the tsarist regime demanded reforms be made.

From 1862 to 1874, a string of military reforms were enacted under the guidance of **Dmitrii Milyutin**. Using the Prussian military system as a model, Milyutin reduced service in the army to fifteen years, modernised training and provided rigorous instruction for officers. The result was a far more professional army and

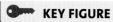

KEY FIGURE

Dmitrii Milyutin (1816–1912)

Military reformer and war minister (1861–81). His most notable achievements were the reorganisation of the army's administration, changes to conscription, the phasing out of the old cadet corps, the introduction of military schools and the establishment of a staff college.

one that was more in line with that of Western rivals. Also of importance to the government was the fact that it now had an army that, in theory, could be relied on to help maintain civil order at home as well as fight wars overseas.

Other reforms

During the reign of Alexander II there were other key reforms, most notably in the field of education and the Church (see pages 100–2 and 115). However, it would be difficult to link the origins of these changes to the Crimean War. One economic development of note that was undoubtedly stimulated by the conflict was the expansion of the railway system (see pages 79–80). The war had revealed how slowly Russia had been to mobilise resources compared with the enemy. Thus, railway development became a priority. Using foreign loans, nearly 2 billion roubles were spent on constructing over 20,000 km of track from 1861 to 1878. In a relatively short space of time, Russia had a transport system that boosted its ability to deal with the logistical problems of expanding, protecting and maintaining an empire.

The changes and most of the reforms of Alexander II's period of rule undoubtedly appear to be linked to the Crimean War. But, it is still important to consider whether such changes would have occurred without the war. Also, although Russia seemed to enter a more liberal phase of government post-Crimea, autocracy remained firmly in place (see page 13).

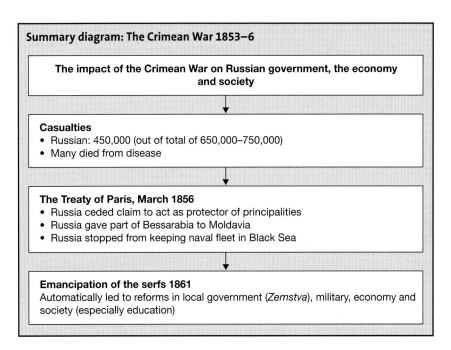

Summary diagram: The Crimean War 1853–6

The impact of the Crimean War on Russian government, the economy and society

Casualties
- Russian: 450,000 (out of total of 650,000–750,000)
- Many died from disease

The Treaty of Paris, March 1856
- Russia ceded claim to act as protector of principalities
- Russia gave part of Bessarabia to Moldavia
- Russia stopped from keeping naval fleet in Black Sea

Emancipation of the serfs 1861
Automatically led to reforms in local government (*Zemstva*), military, economy and society (especially education)

The Russo-Turkish War 1877–8

▶ *How valid is the view that the Russo-Turkish War had a limited impact on the development of the Russian Empire?*

Long-term origins

By the 1870s, Russia was finding difficulty in maintaining friendly relations with Austria. Both had an interest in the Balkans and, more generally, the Eastern question. Austria was especially concerned at the increase in Slav nationalism, which appeared to be seriously destabilising the Ottoman Empire. The Austro-Hungarian Empire had a significant Slavic population and there was a fear that they would be influenced by what was happening in other Slavic communities. Russian interest in the Balkans revolved around religious issues (that is, the need to protect Orthodox Christians living in the region) and the strategic importance of the Black Sea and Mediterranean.

The 1870s also witnessed a rise in Russian nationalism and **pan-Slavism**. One of the main influences was the Slavonic Benevolent Committee (SBC) led by **M.P. Pogodin**. Some very prominent members of the Russian intelligentsia belonged to this body, including Dostoevsky, Fadeev, Aksakov and Ignatiev. By 1877, it had over 1000 committed members but was probably more significant in terms of the pressure it was exerting on senior politicians to adopt a foreign policy that focused on uniting Slav peoples.

Short-term origins

In the middle of 1875, Herzegovina, closely followed by Bosnia, rebelled against the Ottomans (see Figure 3.1, page 130). By the spring of 1876, they were joined by Bulgaria and, in the summer, Serbia and Montenegro actually declared war on Turkey. A Russian plan to stop the crisis escalating was presented to the warring parties. Land, tax and religious reforms were promised to the Balkan states (to be administered by Turkey) but this package was unacceptable to the other Western states, especially Britain. The British prime minister, Disraeli, was wary of Russia trying to manipulate a situation to benefit its own interests. The plan was never implemented and the war raged on.

The Russian people continued to provide support for their Slav compatriots. Pressure on the Russian government to take more direct action grew from different quarters. The SBC, the Orthodox Church, the military and individuals such as Dmitri Tolstoy all campaigned for the tsar to be more belligerent. Connected to this was the Ignatiev initiative, which resulted in the Russian ambassador in Constantinople intimating to the Serbs that they could rely on Russian military support if the war intensified.

 **KEY TERM**

Pan-Slavism The movement to unite all Slavic peoples as one nation.

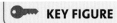 **KEY FIGURE**

M.P. Pogodin (1800–75)
A well-known and highly respected professor of Russian history.

By the autumn of 1876, it was evident that the Serbs were losing the war. Russia threatened to attack Turkey unless a truce was called. Their wish was granted and a six-week armistice was granted.

After the armistice had finished, Turkey returned to taking an aggressive stance against the Serbs. Mostly as a result of Russian public opinion, Alexander II declared war on Turkey in April 1877. The decision was aided by Austria agreeing to remain neutral as long as it could have jurisdiction over Herzegovina and Bosnia. The war was welcomed by Russian intellectuals, particularly the radicals and liberals. They saw the war as an opportunity to release fellow Slavs from the tyranny of an imperialist oppressor.

> ### The course of the Russo-Turkish War: main events
> - Russian forces faced difficulties in the early stages of the war, especially in Bulgaria and the Caucasus. Nevertheless, despite experiencing thousands of casualties, the army advanced.
> - It is worth noting that the army was still in a period of transition after the Milyutin reforms. Weaknesses that had been apparent in the Crimean War had not been fully eradicated.
> - There were two exceptions to the above. The engineering section of the army shone; it was crucial to the successful crossing of the Danube and to the capture of Plevna. The Russian navy was also very successful in using steam-powered vessels to destroy the Turkish fleet.
> - Early in 1878, Turkey agreed to an armistice.

The impact of the war

In March 1879, the Treaty of San Stefano was signed between Russia and Turkey. It stipulated the following:

- Russia was to regain South Bessarabia, which it had lost during the Crimean War.
- Russia also made substantial territorial gains in the Caucasus.
- Turkey was forced to pay a **war indemnity** to Russia.
- Recognition was given to the independence of Serbia, Montenegro and Romania. Serbia and Montenegro also made their own territorial gains.
- Turkey was served the task of carrying out reforms to benefit Herzegovina and Bosnia.
- A 'large' Bulgaria was established.

Unfortunately for Russia, the conditions of the treaty offended and worried Austria-Hungary and Britain. Russia feared that those who were upset might decide to provoke a bigger, more costly conflict over the Balkans. The tsar therefore decided to accept an offer from the German chancellor, Bismarck, to

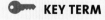 **KEY TERM**

War indemnity A sum of money paid by one nation to another as a result of losing a war.

broker a bigger peace conference in Berlin. The Congress of Berlin was held in mid-1878. The following was decided:

- Russia was allowed to retain its right to South Bessarabia and gains in the Caucasus.
- Austria-Hungary was to govern Herzegovina and Bosnia.
- Britain took over the administration of Cyprus to strengthen its interests and influence in the Balkans.
- Bulgaria became smaller.

Although Russia gained territory and money (from the indemnity) and saw the Ottoman Empire further weakened, Russian nationalists were very unhappy at what happened in Berlin. For the pan-Slavic supporters in particular, the concessions made to Austria-Hungary and Britain were unacceptable. They saw this as amounting to a loss of world status. Alexander II found it very difficult to deal with the unrest that this created and some historians have argued that this one event was responsible for his assassination in 1884.

Summary diagram: The Russo-Turkish War 1877–8

The impact of the Russo-Turkish war on Russian government, the economy and society

Impact on government (1)
Treaty of San Stefano 1876
- Russia regained lost regions of Bessarabia
- Turkey paid war indemnity to Russia
- Large Bulgaria created
Conditions threatened relations with Austria-Hungary and Britain

Impact on government (2)
Congress of Berlin 1878
- Russia retained rights to Bessarabia
- Austria-Hungary and Britain gained territorial rights
- Small Bulgaria created
Russian nationalists unhappy with concessions: caused unrest

Impact on economy
Revealed Russian industrial progress (engineering, steam power)

Impact on society
Some social unrest due to conditions resulting from Congress of Berlin

The Russo-Japanese War 1904–5

▶ *How far did the Russo-Japanese War differ from the wars that
preceded 1904 with respect to the impact on the development of
the Russian Empire?*

Long-term origins

In 1894, Japan fought a limited war against China with the aim of gaining
territory already under Chinese control. Japan won and was 'rewarded' by
obtaining land around Port Arthur together with a war indemnity. Russia
and the other Great Powers were worried that Japan might expand further to
threaten their own economic interests in the east. Using skilful diplomacy, the
Great Powers were able, in a fairly short space of time, to persuade Japan to
return Port Arthur to the Chinese. But the situation was further complicated by
the facts that Russia gave money to China to pay off its war debts and that China
was compliant in allowing Russia to construct the Chinese Eastern Railway
across Manchuria (therefore expanding Russian influence in the area).

In 1897, Germany invaded Kiaochow, in eastern China, and the other Great
Powers demanded a share of the spoils. France became more active in the south
of China and Britain looked to consolidate its interests in central China. Russia
was wary of the Western Europeans expanding their influence in this way.

Russia was able to negotiate a 25-year lease of Port Arthur from China and
turned it into a naval base. The latter was then joined to the Chinese Eastern
Railway via a branch line. Japan obviously felt threatened by this as the influence
of the Great Powers increasingly started to impinge on Japan's own sphere of
interest. In particular, Port Arthur was strategically placed and gave the Russians
great scope for controlling the seas between China and Japan.

The Chinese grew angry at the incursions of the Great Powers into their
territory. Unrest in China resulted in the **Boxer Rebellion**. As the Russians
started supporting the Western Europeans during this time (despite reservations
about their intentions in China), especially with the help of the navy based at
Port Arthur, a mini-war between Russia and China broke out. Russia easily
defeated the Chinese but, as a result of Japanese intervention, Russia backed
down from insisting on too severe a peace treaty. In fact, Russia agreed to
withdraw forces from Manchuria by 1903. Russian leaders seemed happy
enough with the military victory, which they believed showed that their forces
were superior to any oriental army.

Russia and Japan continued to reveal an interest in occupying and controlling
Korea. Some historians have argued that Japan was willing to work a trade-off
that would have allowed Russia to stay in Manchuria while Japan took over
Korea. However, it is not clear what exactly the Russian government wanted.

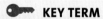 **KEY TERM**

Boxer Rebellion A seven-
week siege of foreign
embassies in Peking (now
Beijing) by Chinese rebels.

Some ministers, such as Plevhe, minister of the interior, seemed to be pushing for an outright war with Japan to settle disagreements once and for all. This would have had the added bonus of deflecting the attention of the Russian public away from mounting social problems. Others, worrying mainly about financial cost and lack of preparedness, were against a war. They included **Kuropatkin** and **Lamsdorff**; there is more disagreement over the stance of Witte who held, at this time, the important position of minister of finance. Japanese attempts at diplomacy over the Korean issue were rebuffed by the St Petersburg administration. Partly as a result, Japan, in 1902, formulated an alliance with Britain. As France was an ally of Britain, the French were unlikely to take sides with Russia if a war between Russia and Japan was to break out.

Short-term origins

Russia reneged on its promise to withdraw troops from Manchuria, which angered the Japanese. In February 1903, Japan retaliated by launching a night attack on the Pacific Squadron at Port Arthur. This escapade was something of a shambles but it did result in damage to three Russian ships. It also seemed to have a negative effect on Russian morale.

Japan then proceeded to blockade Port Arthur. Preparations were made by both parties for a major sea battle to occur.

The impact of the war

General

Similarly to the Crimean War, the disastrous outcome of the Russo-Japanese War led to doubts being expressed about the ability of the tsar to maintain Russia's world status and concerns about the effectiveness of autocracy in general. Also, in comparison to the Crimean War, the conflict with Japan was followed by significant reform. This was because the Russo-Japanese War seemed to spark far more social unrest in the Russian homeland, which in turn influenced the nature of the reforms enacted by Nicholas II.

The Treaty of Portsmouth, August 1905

This resulted in the following:

- Russia was forced to withdraw from Port Arthur, south Sakhalin and south Manchuria.
- Russian leaders had to acknowledge Japanese sovereignty in Korea.

Reforms

The war revealed that Russian military leaders had a lack of knowledge, understanding and skill in dealing with an enemy that, on paper, was vastly inferior. The Russian public associated military incompetence of this scale with the tsar himself; this appeared to fuel discontent at home rather than

KEY FIGURES

A.N. Kuropatkin (1848–1925)

Military reformer and war minister (1898–1904). His military approach to the Russo-Japanese War was to adopt attritional tactics, delaying an offensive until logistical issues could be resolved; his indecisive and cautious approach is often cited as the reason for the Russian military defeats.

V.N. Lamsdorff (1841–1907)

One of Nicholas II's most valued ministers (foreign minister 1900–5). Lamsdorff worked alongside Witte to negotiate the terms of the Treaty of Portsmouth.

The course of the Russo-Japanese War: main events

- Battle of Yalu. The Japanese moved north from Korea to confront Russia in southern Manchuria. Outnumbered by about three to one, Russian forces were well beaten. This was an enormous shock to the tsar and the other Great Powers.

- The siege of Port Arthur continued, isolating about 60,000 Russian troops. In December 1905, the port eventually surrendered.

- May 1905: Rozhestvensky's Baltic Squadron, on its way to relieve Port Arthur, came up against Admiral Togo's fleet at Tsushima Straits. This proved to be another terrible defeat for Russia and emphasised the technological superiority of the Japanese navy.

- 1905: the final straw for Russia came with a humiliating defeat at Mukden. This prompted peace talks and the signing of a treaty.

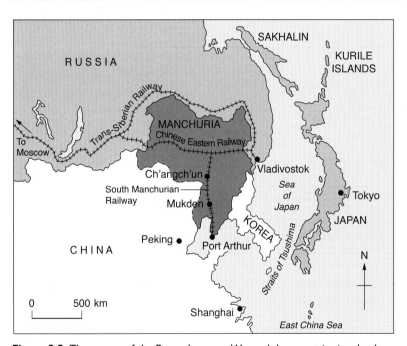

Figure 3.2 The course of the Russo-Japanese War and the countries involved.

extinguish it, which had been one of the key aims of the war. In fact, some historians believe that the social unrest that occurred in 1905 was tantamount to a revolution. Thus, Nicholas II, rather reluctantly, introduced an element of democracy to Russia by setting up the *Duma* (see pages 28–9). The hope was that the public would be convinced that the tsar was willing to become more accountable for his actions and those of his advisers. It is unlikely that this would have happened without the war, as the tsar was a staunch adherent of 'Autocracy, Orthodoxy and Nationality'. This is reinforced by the fact that in a very short space of time the powers of the *Duma* were greatly diminished.

Despite the expansion of Russia's rail network since the Crimean War, the Russo-Japanese conflict revealed serious communication and transport weaknesses. The Trans-Siberian Railway, still unfinished, had failed to solve the logistical problem of getting troops and supplies to war zones quickly and efficiently. The result was further investment in the transport infrastructure and, more generally, in industry. Ironically, such developments also led to rapid urbanisation and mounting public health problems. Poor working and living conditions produced an increasingly discontented populace; reforms were enacted with the promise of raising living standards but they appeared to do the reverse.

Summary diagram: Similarities and differences in the effects of the Crimean, Russo-Turkish and Russo-Japanese wars on the development of Russian government

Similarities	Differences
• Russia lost to enemies that, on paper, they should have defeated • The Russian people were critical of leaders and took to the streets to protest • The wars all led to programmes of reform • Some of the reforms were designed to change the way Russia was governed but autocracy remained in place after each conflict • The wars were costly but not as damaging to the economy as later wars proved to be	• The Crimean War was different from the others in that Russia had to fight Britain and France as well as Turkey • The level of social unrest that followed the Russo-Japanese War was much higher than that which led on from the other two wars. Some historians go as far as to say the protests of 1905 constituted a revolution • The Russo-Turkish War had the least significant impact on the development of Russian government

---

 # The First World War 1914–18

▶ *To what extent was the First World War responsible for the Russian Revolution of 1917?*

Long-term origins

KEY TERM

Prussia The most important German state before the unification of Germany in 1871.

For most of the nineteenth century, Russian foreign policy was dependent on the maintenance of friendly relations with **Prussia** and Austria-Hungary. This fell apart when the unified Germany under Wilhelm II failed to renew the Reinsurance Treaty of 1887 (a treaty between Russia and Germany whereby both parties agreed not to support a third party with whom either might fall into conflict). Russia was then pushed to seek new allies and subsequently formed an alliance, in 1894, with France. This was logical given that the other great European power, Britain, remained wary of Russian designs.

Relations with France were further strengthened after the Russo-Japanese War as Russia actively sought allies in case further conflicts with Japan occurred.

Given the cordial nature of relations between France and Britain, it was not long before France, Britain and Russia joined together to form the Triple Entente to counter the threat of the growing partnership between Austria and Germany (the Central Powers). As the latter were stronger, in a military sense, than Russia, some historians have argued that the Triple Entente was not the best arrangement for the tsar to agree to.

The continued break-up of the Ottoman Empire worsened the relationship between Austria-Hungary and Russia. Both had an interest in the Eastern question, with Austria-Hungary looking to protect its own empire from Balkan nationalist influence and Russia seeking to support Slavic Balkan states when necessary. In 1908, Russia made a deal with Austria-Hungary that once again allowed Russian shipping free movement through the Straits (see Figure 3.1, page 130) in exchange for Russian support for the Austrian annexation of Bosnia-Herzegovina. Two problems arose from this:

- Serbia believed that Bosnia-Herzegovina was Serbian and that, as a Slavic country, its claims deserved support from compatriot Slavs (especially Russia).
- The other European powers rejected the idea of allowing Russia easy access through the Straits.
- Germany reacted by stating that it would support Austria-Hungary if the so-called Annexation Crisis got out of hand.

The tsarist regime felt humiliated by and helpless at the German response; Russia was simply not prepared enough to take on the Central Powers and win.

The Balkan Wars of 1912–13 (see box) were also a disappointment to Russia. The hope had been that the **Balkan League** would deal a serious blow to the prestige and status of Austria-Hungary but instead they squabbled over gains made from the Turks. Bulgaria, in particular, was weakened by this episode; this was serious for Russia as Bulgaria was seen as the Slav state most in line with Russian thinking and planning.

The Balkans crisis was significant in that it illustrated that Russia was not in a position to dictate how serious conflicts between the European powers could be resolved. It once more revealed a degree of political and military impotence, which angered people at home and did not bode well if disagreements over the Balkans escalated.

 **KEY TERM**

Balkan League An alliance, put together between the spring and autumn of 1912, between Serbia, Bulgaria, Greece and Montenegro.

Balkan Wars of 1912–13

These came in two phases. First, the Balkan League went to war against Turkey with the hope of getting the Turks to withdraw from Macedonia so that the latter could be divided up among League members. The Turks were defeated and signed an armistice in December 1912. Second, immediately after the armistice, Bulgaria claimed that it was being cheated out of territory handed over by the Turks by another member of the League, Serbia. Bulgaria then attacked Serbia. Greece, Romania and Turkey went to the aid of the Serbs and the Bulgarian forces were defeated. Bulgaria was forced to hand over all of the gains made during the first war.

Short-term origins

In June 1914, Archduke Franz Ferdinand of Austria-Hungary was assassinated by Gabriel Princip, a member of a Serbian nationalist group. From this point in time it was virtually impossible for Russia not to get involved in a disagreement that was likely to grow into a much bigger conflict. Russia had an obligation to protect Serbia, a fellow Slavic state, against possible Austrian retaliation. There was also the prospect that the incident would galvanise Austria-Hungary into using a war against Serbia as a springboard for making other gains in the Balkans, which would have been detrimental to Russian interests. Thus, it was not surprising that, when Austria-Hungary declared war on Serbia in July 1914, Russia reacted by issuing a **mobilisation order**.

Mobilisation caused a dilemma for Russian politicians and military leaders. A partial mobilisation, in defence of the Slavic countries in the south-west, would have left Russia vulnerable to attack by Germany in the west. As the Russian railway system was still inadequate in that links to the west were undeveloped, it would have been very difficult, at short notice, to move troops to defend against a German incursion. On the other hand, there were those who argued that full mobilisation was too antagonistic and that Russia might find itself embroiled in a war on a scale that was catastrophic.

The full mobilisation order of 30 July was designed to act as a deterrent but it did not prevent both Germany (1 August) and Austria-Hungary (5 August) from declaring war on Russia. This was quickly followed by the implementation of the German **Schlieffen Plan** and further built on by the establishment of an **Eastern Front**. This rapid escalation of the conflict was what the bulk of Russian leaders had feared the most.

KEY TERMS

Mobilisation order
The order by the government for the military to be organised to go to war. A part mobilisation refers to some of the military being prepared for a limited conflict. Full mobilisation means that all of the military would be in a state of readiness to go to war.

Schlieffen Plan The plan put together in 1905 by the chief of the German General Staff, General Count Alfred Von Schlieffen (1833–1913), to act partly as a blueprint for a German attack in the West.

Eastern Front Where the German and Austrian-Hungarian forces met the Russian forces in Eastern Europe.

The course of the First World War: main events

- August and September 1914: an initial Russian victory at Gumbinnen in Prussia was followed by disastrous defeats at Tannenberg and the Masurian Lakes, also in Prussia.

- February 1915: Russian forces were pushed back from East Prussia but in March managed to take Memel in Prussia.

- August 1915: Nicholas II took personal command of the Russian forces much to the consternation of many of his advisers. The Russian retreat was temporarily halted but by September, Nicholas was forced to abandon Vilna.

- February 1916: a glimmer of hope emerged as Russian troops took Ezerum from the Ottomans.

- June 1916: the Brusilov Offensive was launched with the intention of gaining lost ground and appeasing discontent that was spreading at home. There was some initial success but the Germans easily snuffed out the threat.

- June and July 1917: an all-out attack on Austrian forces was made but by the end of July the Russians were once more in retreat.

- August 1917: Russia withdrew from the strategically important port of Riga in Latvia.

- December 1917: peace talks at Brest-Litovsk resulted in the signing of a treaty (1918). Trotsky claimed that the conditions amounted to a *diktat* (see pages 196–9).

The impact of the war

A useful way of analysing the impact of the First World War on the development of the Russian Empire is to consider two schools of thought: one is the so-called 'optimist' school, the other the 'pessimist' school.

The optimists

The optimists argue that tsarism and autocracy, by definition, were extremely resilient to the forces of change. It needed a dramatic and unique event to change the nature of Russian government completely. The First World War fitted the bill perfectly. The optimists claim that Russia was never able to get to grips with the demands of the world's first industrial war (that is, the first large-scale war to be fought using the products of industrialisation) and it was inevitable that the Russian people would point the finger of blame towards those who had led them into the conflict. Furthermore, without the war, the tsar would have coped with the demands for further constitutional reform and, gradually, changes to government would have occurred which would quieten the critics. This was already a trend that had started after 1905, and there was little reason to believe that further progress would not be made.

The optimist line of thought about the impact of the war is neat and cogent. Military failures resulted in economic pressures, which in turn had a negative impact on the daily lives of Russians on the **Home Front**. The consequence was that impetus was given to levels of social unrest not witnessed before. The scale and degree of coordinated protest were such that the authorities could not cope and only a drastic change in government averted a state of anarchy (that is, the replacement of tsarism with the Provisional Government. See the depth study section on pages 169–70 for more detailed discussion of the impact of the war on the new government).

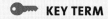

KEY TERM

Home Front What was happening domestically during the war, especially with respect to the wartime work civilians were involved in.

Military failures

Military historians seem to agree that the best chance of Russian military success was at the start of the war. However, the terrible defeats at Tannenberg and the Masurian Lakes meant that the morale of the Russian troops was severely dented. Russian soldiers had actually fought well but they were let down by the poor strategic decision-making of Generals Samsonov and Rennenkampf. The Russians lost twice as many troops as the enemy during these early campaigns and the hope at home that Russia would score an early victory waned. Russian casualties for the whole of the war were around 8 million, including 1.7 million dead and 2.4 million captured.

By the end of 1915, Stavka, the command centre for the Russian army, blamed the lack of military progress on the 'shells crisis'. The implication of this was that industry was struggling to keep up with the demands of the army and, therefore, workers had to put much more effort into increasing munitions production. The truth of the matter was that industry was already working near to full capacity. As the historian Norman Stone has argued (1998), the problem was not that there was a deficit of munitions but it was more a case that military administrators did not have the ability to cope with the logistical challenges posed by the war. This was made worse by communication and transport problems (similar to those that existed in the Crimean and Russo-Japanese Wars). It was not surprising that stockpiling of supplies occurred; piles of foodstuffs rotted away and, at Archangel (in northern Russia), the mountains of hardware were so great that they started to sink into the ground.

Further defeats and the subsequent Great Retreat in 1915 (see page 144) prompted Nicholas II to take the unprecedented step of taking personal control of the armed forces. By early 1916, it looked as though Russian military prospects had picked up. However, the tsar's decision to leave the capital (renamed Petrograd at the start of the war) left a political vacuum. The tsarina, Alexandra, was left as a temporary *de facto* ruler. This was not popular with the *Duma* and supporters of the tsar, partly due to Alexandra's German background but also because of her 'friendship' with Rasputin (see pages 29–30). All of this resulted in mounting criticism of Nicholas and a window of opportunity for those who wanted to push for a more liberal political set-up.

Although Russia's war effort seemed to improve throughout 1916, the failure of the Brusilov Offensive and the emergence of **attrition warfare** gave indications that the tsar was not capable of bringing the conflict to a satisfactory end. By the time the tsar was forced to abdicate, it was not inevitable that Russia would be defeated by Germany. Nevertheless, the domestic upheaval that proceeded throughout 1917 meant that the war was unlikely to turn in Russia's favour and the Bolshevik decision to withdraw from the conflict in 1918 was, for many, sensible and logical. Not all agreed with this; patriots (mainly conservatives and supporters of the tsar) and a host of others of various political persuasions wanted a continuation of the war to the bitter end. This further supports the view of the optimists that the impact of the war was crucial in determining the development of Russian government.

Economic and social factors

The financial burden of the war was huge, although this only became apparent from the middle of 1916 onwards. The total cost was in the region of 3 billion roubles, which far exceeded levels of government expenditure during peacetime. In 1913, for example, government expenditure was about 1.5 billion roubles. The cost was met partly through borrowing (foreign loans, **War Bonds**), increases in tax (income, excess profits) and printing more money. Such measures worked to an extent; for most of the war, enough money was invested in Russian industry to enable it to meet the projected demands of the military. It also meant that Russian workers were fully employed and received a regular and slightly higher

KEY TERMS

Attrition warfare Where no progress is made by either side during a war but both sides continue to wear each other down until one gives way.

War Bonds Government savings certificates issued during wartime to the public with a promised fixed rate of return after the war. They had the important psychological impact of making people feel that they were making a valid contribution to the war effort.

income than usual. However, the latter was offset by rampant inflation, the inevitable consequence of an increase in the circulation of money. Prices had risen 400 per cent by 1917 from the start of the war, and, as is always the case with inflation, those on fixed incomes suffered greatly.

Even if peasants and workers were able to at least maintain a decent level of real income, the likelihood of being able to spend it on even the bare necessities reduced as the war progressed. This was especially the case after 1916 with respect to food supplies. Throughout the war period, the average output of cereals was higher than it had been during the first decade of the twentieth century. But, a rapidly rising population, food requisitioning by the army, a fall in the availability of fertilisers and transport problems all worked together to create food shortages. Some historians have pointed out that this was largely a regional problem; those in Petrograd suffered more than others, with, for example their bread ration falling by 25 per cent in the first three months of 1916. But regional variation is not particularly important as the social unrest that resulted from high prices and shortages gathered momentum in the places where it was likely to have the greatest impact – the growing towns and cities in the west of Russia.

For the optimists, adverse wartime conditions on such a scale had never existed before. It was not surprising that such unique circumstances united those who suffered the most hardship to challenge the ruling elite and demand a far more representative form of government.

Political consequences

Military weaknesses and mounting economic problems gave fuel to the critics of the tsar. Under pressure from military advisers, the Progressive Bloc in the *Duma* (see page 29), friends and relatives, Nicholas decided to abdicate from the throne. Romanov rule was replaced by the unelected Provisional Government. Optimists believe that the continuation of the war made it impossible for the temporary government to deal with the burning issues of land reform, the modernisation of industry and the call for a Constituent Assembly. Thus, the war gave an opportunity to revolutionaries to overthrow the government completely and install their own form of direct rule. As the historian Stephen Lee has pointed out (2006), the war was obviously '… a turning point – which actually turned twice'.

The pessimists

The pessimists argue against the First World War being a significant turning point for the following reasons:

- The tsar had been struggling for some time to deal with the demands for a constitutional government. The *Duma* had developed a progressive bloc before the war; this was acknowledged by Nicholas II, which was why he restricted the composition and freedoms of the *Duma*. Generally, Nicholas had proved to be an incompetent leader and it was only a matter of time before a serious challenge was made to depose him. The war is seen by pessimists as an event that simply speeded up his demise.

- The rise of the working classes as a distinct form of opposition to autocracy had also gained momentum. It went hand in hand with large-scale industrialisation and urbanisation, which could be traced back at least to Witte's 'Great Spurt' (see pages 81–2). Greater working-class consciousness was reinforced by the legalisation of political parties that represented their interests, the growth of trade unions and the setting up of soviets. Again, the war accelerated these trends and was not responsible for the emergence of working-class agitation.

The pessimists' view is clearly one that sympathises with the efforts of the working classes to gain greater concessions and freedoms over a long period. It is a pro-Bolshevik standpoint but fails to fully explain why, given the failure of the July Days (see page 31), the Bolsheviks were able to seize complete control in October 1917. This could not simply have been the inevitable consequence of class struggle that had been going on for some time.

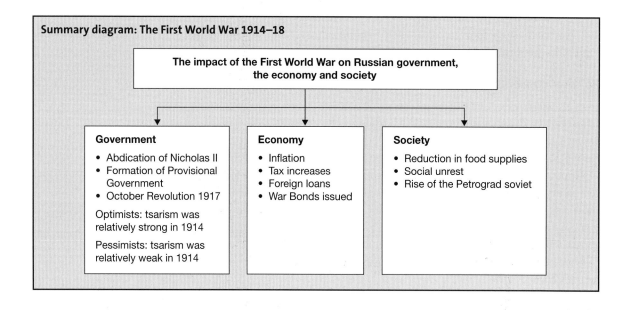

Summary diagram: The First World War 1914–18

The impact of the First World War on Russian government, the economy and society

Government
- Abdication of Nicholas II
- Formation of Provisional Government
- October Revolution 1917

Optimists: tsarism was relatively strong in 1914

Pessimists: tsarism was relatively weak in 1914

Economy
- Inflation
- Tax increases
- Foreign loans
- War Bonds issued

Society
- Reduction in food supplies
- Social unrest
- Rise of the Petrograd soviet

The Russian Revolution 1917

▶ *How does the revolution compare with the other wars with respect to the impact on the development of Russian government?*

The origins, course and consequences of the revolution have been discussed in Chapter 1. However, it is worth making some further general points about the conflict:

- The revolution can hardly be described as a war; the final overthrow of the Provisional Government and the short-lived Constituent Assembly was achieved with very little force and bloodshed.
- The origins of the revolution are obviously quite complex. It is still useful to consider the causes of the conflict in the traditional way (that is, long term and short term). What triggered the final takeover by the Bolsheviks is probably the most contentious part of the story and is inextricably tied up with the impact of the First World War.
- It is reasonable to argue that the course of the revolution ran from March 1917 until October, although some would argue that it is important to include the initial attempts by the Bolsheviks to consolidate power. This would mean that the revolution merges into the Civil War.
- The impact of the revolution at first glance seems obvious. The Bolshevik seizure of power was truly revolutionary in that it put an end to government by a regime associated, via the *Duma*, with Russia's autocratic past. The promise, at the time, was that the Provisional Government would be replaced initially by the dictatorship of the proletariat, which would eventually give way to a stateless society, that is, communism. If this had succeeded, then the consequences of the revolution would have been truly momentous, not just for Russia but probably for the rest of the world. However, for a variety of reasons, the dictatorship *of* the proletariat was transformed into a situation whereby Lenin dictated *to* the proletariat, and the rest of Russian society. Dictatorship under Stalin, akin to that which emerged in other parts of Europe during the inter-war period, became a form of totalitarianism. It could be argued that this was an extreme form of autocracy. It is no wonder that this has led to claims that the tsars were simply replaced with Red Tsars; leaders who were different in appearance and background but almost identical in terms of how they ruled. This would mean that the revolution, in conjunction with the First World War and the Civil War, did not really result in major changes to the governance of Russia even though the events themselves appeared dramatic.

Summary diagram: The Russian Revolution 1917

The short-term and long-term impact of the Russian Revolution 1917 on Russian government, the economy and society

Impact	Government	Economy	Society
Short term	• Overthrow of the Provisional Government • Bolshevik seizure of power (or popular uprising?)	• Link to Civil War resulted in economic dislocation	• Link to Civil War resulted in disruption to social institutions • Dictatorship of the proletariat (or proletariat dictated to?)
Long term	• Dictatorship of the proletariat (or proletariat dictated to?) • Dictatorship • Totalitarianism	• Dictatorship and totalitarianism led to centralised planning and control	• Dictatorship and totalitarianism led to centralised planning and control of social institutions

6 The Russian Civil War 1917–21

▶ *Did the Civil War help or hinder the development of Russian government?*

Origins

The origins of the war can be traced to Russia's involvement in the First World War and the Russian Revolution. What this also indicates is that the Civil War was, indirectly, the result of a culmination of events that led to the other two wars mentioned above. This makes using the long- and short-term framework for analysing wars inappropriate in the case of the Civil War; it does not have a distinct, separate set of causes as the other wars do.

The Bolsheviks' seizure of power in October 1917 sparked chaos throughout what was still the Russian Empire. Different political and regional groups reacted according to their individual wants and needs; some saw the October Revolution as an opportunity to launch a counter-offensive against the Bolsheviks while others moved to attempt to gain long-awaited independence from Russian central government. The one single event that probably signalled the start of the war was Kerensky's Petrograd offensive (see page 151). This was suppressed with relative ease but other shows of resistance proved more challenging. The fact that the Civil War lasted over four years gives testament to the scale and magnitude of the forces that were determined to overthrow Lenin and his comrades.

The course of the Russian Civil War: main events

- November 1917: Kerensky's and General Krasnov's offensive was brought to a halt.
- Spring 1918: opposition from Cossacks in the region of the Don and the Urals was nullified.
- April 1918: having defeated General Kornilov's volunteer army, Lenin proclaimed that the war was about to end. Foreign intervention occurred in this month when British marines were sent to support those opposing the Bolsheviks.
- May 1918: the Czech Legion on its way back to Vladivostok revolted and became a focus for those who wanted to add extra military muscle to their efforts against the Red Army. The Socialist Revolutionaries (SRs), in particular, were keen to ally with the Czechs.
- July 1918: the tsar and most of his family were executed by the *Cheka* at Ekaterinburg.
- August 1918: Trotsky signalled his intent in ensuring the cohesiveness of the Red Army by executing deserters. The Bolsheviks became concerned at the arrival of more foreign troops, this time from the USA.
- September 1918: the Directory government emerged at Ufa. It was made up primarily of SRs and Czechs. By this time, opposition fighting forces were known as the White armies.
- November 1918: Admiral Kolchak announced himself as supreme ruler (of the White armies).
- December 1918 to the end of 1920: White armies fought against the Reds. The Red Army, based mainly in Moscow, initially soaked up attacks from the Whites from all directions. From October 1919 onwards, the Red Armies scored notable victories over the Whites (for example, against General Deniken, leader of the White Volunteer Army, at Orel, and General Yudenich, leader of White forces made up of prisoners of war released by Germany, at Petrograd). By the depths of winter, the Red Army had started to advance. In January 1920, Admiral Kolchak resigned (and was subsequently executed by the Bolsheviks). Certain regions, such as the Ukraine, also demanded to be freed from central control, as they believed they should be allowed to develop a separate national identity. These regions constituted the nationalist forces that were an extra thorn in the side of the Reds. By February, there were signs that the resistance from the nationalists was receding (for example, Estonia signed a peace agreement with *Sovnarkom*. (See page 33 for discussion of the role of *Sovnarkom*.)

- April 1921: Polish armed forces attacked Russia and reached as far as Kiev in the east. Russian forces counter-attacked and pushed the Poles back to Warsaw. Another counter-attack in August, this time by Poland, resulted in the Red Army retreating. The Russo-Polish conflict eventually came to a halt in October 1920 when the Treaty of Riga was signed.
- November 1921: Red forces drove out the last of the White troops from southern Russia.
- Throughout 1921, groups of armed peasants formed to oppose the Bolsheviks. They were known as the Green armies. Their aim was to gain more freedoms from Bolshevik leaders.

The impact of the war

Defeat in the Polish campaign brought a similar kind of humiliation to the Bolsheviks as the Crimean War and Russo-Japanese War did to the tsars. Once again, a Russian army was defeated by another army, which, on paper, was vastly inferior. Coupled with this, foreign intervention during the war on behalf of the Whites and a general mistrust of the Bolsheviks by Western European governments put Lenin on the defensive. Although Comintern and the concept of '**world revolution**' were not abandoned, the Bolshevik government moved towards a foreign policy centred on developing peaceful relations.

 **KEY TERM**

World revolution The idea that communism would not be confined to the Soviet Union but would be spread throughout the world.

The war influenced the nature of Russian government in so far as victory had been achieved through a particular kind of discipline, administration and management. The post-war communist government consisted of men who had served in the Red Army, the *Cheka* and other bodies. This experience was carried over into the running of the new Russia. The emphasis was on orderliness, trustworthiness, comradeship and loyalty to the party.

The militaristic approach to government is well illustrated by the introduction of War Communism (see pages 84–5). The effects of this, along with the actions of the *Cheka*, caused divisions within the party and a move away from the use of 'terror' to control the populace. The New Economic Policy (see pages 85–6) was introduced to bring stability to government even though it appeared to be in contradiction of all that the communists stood for.

It is also fair to say that the war led to power being even more centralised than before. Power revolved around the Politburo and Orgburo (see pages 33–4). This meant that these very tightly knit party sub-committees became the main organs of government.

Summary diagram: The effects of the wars of 1914–21 on the development of Russian government

> **First World War**
> - Heavy military losses
> - Shells crisis
> - Tsar in command of the military
> - Overlap with Russian Revolution
> - Peace treaty signed with Germany before end of war

> **Russian Revolution**
> - Strikes and protests in February 1917
> - Installation of the Provisional Government
> - Overthrow of Provisional Government in October 1917 by the Bolsheviks
> - Overthrow of Constituent Assembly
> - Overlap with Civil War

> **Civil War**
> - Reds vs Whites and Greens
> - War Communism and the *Cheka*
> - New Economic Policy replaced War Communism
> - Victory for Reds but no success over Poland
> - Militarism of war shaped nature of post-war government

The Second World War 1939–45

▶ *Why did the Second World War not affect the nature and function of Russian government as much as the First World War?*

Long-term origins

Russia's involvement in the lead-up to the Second World War can be dated to Hitler's accession to power in 1933. Despite the wariness of the Third Reich towards building strong relations with Russia, the **Treaty of Berlin** was renewed and diplomatic visits continued. However, the Nazi regime remained anti-communist.

By the end of 1933, however, a change in relations occurred as Russia became increasingly concerned about indications that Germany intended to expand into other territories. This was made worse in January 1934 when Germany signed a non-aggression pact with Poland. Poland bordered Russia and the implication was that Germany and Poland would somehow form an alliance to invade Russia. In May 1934, Russia responded by ending all Polish and Baltic non-aggression treaties. This was to signal its intent to fight back against its East European neighbours if they collaborated with Germany. To add to mounting tensions, in September 1934, Russia was admitted to the **League of Nations** just as Germany and Japan opted out.

In 1935, a German–Soviet trade agreement was formulated (in another attempt to improve relations) only to be countered by mutual defence treaties with France and Czechoslovakia (May 1935) and a united fascist stance taken by the Seventh Comintern Congress (July 1935).

The Spanish Civil War (1936) was something of a turning point for the development of Russian government in the way it affected relations with the other international powers. Stalin's decision to support the Spanish government against the nationalist rebel Franco was, in itself, not an issue. The dilemma for the Russian leader was in deciding on the type and scale of support to be offered. In the end, it consisted of the following:

- The NKVD provided military and technical advisers.
- Backing was given to the setting up of anti-fascist International Brigades.
- Disloyal Spanish leftists were discredited.

The limited nature of the support had the effect of, on the one hand, not causing too much of a backlash from Hitler (who was supporting Franco) and, on the other, preventing a quick victory for Franco and, therefore, a potential strengthening of Western fascism. Despite Russia's attempt not to upset Germany too much, Hitler still moved forward to form an Anti-Comintern alliance in conjunction with Italy and Japan.

 **KEY TERMS**

Treaty of Berlin Germany and Russia agreed to remain neutral if either was attacked by a third power.

League of Nations An international body set up in 1919 to keep international peace through the settlement of disputes by arbitration.

In the light of the ***Anschluss* of Austria**, in 1938, Stalin pushed the view that Germany was increasingly a challenge to Russian security. The *Anschluss* strengthened German forces and resources and confirmed to Russia that Germany was prepared to march into other countries and take them over. This perceived threat was heightened by mounting anti-Soviet feeling in Britain and France due to knowledge of Stalin's 'purges' (see page 55) and his anti-appeasement stance. On top of this, the **Munich Peace Conference** of September 1938 excluded Russia and Czechoslovakia. It was no wonder, then, that Stalin proceeded to do deals with Nazi Germany; by the end of 1938 revamped trade agreements were in place, Russia had watered down its commitments in Spain and attacks in the Russian media against Germany virtually disappeared. Stalin justified his policy of dealing directly and firmly with Hitler to the Russian nation by pointing out that **appeasement** was failing, a war had almost started, and that Russia was industrially strong enough to resist invasion. The historian Adam Ulam (1976) has suggested that this policy amounted to a message from Stalin to Hitler along the lines of 'We don't need you, but you may need us; if so you had better hurry up.' Others, such as the historian Walter G. Moss (2005), believe that Stalin's policy simply provided choice and flexibility; Russia could ally with the Nazis or continue to seek a deal with the West.

By the end of 1938, a pact between Russia and Germany became more likely. Hitler's invasion of the **Sudetenland** prompted a promise from France and Britain to help Poland. The importance of this was that in theory, Hitler now faced a war on two fronts (west and east) and therefore was pressured to go to Stalin to make a pact. In August 1939, the famous Nazi–Soviet non-aggression pact was made. Russia and Germany both agreed to stay neutral if either was the victim of 'belligerent action by a third power'. Behind the scenes, **Molotov** and **von Ribbentrop** signed a top secret protocol. Under this agreement, Lithuania and west Poland, Latvia, Estonia, Finland and Bessarabia were placed under Soviet influence.

The reaction to this was mixed. There was some opposition from those outside the Politburo who viewed it as a dastardly deal with the fascists. The core of the Russian leadership, though, hailed it as a success as it provided time to prepare for a hypothetical invasion by Germany and/or Japan.

Short-term origins

After Germany invaded Poland on 1 September 1939, France and Britain declared war on Germany. However, due to the Nazi–Soviet Pact, the period from September 1939 to 1941 was viewed as one of neutrality in Russia.

Neutrality did not prevent Russia from taking further moves to protect itself against attack. Soviet troops were sent to eastern Poland with the intention of protecting the Ukraine and Belarus. The Baltic States were persuaded to allow the stationing of Soviet troops on their soil to act as a line of defence for Petrograd and Leningrad. Finland refused a similar demand, resulting in the Winter War (November 1939 to March 1940). The significance of this for the Russian government was that war once again highlighted military weaknesses; there were somewhere near 50,000 Soviet deaths as a result of this very limited military conflict. Nevertheless, Finland ceded border space to the Russians and this set a precedent for the Baltic States to be forced to become part of the USSR by the summer of 1940. Dissidents within newly occupied territory were brutally dealt with, as illustrated by the **Katyn Forest massacre** (see page 187).

(see page 187)

> # The course of the Second World War: main events
>
> - July 1941: in response to the implementation of Operation Barbarossa, Stalin ordered a **scorched earth policy** to be put in place. However, German forces moved forward with speed.
> - September 1941: Kiev was taken and Leningrad encircled. The siege of Leningrad by the German army lasted for two years; the city was completely cut off from the rest of Russia.
> - October 1941: the main attack on Moscow was launched. German forces were held at bay as they struggled to cope with severe winter weather. By December, the Russians had started a counter-offensive. Stalin ordered Russia to be defended 'to the last drop of blood'.
> - May 1942: German troops moved away from Moscow and focused on attempting to take control of the oilfields in the Caucasus. To be sure of succeeding, the German army under General von Paulus had to take Stalingrad.
> - August 1942: the Battle of Stalingrad started. Von Paulus had some initial success in surrounding the city. Gunfights on the streets of Stalingrad ensued. But, by the beginning of 1943, Soviet forces had launched a counter-offensive. In February, the German army was forced to surrender at Stalingrad. However, the battle was infamous in that there were about 1.1 million Soviet casualties and around 500,000 deaths.
> - July 1943: a major Russian victory at Kursk occurred. This involved the 'greatest tank battle in history' and signalled the start of a continuous German retreat. It was clear that the Germans had overstretched their resources, having tried to launch an invasion along a military front that ran about 2000 miles from north to south.
> - November 1943: Kiev was retaken.
> - January 1944: the siege of Leningrad ended but only after citizens endured wide-scale starvation resulting in around 1 million deaths.
> - June 1944: the full Russian counter-offensive was launched with the intention of pushing the German army back to its homeland. Warsaw was soon captured by the Russians (January 1945), swiftly followed by Vienna (April 1945). The Red Army pushed on through Germany. The Battle of Berlin (April–May 1945) resulted in defeat for the entire German forces. Germany surrendered in May 1945.

KEY TERMS

Katyn Forest massacre
The execution of around 5000 Polish officers by the Red Army in the forest of Katyn, Smolensk, on the eve of the German invasion.

Scorched earth policy
Stalin ordered that all material objects of worth should be destroyed as the Russian forces retreated, to stop them falling into the hands of the enemy.

Wariness of possible German invasion grew again by the spring of 1940. Stalin's response to the Nazi defeat of Denmark, Norway, the Netherlands, Belgium and France was to state that Hitler would move on to 'beat our brains in'. With the signing of the **Tripartite Pact** in September 1940 and the German failure to win the **Battle of Britain**, it appeared that an attack on Russia was imminent.

In December 1940, approval was given by Hitler for Operation Barbarossa, an all-out attack on Russia. Before it was launched (planned for 15 May 1941), Russia managed to sign a pact with Japan, mainly in the hope of buying more time. Germany, in theory, would have been wary of attacking Russia if the latter had Japan on its side. On 22 June 1941, the attack finally started.

The impact of the war

Social effects

The human cost of the war to the nation was enormous. Over 27 million Russians were killed. Civilians constituted two-thirds of this total; 1 million alone died during the siege of Leningrad and there were 1.1 million casualties as a result of the Battle of Stalingrad. Politicians in the post-war years were thus faced with the problem of a shortage of all types of labour, which was essential if Russia was to move successfully into the new technological age.

During the war, 5 million prisoners were taken by the Germans. A significant number switched sides; the historian Anthony Beevor (1998) has indicated that around 50,000 Russian citizens fought on the side of Germany at the Battle of Stalingrad. Stalin viewed all prisoners of war as traitors and if they managed to return home they were treated harshly. Despite the patriotic fervour that was whipped up, there was still desertion from the armed ranks. About 13,000 deserters were shot.

During the counter-offensive and the March on Berlin, Russian troops reportedly raped over 2 million women. When challenged over the behaviour of the typical Russian soldier, Stalin allegedly retorted with 'what is so awful about his having fun with a woman?'

Stalin's treatment of prisoners of war, deserters and non-Russian women did little to enhance the relations with the Allies both during wartime conferences and afterwards, when proposals for economic aid and reconstruction were discussed.

Economic effects

The government had a huge challenge in addressing the damage to the industrial and rural infrastructure. Much physical damage was caused both by the German military through shelling and by Stalin's scorched earth policy. Factories, production plants, mines, dams, roads, bridges and the railway were all badly affected. Such physical damage was made worse by the fact that during the war many industrial enterprises had to be relocated to the Urals, Volga basin and Central Asia to be protected. However, these were not necessarily the best areas for the organisation of efficient and effective production. Also, many factories had to be reconverted from munitions production back to their original function. All of this was a costly business, especially given that the government ran a command economy and was therefore responsible for all industrial enterprise.

The Soviet government's reconstruction programme revolved around a fourth Five-Year Plan (1946–50). The specific aim of this was to get the Soviet economy back to growth levels achieved immediately before the war. The plan would then be followed by two others, which would accelerate the development of heavy industry. As with the first three Five-Year Plans (see pages 87–8), the production of consumer goods was neglected. Interestingly, the targets set by the fourth plan were achieved after three years, way ahead of schedule. This was due to a number of reasons including:

- the availability of 'free' labour (up to 4 million prisoners of war, Soviet prisoners and conscript labour)
- unilateral trade agreements (agreements that only favoured Russia)
- external financial aid (from the **United Nations**, the USA in the form of **lend–lease**, Britain and Sweden)
- the commitment of the Russian people; ordinary Russian workers continued to labour for excessively long hours and under very challenging conditions to increase production and productivity in all of the staple industries.

There were a number of weaknesses in Stalin's post-war economic strategy, though:

- The biggest flop was his continuation of 'gargantuan' projects. Great amounts of capital were ploughed into schemes such as the Volga–Don Canal but with very little economic return.
- Agriculture also suffered, mainly through neglect. The war years had seen a reversion to a kind of small-scale ownership of land plots and a crumbling of some collective farms. Those who acquired private plots were soon hit by exorbitant taxes. The collectives suffered from shortages of labour and materials. The inevitable consequence was a famine in 1947 (see page 110) and rural unrest.
- Khrushchev, as minister for agriculture, attempted to resolve some of the problems through farm amalgamation (joining farms together to make bigger farm units to share costs and raise production), but this had a limited impact.

Political effects

Impact on the structure of government

The war had very little impact on the structure of government. During the conflict, Stalin became the chairman of the State Defence Committee, which had absolute control over the lives of Soviet citizens. He also took the role of

KEY TERMS

United Nations
An organisation that formally came into being in June 1945 that was designed to maintain world peace.

Lend–lease The US Congress passed an Act in March 1941 that allowed the president to lend or lease equipment to countries 'whose defense the president deems vital to the defense of the USA'.

supreme commander of the military, just as Nicholas II had done during the First World War. The difference was that Stalin actually took advice from his advisers and even relied on others, deemed to be military experts, to make key strategic decisions. In fact, it would be incorrect to assume that the government became even more totalitarian. That would have been difficult given the high degree of control already in place. Besides, all governments of those countries directly involved in the war passed measures that gave them total authority. Unsurprisingly, until his death, Stalin retained the two key political posts in Russia; those of head of government (he actually took the premiership from Molotov during the war) and party secretary.

The Politburo

The composition of the Politburo also remained roughly the same. In 1948, the prominent members included Stalin, Molotov, Voroshilov, Kaganovich, Mikoyan, Andreyev, **Zhdanov** and Khrushchev. All of these characters were part of the Politburo in existence ten years earlier.

Party membership

Despite the extremely high number of war casualties, the numbers joining the Communist Party actually increased during the war from 3.76 million in 1941 to 5.8 million in 1945. Much of this rise was due to additions from the military who were rewarded for their gallantry with official party membership. By the time of the Nineteenth Party Congress, called in 1952 (for the first time in thirteen years), party numbers had declined, although this did not seem to affect the main function of the party. It continued as an administrative tool, especially when it came to economic affairs.

The NKVD

The NKVD was very active during and after the war. It was involved in the policing of prisons and the deportation of national minorities while the conflict ensued. The secret police were particularly harsh on Balkans, Chechens, Karachans and Crimean Tatars, all of whom were accused of collaborating with the Nazis. After the conflict, the NKVD reverted to purging the party and other groups of dissidents. Of special note was their involvement in the resolution of the **Leningrad affair**, which resulted in over 200 supporters of Zhdanov being purged.

Foreign policy and changes to the composition of the USSR

Soviet foreign policy was significantly affected by the war. By joining the **Grand Alliance**, Stalin believed that he placed Russia in a very strong bargaining position over making territorial gains. His main objective was to keep the frontiers established under the Nazi–Soviet Pact. The wartime conferences at Tehran (November to December 1943) and Yalta (February 1945) confirmed Russia's claims. Poland was forced to concede most of the Ukraine, Belarus and Lithuania to Russia but gained some German territory as recompense.

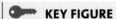

KEY FIGURE

A.A. Zhdanov (1896–1948)

An important member of the Politburo from 1935 to 1948. Zhdanov was groomed to be Stalin's successor but his alcoholism resulted in an early death (and before Stalin passed away).

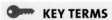

KEY TERMS

Leningrad affair A purge of the friends and colleagues of Zhdanov after his death in 1948.

Grand Alliance The wartime alliance of Britain, France, Russia and the USA.

Figure 3.3 Russian territorial gains as a result of the Second World War.

The more crucial point about this agreement was the addendum that Stalin was to be allowed to influence the nature of government in these areas, that is, to insist that they were ruled by communist regimes. As the Red Army pushed the German forces back they naturally occupied a string of other Eastern European countries (including Czechoslovakia, Hungary and parts of the Balkans).

As early as October 1944, the British Prime Minister Churchill agreed that Russia could maintain these areas as a 'sphere of influence' after the war. For Stalin, this was critical in helping to maintain a physical barrier between the West and the western Russian border. Others in the West viewed the Russian territorial gains as the start of a Soviet expansionism with the long-term intention of promoting communism throughout the whole of Europe. Churchill

🔑 KEY TERMS

Iron Curtain An imaginary border between Russian-dominated Eastern and Western Europe.

Kurile Islands and South Sakhalin The Kurile Islands, in Russia's Sakhalin Oblast region, are a volcanic archipelago that stretches approximately 1300 km north-east from Hokkaido, Japan, to Kamchatka, Russia, separating the Sea of Okhotsk from the North Pacific Ocean.

Berlin Blockade In June 1948, the Western powers combined to introduce a new currency in the zones under their control. Russia saw this as an attempt to show how capitalism could bring prosperity to Berlin and retaliated by blocking all communication links with the Western part of the city. The blockade was eventually lifted in May 1949.

Berlin Wall A wall erected in 1961 by Russia in Berlin to formally separate the East from the West. The aim was to stop people escaping to the Western zones. The wall was taken down in November 1989.

was to later refer to the barrier as an **Iron Curtain**; some claim that this point marked the start of the Cold War.

War against Japan

Stalin's agreement to enter the war against Japan was rewarded with further territorial concessions. Russia was given the **Kurile Islands and South Sakhalin**. Coupled with the Eastern European land, this meant that the Soviet Union had gained responsibility for a further 24 million people.

The issue of post-war Germany

The issue of what should happen to Germany after the war caused the Soviet leadership difficulties. Germany as a whole, but also Berlin in particular, was divided into zones, which were to be occupied by the Allies until a stable German government could be set up. Russia had jurisdiction over the Eastern zones, but there was mutual suspicion and tensions between the occupying forces right from the start. The **Berlin Blockade** of 1948 and the erection of the **Berlin Wall** worsened relations between Russia and the West. The result of this was that the key problem of unifying Germany was not resolved until communism started to collapse throughout Europe over 40 years later.

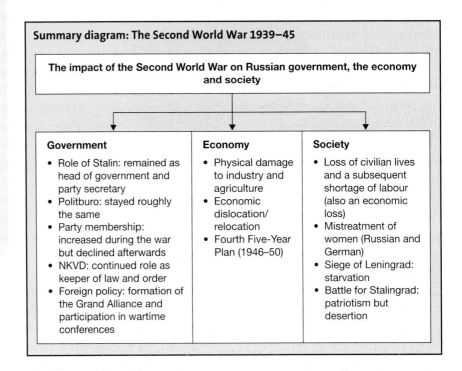

Summary diagram: The Second World War 1939–45

The impact of the Second World War on Russian government, the economy and society

Government
- Role of Stalin: remained as head of government and party secretary
- Politburo: stayed roughly the same
- Party membership: increased during the war but declined afterwards
- NKVD: continued role as keeper of law and order
- Foreign policy: formation of the Grand Alliance and participation in wartime conferences

Economy
- Physical damage to industry and agriculture
- Economic dislocation/relocation
- Fourth Five-Year Plan (1946–50)

Society
- Loss of civilian lives and a subsequent shortage of labour (also an economic loss)
- Mistreatment of women (Russian and German)
- Siege of Leningrad: starvation
- Battle for Stalingrad: patriotism but desertion

The Cold War 1947–64

▶ *'The Cold War had limited impact on the development of Russian government, society and the economy.' How far do you agree with this view?*

Definition

The Cold War, according to the historian Chris Cook (1998), is the term given to the 'protracted state of tension between countries falling short of actual warfare'. 'Actual warfare' refers to physical combat: 'hot' war. Ironically, some of the most notable features of the Cold War related to 'hot' wars (or 'proxy' wars), for example, in Korea (1950–3) and Vietnam (1946–54 and 1961–75). The Soviet Union did not play any direct role in the 'hot' conflicts; it appeared more concerned to win the ideological battle.

The words 'Cold War' were made popular from 1947 onwards by the US journalist Walter Lippmann. The term seems to have been used by US politicians when the Truman Doctrine was announced in March 1947 (see page 163) and also during discussions over the implementation of the **Marshall Plan** in the summer of 1947 (see page 163).

Note that the Cold War lasted from 1947 to 1991 but discussion of the period after the demise of Khrushchev is beyond the remit of this book.

Long-term causes of the war

Conflicting ideologies

A main cause of the war concerned the conflicting political ideologies held by the main players. The regimes of both Stalin and Khrushchev were based on Marxism–Leninism, which espoused state control of the means of distribution, production and exchange on behalf of the Russian people. In turn, state control amounted to a dictatorship, with no element of democracy. This was, of course, diametrically opposed to the ideologies that predominated in the West. The USA stood for liberal democracy and free-market capitalism; to the Soviet Union this meant a bourgeois system similar to that which had emerged in tsarist Russia.

Immediately after the Second World War, during a speech in February 1946 to the Supreme Soviet, Stalin blamed the conflict on the '**monopoly capitalism**' of the West. This was identical to the claims made by Lenin about what he believed to be the root cause of the First World War. For Stalin, the outcome of the Second World War was a success as it emphasised the strength of the Soviet economy and system of government. According to the Soviet leader, without the discipline and collaboration engendered by a communist system of government the Nazis would never have been defeated.

 **KEY TERMS**

Marshall Plan
A programme to help European recovery after the Second World War which was put forward by the US Secretary of State General George Marshall (1880–1959). He believed that the USA should 'assist in the return of normal economic health in the world without which there can be no political stability and no assured peace'.

Monopoly capitalism
The profit-making motives that dominated the economies of Western Europe.

The Soviet war victory became a justification for the Soviet 'way' to be consolidated (mainly through new Five-Year Plans) and promoted. But this did not mean that Stalin and Khrushchev were intent on expansionism. The Russian leaders seemed to recognise that they would not be able to govern a state that could compete on equal terms with the USA in the developing world free market. Therefore, the 'sphere of interest' in Eastern Europe that Russia valued so highly was as much for purposes of economic growth as it was for political stability. Western politicians did not seem to understand this or at least chose to ignore it.

Short-term causes of the war

US mistrust of the USSR

After 1946, the USA's mistrust of the USSR grew swiftly. The main reasons for this were as follows:

- the association of Russia with a newly established communist regime in North Korea
- the discovery of a communist spy network in Canada
- the Kennan 'long telegram'
- Churchill's Iron Curtain speech.

The last two factors appeared to be especially influential.

The Kennan 'long telegram'

On 22 February 1946, George Kennan, a US diplomat, sent a lengthy telegram message to the European Division of the US State Department expressing his concerns about Soviet foreign policy. Kennan was an acknowledged expert on Soviet affairs, having been in constant contact with Russian dissidents who had managed to escape from Russia and set up base in Riga. Kennan believed that Russia was not a 'fit ally or associate, actual or potential' for the USA. The Soviets had aggressive tendencies based on 'basic inner Russian necessities' and a 'traditional instinctive sense of insecurity'. The result of this was a 'patient but deadly struggle for total destruction of a rival power. Never in compacts or compromises with it.' The Soviet Union would do all it could to strengthen the Soviet bloc and challenge capitalism. Kennan argued that US concessions that might be made to Russia would not work. The only solution was to actively contain communism. Because of Kennan's expertise, his telegram had a significant impact on the thinking of senior US politicians.

Churchill's Iron Curtain speech

This speech was made on 5 March 1946 at Fulton, Missouri, USA. Churchill's views echoed those of Kennan. To create anxiety in the West purposefully, Churchill claimed that 'from Stettin in the Baltic to Trieste in the Adriatic, an iron curtain has descended across the continent'. The spread of Soviet influence had made it a military force to be feared. Churchill played on the idea that any country taken over by communism would result in a complete loss of freedoms for its people.

The Truman Doctrine

Another expression of fear of communism came in the form of the Truman Doctrine, announced in March 1947. Referring to the prospect of communist governments being installed in Greece and Turkey, US President Truman declared that 'it must be the policy of the United States to support free peoples who are resisting subjugation by armed minorities or by outside pressures'. Soviet politicians were antagonised by this statement as they found it very threatening.

The Marshall Plan

The Marshall Plan for the economic recovery of Europe was presented by the USA in June 1947. It was rejected by the Soviet foreign minister, Molotov, as the Russians believed that it was a scam to spread capitalism. Such a snub simply created further ill feeling against the Soviet Union from the West.

Cominform

The Soviets responded to the above developments by setting up, in September 1947, the Communist Information Bureau (Cominform). The aim of this body was to reject the West's offer of financial help and to coordinate economic recovery for Eastern Europe through a programme of cooperation. Cominform was not a great success and it probably created more problems for the Eastern bloc countries than it solved. It also served to heighten tensions and, along with the Truman Doctrine and the Marshall Plan, marked the start of the Cold War.

The impact of the war

The Cold War had very little direct effect on the structure and function of Russia's government. However, de-Stalinisation (see pages 21–2) was an attempt by Khrushchev to present Russia in a more positive light to the rest of the world. This was especially important at a time when the USA was determined to enforce its **containment policy** towards Russia. American politicians never wavered from trying to prove that communism was evil and would easily spread if allowed to. In this way, Khrushchev's political ideology was partly determined by the Cold War.

 **KEY TERM**

Containment policy
The policy of attempting to stop communism spreading throughout the world.

The nuclear arms race and space race were very expensive. Before 1964, the Russian government managed to cope, but high levels of investment in heavy industry to meet military requirements were to the detriment of consumer industries. The knock-on effect was that living standards appeared much lower than in the West. Russian people were not afraid to express their discontent but, as was always the case, protests were ruthlessly dealt with.

North Atlantic Treaty Organisation (NATO) Members of this group agreed to support each other if they were attacked by an aggressor. Those who belonged were anti-communist and it was obvious that NATO was designed to combat the perceived threat from the Soviet Union.

Suez Crisis The Suez Canal was nationalised by President Nasser in 1956. France and Britain, alarmed by Egypt's growing ties with communists, planned to take control of this important shipping route.

The course of the Cold War before 1964: main events

- March 1947: the Truman Doctrine was announced; in the summer, the Marshall Plan for European economic recovery was unveiled.
- September 1947: Cominform was set up.
- June 1948: start of the Berlin Blockade.
- April 1949: **The North Atlantic Treaty Organisation (NATO)** was founded.
- May 1949: end of the Berlin Blockade.
- June 1950: Korean War started.
- November 1952: the USA exploded its first hydrogen bomb.
- August 1953: the Soviet Union announced the explosion of its first hydrogen bomb (the test took place on 8 August).
- May 1955: the Warsaw Pact was formed. This involved the signing of a peace and security treaty by the Soviet Union, Albania, Bulgaria, Hungary, East Germany, Poland, Romania and Czechoslovakia.
- April 1956: Cominform was disbanded.
- October 1956: the Hungarian Revolution (see pages 213–14)
- November 1956: the Soviet Union cut off diplomatic relations with Israel and warned France and Britain about the consequences of their behaviour during the **Suez Crisis**; Russian leaders hinted at possible missile attack.
- October 1957: *Sputnik 1* was launched by Russia and signalled the start of the space race. *Sputnik 1* was the world's first artificial satellite. The launch led to new political, military, technological and scientific developments.
- September 1959: Khrushchev flew to the USA for the first time and held negotiations with President Eisenhower; demands over Berlin were withdrawn.
- May 1962: a US U-2 spy plane, piloted by Gary Powers, was shot down while flying over Russia. Khrushchev demanded an apology from Eisenhower.
- June 1961: Khrushchev demanded the demilitarisation of Berlin during negotiations with US President Kennedy in Vienna.
- August 1961: the construction of the Berlin Wall was started.
- September 1962 to January 1963: the Cuban Missile Crisis. This was a major Cold War confrontation between the USA and the USSR. After the Bay of Pigs Invasion (in Cuba) by the USA, the USSR increased its support of Fidel Castro's Cuban regime. By the summer of 1962, Khrushchev decided secretly to install ballistic missiles in Cuba. When US reconnaissance flights revealed the secret construction of missile launching sites, President Kennedy publicly denounced the Soviet actions. In October 1962, Kennedy imposed a naval blockade on Cuba and said that any missile launched from Cuba would be met with a full-scale retaliatory attack by the USA against the USSR. On 24 October, Soviet ships carrying missiles to Cuba turned back to Russia. Khrushchev then agreed on 28 October to dismantle the missile sites. The crisis ended as suddenly as it had begun. The USA ended its blockade of Cuba on 20 November and promised not to go ahead with a planned invasion of the island.
- June to July 1963: rapid deterioration in Sino-Soviet relations after China accused Soviet leaders of 'restoring capitalism' and abandoning Marxism.

A number of the 'hot spots' during the Cold War took Russia to the brink of a major military conflict with the USA. The Cuban Missile Crisis in particular showed that Russian politicians were not afraid to flex their muscles. This incident also showed that the Soviets were willing to back down to prevent disagreements getting out of hand. The USSR was not financially strong enough to participate in another full-blown war.

Summary diagram: The effects of the Second World War and the Cold War on the development of Russian government

Second World War
- High casualties and war atrocities
- Soviet resilience and victory
- Reconstruction through the fourth Five-Year Plan
- Minimal impact on internal function and structure of government
- Greater impact on foreign relations – cordiality changed to tension and the prelude to the Cold War

Continuity and overlap
Second World War merged into the Cold War

Cold War
- Minimal impact on internal function and structure of government – similar to Second World War
- High financial cost borne by the bulk of the population
- Heightened international tensions, although eased by start of *détente*

Chapter summary

Trotsky famously claimed that 'war is the locomotive of change'. In other words, war was seen to act as a catalyst. However, this begs a number of questions. Did the wars during the period simply accelerate developments already underway or did they initiate change? For example, the Crimean War and the Russo-Japanese War seemed to lead to reforms that were already under consideration. On the other hand, the First World War, in conjunction with the Russian Revolution and Civil War, resulted in a fairly sudden and complete change in the way Russia was ruled.

Wars undoubtedly led to political change, which was often linked to economic and social developments. On occasion, leaders committed Russia to wars in the hope that political, economic and social problems would somehow be resolved. Such action often backfired and resulted in Russian forces underestimating and being unprepared for the conflict they faced. In the case of the Crimean War, Russo-Japanese War and, to an extent, the First World War, there were dire consequences for rulers. The nature of autocracy was challenged, concessions had to be made and the First World War was a key factor in the fall of the Romanov dynasty. Russia fought in other wars due to changing international circumstance and a threat to internal security. Where this was the case, the Russian military was better prepared and more determined to win through. This was especially true of the Second World War (but not the case with the First World War), although research since 1991 has suggested that the centralised planning that happened under Stalin might have hindered Russia in its preparations.

Another way of looking at the effects of war is to focus on the type, nature and extent of military conflict. Some historians quite simply argue that limited wars (the Crimean War, Russo-Turkish War and Russo-Japanese War) had, by definition, a limited impact. The financial cost and human cost were less than in the total wars (those wars involving civilians as well as military forces) and the response of governments with respect to post-war reform and reconstruction was less far reaching. Revolution obviously resulted in a complete overhaul of the Russian political system, although some historians downplay the impact by claiming that one form of autocracy was simply replaced by another. Thus, it would appear that some wars had more of an impact than others depending on the nature of the war.

Wars clearly altered the way governments thought and behaved, as revealed by policies in existence before and after the wars. However, whether policy change would have been enacted without war is a matter for conjecture. This is where the counter-factual approach to historical study becomes useful. Perhaps the impact of wars in general on the development of Russian government has been exaggerated. Given that the nature of rule remained strictly authoritarian, this would certainly seem to be the case.

Refresher questions

Use these questions to remind yourself of the key material covered in this chapter.

1   How was the Crimean War connected to the Emancipation Edict of 1861?

2   What evidence is there that Alexander II's reforms were influenced by the Crimean War?

3   What was the impact of the Russo-Turkish War on the composition of the Russian Empire?

4   Why did Nicholas II go to war with Japan in 1904?

5   What was the impact of the Russo-Japanese War on Russian government?

6   What was the impact of the First World War on the Russian economy and society?

7   What was the connection between the March Revolution of 1917 and the formation of the Provisional Government?

8   How far was the First World War responsible for the collapse of the Provisional Government?

9   How did the October Revolution of 1917 change the nature of Russian government?

10 What was the impact of the Russian Civil War on the composition of the Russian Empire?

11 What was the connection between the Civil War and changes to Russian economic policy?

12 What was the link between the USSR's involvement in the Second World War and the start of the Cold War?

13 What challenges did Khrushchev face as a result of the Cold War?

14 What was the significance of the Cuban Missile Crisis for the government of the USSR?

In-depth studies and debates

Remember that the examination requires you to study three topics in depth and for this unit they are:

- Alexander II's domestic reforms
- The Provisional Government
- Khrushchev in power 1956–64.

This section will go into more detail about how wars impacted on the politics, economy and society of the Russian Empire and the USSR. Some of the key debates about the impact of wars will be introduced so that you will have enough depth of knowledge to be able to evaluate passages that are set on any of the depth study topics

Key debate 1: how far were Alexander II's reforms due to the Crimean War?

The Crimean War is often cited as being the chief reason behind the issuing of the Emancipation Edict of 1861 and other reforms that followed this. The causal link is based on the following observations:

- The war revealed weaknesses in the way Nicholas I had ruled; the maintenance of serfdom under strict autocratic rule did not seem to fit with staging modern warfare.
- The army was recruited from serfs who were not trained to the same standard as the professional armies of Britain and France. Also, serfs were inclined towards revolt and, given their other responsibilities, were probably not as committed as they might have been.
- Soldiers had been poorly supplied; the production of armaments and uniforms was inadequate. This was a reflection on the way the economy was organised and how Russia had been slow to industrialise.

However, the causal link between the Crimean War and Alexander II's reforms is questionable; 'correlation is no proof of causation'. Some historians have pointed out that there were other reasons for Alexander II's reforms, some of which were linked to what was happening in Russia before the Crimean War. These included:

- Pressure to abolish serfdom as it was seen be some as a form of slavery and an institution that was immoral.
- Growing peasant unrest that could be dated to the 1770s.
- Demands from some politicians and entrepreneurs for more labour to work on projects such as railway routes.
- Population growth which put pressure on a farming system that was geared up to provide subsistence and not surplus. Famines became more frequent as the demand for food outstripped supply.

Thus, arguing that the Crimean War was the main reason for Alexander II's reforms is misleading. It was one of a number of factors that influenced change.

Given the failures of the Russian military during the war it is not surprising that Alexander II prioritised major reforms to the military (see page 134 for details). How far-reaching and effective these reforms were has been a matter of debate:

- Although aspects of the reforms, such as conscription and the reduction in periods of service, were seen as radical, as a package weaknesses were revealed. For example, new training regimes were compromised by the poor level of education of recruits (although this was eventually addressed through the establishment of military schools).
- The historian John Hite (2005) has emphasised that in 1877 the Russian army struggled to defeat 'weak Turkish troops' and later, in 1904–5, Russia was beaten by Japan.
- The reforms were slow to come about; some nobles were only convinced of the need for far-reaching reforms when they witnessed the success of the 'modern' Prussian army in 1866–71.

Some commentators have suggested that it is easy to be critical of the military reorganisation programme with hindsight. At the time, the tsar and other senior members of the aristocracy appeared confident that the reforms would aid the modernisation of Russia. The economic costs of supporting an ineffective standing army were reduced, agricultural efficiency was improved (peasants had more freedom and time to work on the land), soldiers were better trained, and, in the long run, there was an improvement in literacy. Therefore, in context, the military reforms were more radical than some observers have made out.

Key debate 2: how far was the First World War responsible for the downfall of the Provisional Government?

The debate over the impact of the First World War on the Provisional Government can be engaged in by considering the so-called 'optimist' and 'pessimist' perspectives.

For the optimists, the formation of the Provisional Government was not a disaster and it was not necessarily doomed to fail; it was the continuation of the war that meant the new regime struggled to establish its authority. If Russia had pulled out of the war in March 1917, then maybe the Provisional Government would have succeeded, with the added possibility of the reinstatement of the tsar to create a constitutional monarchy.

More specifically, the optimists claim that the war hindered the progress of the Provisional Government as:

- The war had popular support; demands for withdrawal and peace were made on the basis that this would be honourable and unconditional. It was unlikely that Germany would agree to such a deal given the strong military position it was in by March 1917.

- The war was costly in terms of the impact on land, labour (especially soldiers) and capital. The Provisional Government also felt committed to continuing the war given that much had already been invested in trying to win it.
- The Provisional Government had limited support from its allies (Britain and France).
- Challenges such as land distribution and the impact on public health as a result of urbanisation were ignored; continuing with the war became a priority.

When these pressures related to the war are taken into consideration it is not surprising that the Provisional Government struggled to maintain authority. It does seem that the government was unlucky in that it was formed late in the war when much of the damage to the economy and military had already occurred. In this respect, the optimists' view seems to hold some weight. However, critics of this perspective have argued that the Provisional Government was doomed to failure regardless of the war.

The pessimists believe that:

- The peoples of the Russian Empire viewed the Provisional Government as simply a variation on the tsarist regime. In fact, the empire was in danger of disintegrating before the First World War; the new government struggled to contain demands for autonomy from Finland, Poland and the Ukraine (all major agricultural areas).
- Workers had already organised and campaigned for economic and social change before the war. By 1917, the Soviets were in such a strong position that the Provisional Government was compelled to join with them to create a dual authority. This is evidence that the groundswell of popular protest had gained momentum over at least a decade and it was only a matter of time before the proletariat took control of the governance of Russia.
- Kerensky's leadership was suspect especially when it came to dealing with opposition from Kornilov. He was not trusted by the workers and peasants even though he had a socialist background.

The pessimist view is convincing to an extent; it stresses the need to see the revolution of 1917 as an event resulting from a multitude of pressures that built up over a long period of time and there is much evidence to support this. However, it downplays the impact of the First World War by suggesting that it affected Russia in a similar way to previous wars. This washes over the point that the war was the first global, total war and, by definition, would have had a much greater effect than any military conflict witnessed before.

Key debate 3: how effectively did Khrushchev deal with the challenges posed by the Cold War?

The Cold War was already under way when Khrushchev became the leader of Russia. He faced the challenge of dealing with the aftermath of the Korean War, dissent in Eastern Europe against Russian influence and managing a nuclear arms race. How well he dealt with these three issues has been debated extensively by historians.

One perspective, especially at the time, is that Khrushchev was seen to have a number of successes:

- The death of Stalin and the end of the Korean War (July 1953) and Indo-China War (1954) seemed to influence Russian leaders to alter their stance on the Cold War. In Khrushchev's 'Secret Speech' of February 1956, he stated that for Russian foreign policy: 'There are only two ways – either peaceful coexistence [with the West] or the most destructive war in history. There is no third way.' The change of policy can be viewed as a success as the Russian leader was seen to be taking the initiative in attempting to create a more peaceful and secure world.
- Khrushchev supported the signing of the Austrian State Treaty (May 1955). This indicated that Russia was willing to cooperate with the West over dealing with Austria's claims for independence.
- The thaw in the Cold War epitomised by the policy of 'peaceful coexistence' prompted Russia's satellite states to demand more freedom. When this appeared to get out of control, as in the case of Hungary in 1956, Khrushchev, using Russian tanks, was quick to react. The Budapest rising was ruthlessly suppressed, which gained Khrushchev support from the Communist Party in Russia.
- In 1961, Khrushchev proposed to the US government that the West should come out of Berlin. This demand was prompted by the increasing number of East Germans trying to flee to the Western sector. President Kennedy refused to agree to the idea, causing Khrushchev to support the construction of the Berlin Wall. Again, back in Russia this was seen as a bold move to prevent further embarrassment to fellow communist leaders in East Germany.
- Khrushchev's handling of the Cuban Missile Crisis (1962) is sometimes praised as he initially tested Kennedy's diplomatic and decision skills before agreeing to a relaxation of tensions. Some historians have argued that Khrushchev forced Kennedy to compromise rather than call the Russian leader's bluff by invading Cuba and overthrowing Castro. Also, the compromise can be viewed as a Russian success as it resulted in the 'hotline' telephone link between Moscow and Washington. By agreeing on a more direct, quick way of solving disputes, the hotline strengthened the Russian 'peaceful coexistence' stance.

Some critics of Khrushchev, though, have been quick to identify flaws in his approach to dealing with Cold War challenges.

For some, commenting at the time and since, Khrushchev's Cold War policy was too risky. Rather than creating stability it is often viewed as leading to heightened tensions. More specifically:

- Peaceful coexistence was viewed by some communists as a betrayal of ideals; it was perceived as a U-turn with respect to spreading communism internationally. In particular, the Chinese communists accused the Russian leader of being 'too soft on imperialists'; this criticism led to Khrushchev withdrawing military support when the Chinese needed it.
- The historian Martin McCauley (1995) has argued that the Hungarian crisis of 1956 was a 'disaster' that could be blamed on de-Stalinisation. Furthermore, he believes: '… it put back the cause of de-Stalinisation, and hence reform, in Eastern Europe and also weakened the Soviet cause abroad. Communist parties in western Europe lost many members and declined in influence'. The ruthless suppression of Hungarian protesters was viewed as a 'poor advertisement' for communism.
- The erection of the Berlin Wall can also be seen as an oppressive measure and one that worsened relations with the West.
- By taking Kennedy to the brink during the Cuban Missile Crisis, Khrushchev is seen as someone who nearly provoked what would have been a catastrophic nuclear war. Moreover, by agreeing to withdraw missiles from Cuba, the Russian leader was seen by fellow Russian officials as someone who had backed down. This is often cited as being a main factor in Khrushchev's demise.

The debate over Khrushchev's handling of the Cold War seems to hinge on whether he is seen as 'inspirational and innovative' (by trying to instil peaceful coexistence) or 'erratic and impulsive' (by not being consistent) or both.

Study skills: thematic essay question

How to answer turning-point questions

In answering turning-point questions you should remember that this is a themes paper and the mark scheme used by examiners is exactly the same for these types of questions as it is for other thematic essays. This suggests that the approach should be exactly the same as it is for other themes essays, and that the structure should be thematic and not chronological. It is much easier to compare the significance or importance of different turning points if a thematic rather than a chronological approach is adopted.

If we consider the question below, there is a range of wars which might be considered to be the most important turning point in the development of Russia.

'The importance of the First World War, compared with other wars, as a turning point in the development of Russia has been vastly exaggerated.' How far do agree with this statement?

The other wars might include:

- the Crimean War
- the Russo-Japanese War
- the First World War
- the Civil War
- the Second World War.

In theory, an essay could analyse, evaluate and compare each of these events (in order to show synthesis), but it would make for a very cumbersome structure and would be difficult to undertake in 45 minutes.

It would be far easier to adopt a thematic approach which would allow you to compare the impact of the wars. The following themes could be considered:

- political
- economic
- social.

You would then select examples of wars from the period and compare their relative importance in terms of being a turning point for each theme. Then you would move on to make a judgement as to which war was politically, economically and socially the most important, before going on to reach an overall judgement as to which one was the most important turning point.

This means that the skills you have considered in the previous chapters are just as applicable to turning-point questions as to other essays.

Consider the following sample answers to the question.

Example A

As a result of the Russo-Japanese War, Nicholas II also instructed his ministers to speed up industrialisation and to continue to improve the railway system. Without this, Russia would never have been able to compete in a major conflict with the other European powers. But even though this was mostly successful, Russia still struggled to cope with the First World War. During the first part of the war there were heavy defeats for the army at Tannenberg and the Masurian Lakes. The main reason for this was a shortage of munitions. Later, Nicholas took control of the armed forces and there was a decent attempt to launch a counter-attack offensive under General Brusilov. However, this failed and Nicholas was blamed for Russia's poor showing. He was forced to abdicate and was replaced by the Provisional Government. This was significant in that it was the first move towards a Constituent Assembly and the implementation of a democratic system of rule. But the Provisional Government was short lived. It struggled to cope with the pressure it was placed under by the Petrograd soviet, offered little in the way of a solution to problems created by the war and failed to deal with land problems. It was no surprise that radicals took advantage of this situation and moved to overthrow the Provisional Government in October 1917. This clearly makes the First World War an important turning point as it led to a dramatic, irreversible change in Russian government.

Comment

Strengths:

- The paragraph shows good knowledge of Russia's involvement in the First World War.
- The knowledge is used to support explanation of the significance of the war.
- The paragraph offers a reasonable judgement about the importance of the war as a turning point.

Weaknesses:

- There is very limited synthesis or comparison of the First World War with the impact of other wars on the Russian Empire; this makes the judgement about whether it was the most significant turning point rather weak.
- It explains the significance of the First World War, but there is no comparative evaluation and therefore it is more like an answer to a unit 1 or 2 essay.

Example B

One important way in which the First World War can be viewed as a turning point is through the impact it had on Russian government and politics. Russia's poor performance in the early years of the war resulted in Nicholas II deciding to take sole control of the Russian military. In turn, this involved him being away from the centre of political decision-making, leaving control of internal affairs in the hands of his wife Alexandra and her 'adviser', Rasputin. Alexandra was not trusted by the Russian people due to her German background and Rasputin was seen as a negative influence mostly as result of the mysticism that surrounded him. This handing over of responsibility is often linked with the rise in discontent among workers and peasants about tsarist rule and the subsequent abdication of the tsar in March 1917. **This was very different** from how Alexander II handled the end of the Crimean War; he left military matters largely to senior military leaders but directed the peace negotiations to end the war. **Lenin and Trotsky**, in their handling of the First World War once they had seized political power, **also** organised peace negotiations while maintaining political control of the empire. The division between military and political control **was maintained** during the Civil War, with Lenin heading the government and Trotsky directing the Red Army. Despite the advent of totalitarianism, **Stalin also** retained management of affairs of government but trusted his military commanders to do their best to hold back German advances. However, he did intervene more directly during the Battle for Stalingrad in 1944, by ordering that troops should fight to the death. **Khrushchev, like his communist predecessors and Alexander II**, focused on his responsibilities as political leader during a period of war. **There were times though, as with Stalin, that Khrushchev took more direct control** (such as during the Cuban Missile Crisis). Thus, Nicholas II was the only Russian leader who significantly changed his role during a war; it was probably a bad move as it does seem to be linked with a loss of control over worsening economic conditions and rising opposition. He was the only leader during the period who failed to deal with the political challenges engendered by war. In this sense, the First World War, in influencing Nicholas II's decision, was a, if not the, most important turning point in the development of Russia.

Comment

Strengths:

- The whole period is covered from 1855 to 1964.
- A clear view is offered: the First World War was more important than other wars as a turning point in the development of Russia; an interesting angle is adopted on how war affected political leadership.
- There is comparison between the impact of the First World War and other wars on Russian leadership, as shown by the comments in bold type.
- The view taken is explained and justified.
- The importance of the division between military command and central control of government during times of warfare is highlighted; this indicates the thematic rather than chronological approach being adopted.
- The argument about the significance of political as opposed to military control is sustained throughout.
- There is considerable comparison between periods and the significance of a range of wars is evaluated.

Activity

You should now try to write thematic paragraphs which compare the importance of the First World War with other wars in terms of political, economic and social change.

Essay questions

1 How far did wars hinder the development of Russian government during the period from 1855 to 1964?
2 To what extent were the two world wars far more important in the impact they had on Russian governments than any other wars that occurred in the period from 1855 to 1964?
3 'The importance of the First World War, compared with other wars, as a turning point in the development of Russia has been vastly exaggerated.' How far do agree with this statement?

4 'The impact of war on the development of Russian government was never as significant as internal political change.' How far do you agree with this statement?

5 Assess the view that Russian governments always saw war as an opportunity to deflect attention from domestic economic and social problems during the period from 1855 to 1964.

Evaluation and the historical interpretation in-depth question

This section will continue to look at how to evaluate, using the application of 'own knowledge' to one of the interpretations to judge its strengths and weaknesses. In the first paragraph you will have explained the two interpretations and placed them in the context of the wider historical debate about the issue. In the second paragraph you will have evaluated the strengths and weakness of the first interpretation.

Read the interpretation below about the impact of the First World War on the fate of the Provisional Government.

PASSAGE A

The Duma committee which tried to run Russia until its overthrow by the Bolsheviks in the October Revolution made what seems a tragic decision to continue the war, yet at the time it was popular. Apart from Lenin's Bolsheviks who adopted the famous 'Peace, Bread and Land' slogan in the April Theses, all political groups supported the war. Russia's reputation with its allies was at stake; Germans were intensely unpopular and there was little desire for previous sacrifice to be in vain. Too often demonstrations in the summer [of 1917] are shown in documentaries and even in textbooks to be against the war, while their [the demonstrators] banners actually read not 'Mir' (peace) but 'Voina' (war). Lenin was careful not to say too much about peace while the June offensive was being prepared and rumours of his association with the Germans made him unpopular with the troops. However, the failure of the Kerensky attacks in June ended this period of war fever. It did not however bring Lenin into power. The July days failed; revolutionary soldiers were disarmed by loyal troops. The bulk of the forces were still loyal to the Provisional Government by August 1917. It was the attempted Kornilov coup of September, when he launched army units on Petrograd following Kerensky's dismissal of him as commander-in-chief of the army that was a major turning point and revived the Bolsheviks. The attempted coup by Kornilov and the failure of Kerensky at a vital moment to establish clear leadership coupled with the failures in war and the organizational ability of the Bolsheviks all came together. It is doubtful [therefore] if war alone was the key factor in bringing the Bolsheviks to power.

(Mike Wells, Russia and its Rulers 1855–1964, Heinemann, 2008, p. 143.)

Response

The interpretation of the impact of war on the Provisional Government is convincing in many respects. First, it highlights the fact that until quite late on there was much popular support for Russia's continued involvement in the war. Some interesting support for this point is provided in the form of reference to protestors' slogans. Second, the interpretation correctly emphasises Kerensky's poor leadership as a major factor in the downfall of the government. Kerensky was mistrusted by many and during the Kornilov affair was seen to make the mistake of giving extra responsibility and authority to the Petrograd soviet. This had the effect of boosting the confidence of the soviet to challenge for power as well as providing them with military hardware (Kerensky ordered soviet members and workers to be armed). Finally, the interpretation suggests that a monocausal explanation for the downfall of the Provisional Government is unhelpful. The interpretation is strong in providing a balanced view; it emphasises how a number of factors 'came together' to bring the Bolsheviks to power. However, the interpretation is weakened by the fact that although it stresses the level of popular support for the war and provides some evidence for this, the latter is actually quite flimsy. It is difficult to know for sure, due to a lack of documentation, what the opinions of the Russian people across the empire were about the decision to continue in the war. Also, although a multicausal explanation is offered about the demise of the government, no consideration is given to the desires of workers to gain more authority or the role of the soviets. Recent research has suggested that pressure from below, that had mounted over a long period of time, was possibly more important than the war in instigating the downfall of the Provisional Government.

What are the strengths of the response?

- Identify places where the interpretation is evaluated.
- What other information could you use to either support or challenge the view offered?

Now read Passage B on the impact of the First World War on the Provisional Government and consider the following question.

> Evaluate the interpretation in the passage and explain how convincing you think it is as an explanation of the impact of the First World War on the Provisional Government.

Remember: in the examination you will have to evaluate two passages and reach a judgement as to which you think is more convincing, but this exercise will help to develop the required skills.

PASSAGE B

None of the participants in the March Revolution [of 1917] would have chosen the regime that was to come to power in October 1917. Nor should any natural impetus be deduced moving towards a Bolshevik takeover. The Provisional Government could have succeeded in setting up a permanent successor to the Tsarist system. That it failed to do so was due to the continuing impact of the war. This prevented the Provisional Government from addressing popular demands for land redistribution, industrial reorganization and constitutional reform. Instead the real beneficiaries were the Bolsheviks, who were able, in Lenin's words, to 'turn the capitalist war into a civil war'. Historians are now divided as to whether the Bolsheviks launched a minority conspiracy-based coup or whether they led a popular backlash against an unpopular government. But, either way, it was the war that made the crucial difference – in breaking the patterns of traditional loyalties. Without the war the Bolsheviks could not have overthrown the Provisional Government: they had, after all, already shown themselves incapable of threatening its predecessor.

(*Stephen J. Lee,* Russia and the USSR, 1855–1991, *Routledge, 2006, p. 124.*)

Activity

Having looked at both the opening paragraph and two paragraphs that evaluated an interpretation, you should now apply the skills to the passage above. It might be helpful to consider the following questions before you write an evaluative paragraph:

- What is the view of Passage B about the impact of the First World War on the Provisional Government?
- What evidence is there in the interpretation that supports your view?
- What own knowledge do you have that agrees with the view?
- What own knowledge do you have that challenges this view?
- How convinced are you by the view offered in the interpretation? Explain your answer.

Having answered these questions, you are now in a position to evaluate the interpretation. You could also repeat the process for Passage B in the previous chapter.

CHAPTER 4

Russia and its empire, nationalities and satellite states

The composition and extent of the Russian Empire changed over time. There were occasions when a policy of expansionism and Russification resulted in Russian influence extending to the Polish border with Germany and, in the opposite direction, to the Far East. But the empire also shrank at times, mainly as a result of wars and revolution. Changes in central government often led to a rise in nationalist movements in parts of the empire. Russian leaders, whether tsars or communists, dealt with nationalist uprisings either with force or by making concessions. This chapter focuses on how and why the Russian Empire changed. It also considers the consequences of such change for national minorities within the empire and for the satellite states that emerged after the Second World War. The chapter covers the following topics:

★ Nationalities: context and definitions

★ Russo-Polish relations

★ Russification

★ The impact of the First World War and the Treaty of Brest-Litovsk

★ Expansion in Asia

★ Communist advances into Eastern and Central Europe after the Second World War

It also considers the debates surrounding the three in-depth topics:

★ How far were issues relating to the empire and minorities neglected by Alexander II?

★ To what extent did opposition from national minorities lead to the fall of the Provisional Government?

★ 'Courageous failure'. How valid is this assessment of Khrushchev's policy towards minorities, satellite states and Asia?

Key dates

1863	Polish Revolt		1936	Stalin Constitution
1918	Constitution; Treaty of Brest-Litovsk		1939–40	The Winter War and impact on Russo-Finnish relations
1920	Russo-Polish armistice		1945	Yalta and Potsdam conferences
1924	Constitution		1956	Russian invasion of Hungary

Nationalities: context and definitions

▶ *Who were the 'national minorities'?*

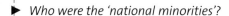

KEY TERMS

Great Russia Also known as Muscovy, the old Russian principality that had Moscow at its centre.

Russian peoples
The Russian peoples are usually considered to be those originating from and living in Muscovy (Muscovites or 'Great Russians'), the Ukraine ('Little Russians') and Belarus ('White Russians').

Baltic Germans
The upper-class inhabitants of Estonia and Latvia who had links with Germany.

In the middle part of the nineteenth century, the Russian Empire consisted of **Great Russia** and 'national minorities' (that is, those who did not originate from the **Russian peoples**). The main national minority groups were from Poland, Finland, the Caucasus and Central Asia and the Baltic provinces (Estonia, Latvia and Lithuania). Russian Jews stand out as a unique national minority in that their geographical location was one that was artificially created and crossed the boundaries of other groups. The significance of national minorities is highlighted in the results of the first Russian census of 1897; for example, it was revealed that minorities made up about 55 per cent of the empire's population in the Ukraine (see Figure 4.1, page 181).

Not all national minorities opposed the ruling elites during both the tsarist and communist periods. As a generalisation, the Finns, **Baltic Germans** and Christian Armenians remained fairly loyal, whereas the Poles, Ukrainians and Tatars were a constant thorn in the side of Russian rulers. From the point of view of the tsars and communists, this did not seem to matter, as they were all treated roughly the same. All leaders, to a greater or lesser extent, aimed to Russify peoples of the empire in what with hindsight proved to be a naïve and unrealistic attempt to create internal stability.

The main objective of the 'uncooperative' national minorities was, of course, to gain autonomy or even to break away from central Russian rule and to gain independence. The experience of each national minority group in attempting to achieve autonomy and independence varied according to time and place.

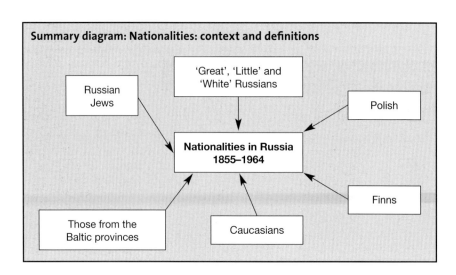

Summary diagram: Nationalities: context and definitions

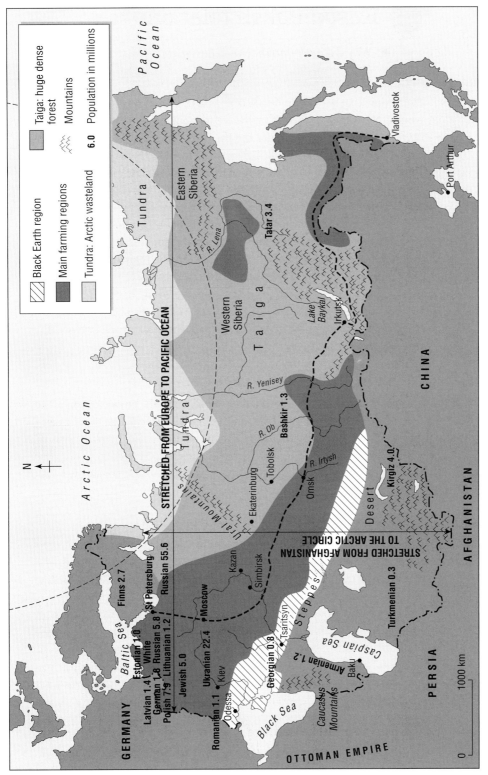

Figure 4.1 The Russian Empire in 1900 showing the population of national minorities.

Russo-Polish relations

▶ *Why were relations between Russia and Poland fraught with difficulty from 1855 to 1964?*

By the time that Alexander II took over as tsar, Poland was firmly under Russian control. Nevertheless, located on the western edge, Poland had never 'obviously' been part of the Russian Empire and the Poles had a long history of attempting to break away from tsarist rule. For example, in 1830, there was an attempted coup against Russian rule resulting in independence, albeit for a short period of time (the rebel movement was divided with not all Poles wanting to break away). After further decades of repression, many Poles grew hopeful that Alexander II's reformist attitude would lead to an improvement in their position. The new tsar, though, was wary of the situation in Poland and, for a while, measures to prevent insurgency that had been in place before the mid-1850s were retained. For example, Russian artillery squads based in Poland were not directly issued with shells to prevent munitions getting into the wrong hands. If military conflict broke out the artillery would have to wait for the shells to be released from heavily guarded storage facilities far detached from artillery bases (thus delaying mobilisation).

The Polish Revolt 1863

The initial reforms made by Alexander II, including the emancipation of the serfs in 1861 (see pages 118–19), seemed to give renewed hope to the Poles that they would be granted certain freedoms. There was a rise in Polish nationalism which was characterised by increased demands for political autonomy, education reforms (such as the reopening of Warsaw University) and debate over whether serfs in Poland should also be emancipated.

Independence and the role of Wielopolski

Not all Polish people agreed with the idea of full independence. There were those who wanted to break away from Russian control completely and also to reclaim territory in the east that had been lost by Poland to Russia in land partitions made in the eighteenth century. On the other hand, there were other individuals and groups that campaigned for partial independence. The latter were led by **Marquis Aleksander Wielopolski**, appointed as prime minister of Poland in 1862 (lasting until 1863). Wielopolski was greeted with suspicion by staunch nationalists who viewed him a tsarist lapdog. Indeed, the prime minister's push for reforms and the framing of a policy that gave Poland a national identity was done only with Russian guidance and approval.

The rise in Polish nationalism

Opposition from nationalists to the notion of compromise with Russia had started to mount from the middle of 1861. By the summer of 1862, there had

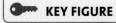 **KEY FIGURE**

Marquis Aleksander Wielopolski (1803–77)

In 1861, he was appointed to the newly created post of head of a commission of religion and education. He accepted Russian rule but attempted to introduce liberal reforms such as a land policy involving the conversion of money rents and legal changes that brought equality between Jews and Christians.

been a swelling of patriotic fervour as witnessed by an increase in the number of mass meetings and demonstrations. Protest extended to an attempted assassination of Wielopolski and his **viceroy**, Grand Duke Konstantin. The prime minister retaliated by introducing the forced conscription of young male Poles into the Russian army, the aim being to divert the potential manpower resources away from his opponents. Unfortunately for Wielopolski, the new recruits failed to cooperate and fled to the woods to create bands of renegade rebels. A platform was laid for an attempt at a full-blown insurrection.

The course of the revolt

From January 1863 to spring 1864, the Polish government faced rebellion on a wide scale. Although there were no major military confrontations, the rebels threatened the stability of government through the adoption of guerrilla warfare. There is some evidence that the rebels were supported by the Russian Land and Liberty movement and even had the help of some sympathetic Russian military officers. For example, the rebel leader, **Jaroslaw Dabrowski**, was an officer trained and deployed in the Russian army. However, the nationalist movement failed to get total support from the majority of the population (that is, the peasant class). Some significant destruction and disruption did occur in the countryside but by the middle of 1864 the Russian army had stepped in to regain control. Rebel leaders were captured and executed.

The reaction from the authorities to the rebellion was mixed. Interior and Foreign Minister Gorchakov wanted Poland to be continued to be ruled by the Polish aristocracy under the control of the Russian tsar. In opposition to this, the war minister, Milyutin, wanted the Polish gentry to be purged as he believed that they had lost the support of the countryside and had even conspired with peasant ringleaders to bring down the government. His view was that Russian officials needed to be brought in to carry out administration and governance at grass-roots level; Poland would then be converted into part of the bigger **nation-state** of Russia.

After Wielopolski fled the country, direct control of Poland was placed in the hands of Milyutin. The war minister immediately put his plan into operation:

- Hundreds of members of the Polish nobility were exiled to Siberia; their estates were transferred to incoming Russian officials who were to take over the duties of the nobles.
- Polish peasants were emancipated and gained even more favourable terms than their Russian counterparts had done in 1861. They gained freehold rights to allotted lands and paid for this through a reformed taxation system. The latter resulted in all landowners paying tax (not just peasants) to compensate those who had property redistributed.
- Rural district councils were set up (similar to the *Zemstva*) and were to contain members from all sections of Polish society.

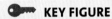

KEY TERMS

Viceroy A person sent by a ruler (usually a monarch) to govern part of a region or an empire.

Nation-state An organised political community (or country) consisting of people sharing the same language, culture and history.

KEY FIGURE

Jaroslav Dabrowski (1836–71)

A Polish left-wing independence activist and military general. His involvement in the planning of the rebellion that broke out in January 1863 and a plot to kill the tsar led to his being exiled to Siberia. In 1865, he managed to escape and ran away to France.

According to the historian Geoffrey Hosking (2002), the plan 'laid the basis for a cross-class Polish civic consciousness which remained absent in Russia itself'.

The Milyutin plan had a number of important consequences for Poland:

- The level of nationalism diminished along with the level of autonomy that the Poles had experienced before the revolt. Poland officially became the 'Vistula region' of Russia.
- Russian became the official language of administration and governance. It was taught in schools to ensure that its role was consolidated.
- The Catholic Church was not allowed to communicate with the Vatican, in an attempt to diminish its authority; it was believed that a number of bishops had been sympathetic to the rebels.

What this amounted to was the start of the process of Russification that was to spread to other territories similar to Poland (see page 190). Russification ensured that until the end of 1915 Poland was considered an integral part of Russia.

By the 1890s, Poland had revealed its importance in fuelling Russian industrialisation. A Polish proletariat emerged that showed an interest in and enthusiasm for Marxism and socialism. In 1892, a Polish Socialist Party (PPS) was formed, closely followed in 1893 by the setting up of a Social Democratic Party. Also of note was the re-emergence of nationalists who formed the National Democrats group. Polish politicians elected from these parties went on to make important contributions to the first and second *Dumas* (see page 28), although along with other national minorities, their representation fell by 1914.

The impact of the First World War on Russo-Polish relations

The First World War was a major turning point for Russian Poles. German successes at Tannenberg and the Masurian Lakes in August and September 1914 provided the impetus for a rapid advance into Russian territory. By September 1915, German and Austrian advances meant that Russia was forced to give up jurisdiction over Warsaw and Vilna, the centres of the Vistula region. Poland was free from Russian rule, although official independence was not granted until 1918 with the signing of the Treaty of Brest-Litovsk (see pages 196–9).

The Russo-Polish War 1920

The Russian Civil War (see pages 150–2) created the prospect of Poland losing its newly found freedom, but the Red Army suffered a major defeat in 1920 in its attempt to recapture Polish territory. After taking Kiev, the Red Army moved westwards towards Poland. Lenin believed that by invading Poland he would be able to free workers from their tyranny and that this would have a knock-on effect for the proletariat in neighbouring states. However, the Poles

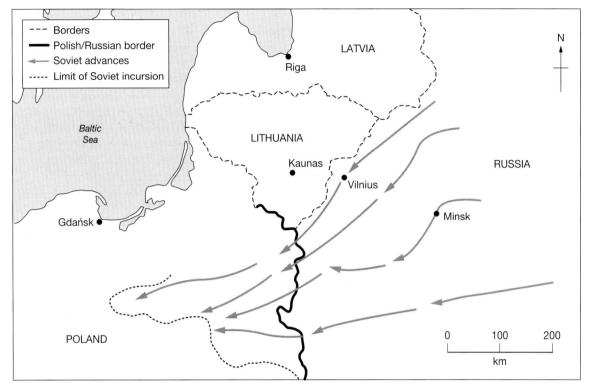

Figure 4.2 Map showing Russian advances into Poland in 1920.

did not welcome Lenin in the way he envisaged; Russian forces were halted outside Warsaw before being forced to retreat. On 16 October 1920, an armistice between Poland and Russia was signed. Polish independence was confirmed and it was agreed that western Ukraine and western Belorussia should come under Polish authority. The freedom and territory gained in 1920 would remain in place until the immediate post-Second World War.

The lead-up to the Second World War and Russo-Polish relations

Russo-Polish relations after 1933 and until 1939 were influenced by the following developments (see pages 153–4 for more details):

- The neutrality pact between Russia and Germany (Treaty of Berlin); this was agreed on by Russia despite the fact that the Nazis were opposed to communism.
- Early signs of Germany's expansionist policy (hinted at by the non-aggression pact between Germany and Poland of January 1934).

- The Russian response to the pact (annulment of Polish and Baltic non-aggression treaties from May 1934).
- Russia's admittance to the League of Nations in September 1934.
- The growing concern, by the end of 1935, that Germany would attempt an invasion of Russia via Poland.
- The formation of the Anti-Comintern alliance.

The Anti-Comintern alliance did not bode well for Poland; it inferred that Germany was considering a direct challenge to Russian authority, possibly through invasion. Geographically, it was only Poland that stood in the way. Besides, Hitler was also developing his **lebensraum** policy. Poland and Czechoslovakia were targeted to become German territory and to provide extra living space for a growing German population.

The late 1930s witnessed the tension between Russia and Germany peaking (see page 154 for details of the following developments):

- The 1938 *Anschluss* of Austria suggested that it would not have taken much for the Nazis to target Czechoslovakia and then Poland for takeover.
- Stalin's purges and anti-appeasement stance alienated the British and French; this, in theory, meant that Russia would be left alone to defend Poland (and then its own borders).
- Russian exclusion from the Munich Peace Conference confirmed that the Soviet Union might be left to its own devices in coping with the Nazi threat.

Thus, the Russian leadership proceeded to broker deals with Hitler. The ultimate deal made by Stalin with Germany was the signing of the Nazi–Soviet non-aggression pact of August 1939 (see page 154). The signing of the pact was, in reality, an admission to Poland by the Russian leadership that the Soviet Union would not interfere in any attempt by Germany to invade Poland. When the invasion occurred on 1 September 1939, Russia took some steps to protect its borders (see page 154). In general, though, to buy time to prepare for a possible German onslaught, Stalin watched the early stages of the Second World War unfold from a distance. His main concern was to redeploy troops to eastern Poland and the Baltic states in the hope that this would deter Hitler from entering Russian soil immediately after the September invasion.

The impact of the Second World War on Russo-Polish relations

By the early stages of the war, the Polish government had decided to flee to London and, with the support of a Polish underground movement, to go into exile. One of the main aims of the London Poles was to ensure that when the

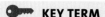

KEY TERM

Lebensraum In German, *lebensraum* means 'living space'. In the 1930s it was a term the Nazis used to describe their expansionist foreign policy.

war came to an end Poland would not endure any territorial loss. The Nazi–Soviet Pact had obviously soured relations between the Polish government and Russia. Matters took a sharp turn for the worse when in April 1943 the German occupying forces in Poland revealed that they had uncovered the mass graves of 4231 Polish officers in a forest at Katyn near Smolensk. Each corpse had his hands tied behind his back and had been killed by a bullet to the head. The Germans suggested that the killings had been carried out by the NKVD in spring 1940. The Russians blamed German soldiers for the massacre. The London Poles pushed for an investigation by the International Red Cross, which caused the Russians to accuse the exiled government of attempting to collaborate with Germany. Russia then ceased all diplomatic relations with the London Poles.

In the summer of 1944, the Russians launched a massive offensive against German forces. The German army was pushed out of Belorussia and the Ukraine. Russian troops were then ordered to proceed to Poland, Slovakia, Hungary and Romania. However, the two main cities in Poland, Warsaw and Lublin, were bypassed. In the former, the **Polish Home Army** (non-communist) was encouraged to rise up and fight against the occupying forces. The Russians seemed to hope that the Home Army would be badly damaged by the German troops; this would leave the Russian army and government with one less challenge to deal with. The Russians knew that they had the momentum in driving out the Nazis, so that in a short while Warsaw would have been free of both a non-communist Polish and German influence. They would then be in a position to install a Soviet-type regime. In tandem with this development was the establishment of the communist-dominated **National Liberation Committee (NLC)** in Lublin, which had been liberated by the Russians during the offensive. Russian politicians believed that it would be this body that would eventually provide the personnel to administer Warsaw. Unsurprisingly, the London Poles feared that they would be excluded from post-war settlements on the governance of Poland and claimed that the NLC would merely constitute a puppet regime.

The wartime conferences: Yalta, Potsdam and the Polish question

In February 1945, the British, US and Russian war leaders met at Yalta to discuss, among other things, what would happen to Poland once hostilities had ceased. By this time, Warsaw had been liberated and was temporarily governed by the Red Army. Stalin demanded that the new Russo-Polish frontier should be established along the so-called Curzon line and that the whole of Poland had to be governed by a Soviet-backed Lublin-style regime. Roosevelt and Churchill acquiesced; the London Poles were abandoned and the new border was agreed to, at least in principle.

 **KEY TERMS**

Polish Home Army
The Polish resistance army that originated from the Union of Armed Struggle (established in September 1939). The Home Army coordinated the activity of over 150 resistance sub-groups; by 1944, the groups probably consisted of over 300,000 men and women. It was answerable to the commander-in-chief in London.

National Liberation Committee (NLC) Set up in Chelm (south-east of Lublin) in July 1944 by the Polish State National Council to oppose the National Government in exile in London. The NLC was supported and controlled by Russia.

In July 1945, a second conference held at Potsdam dealt with the issue of Poland's western border. Stalin persuaded Truman (Roosevelt died on 12 April 1945) and Churchill to accept a western demarcation at the 'Oder–Niesse line', which was well inside ethnic Germany. The Yalta and Potsdam agreements together paved the way for Russia to fully implement a Soviet-style government across the newly reconstituted Poland.

In February 1947, a provisional constitution was instigated which set up a Council of State. The Council had almost total legislative and executive power and was dominated by the Stalinist-influenced **Polish Workers' Party (PPR)**. By August 1948, the PPR was the only party that could be voted for (thus, a one-party state had been established). Those who questioned the move away from any semblance of social democracy, such as members of the Church and trade unions, were arrested. In 1950, for example, over 30,000 workers went on strike at various times, only to find that they were quickly rounded up and sent to the newly built concentration camps at Mielcin and Jaworzno. The clampdown was reinforced by the imposition of Soviet-type economic and social reforms. Most notable was the spread of collective farms.

By 1952, with the imposition of a Soviet-style constitution, Poland was officially renamed the People's Republic of Poland. As the historian Adam Zamoyski has pointed out (2015): '… Poland had been hermetically sealed off from the outside world, and not just by the three hundred kilometres of barbed-wire entanglements and 1200 watchtowers surrounding it'.

Khrushchev and Poland

Revelation of the contents of Khrushchev's 'Secret Speech' (see pages 22–4) provoked a demand from Polish intellectuals for Stalinist politicians in Poland to stand down. Such requests were supported by workers through strike action. Khrushchev largely agreed to their demands; in October 1956, **Wladyslaw Gomulka** was released from prison to take over the leadership of Poland. What followed was an easing of control over the Polish people. For example, peasants were allowed to leave collective farms to set up independent smallholdings and the Catholic Church was once more allowed to teach religion in schools. Generally, until the death of Khrushchev, the Polish experienced elements of relief from the highly oppressive period of Stalinist overrule.

KEY TERM

Polish Workers' Party (PPR) Founded in 1942 and led by Wladyslaw Gomulka. By December 1945, it had around 65,000 members, only about a tenth of the membership of its rival, the Polish People's Party (PSL). In December 1948, the PPR changed its name to the Polish United Workers' Party and, with the backing of Stalin, monopolised party politics.

KEY FIGURE

Wladyslaw Gomulka (1905–82)

A Polish communist who was instrumental in the formation of the Polish Workers' Party (1942). He became a key figure in the Provisional Government of National Unity (1943–8) but was denounced by opponents as a reactionary. In the early 1950s, Gomulka spent time in prison; he was released as a result of de-Stalinisation and was elected as the leader of a new Polish government (1956–70).

Summary diagram: Russo-Polish relations

The Polish Revolt 1863
- Background: the role of Wielpolski; the rise of Polish nationalism
- Nationalists rebelled against Polish government (1863–4)
- Milyutin reforms and start of Russification

↓

The impact of the First World War
Independence gained from Russia (1918)

↓

The Russo-Polish War 1920
- Red Army defeated by Polish forces
- Armistice signed (October 1920); territorial agreements

↓

The lead-up to the Second World War
- Treaty of Berlin (1933)
- Non-aggression pact agreed between Germany and Poland (1934)
- *Anschluss* of Austria (1938)
- Munich Peace Conference (1938)
- Nazi–Soviet non-aggression pact (1939)
- German invasion of Poland (September 1939)

Impact of the Second World War
- London Poles
- Katyn Forest massacre
- Formation of Polish Home Army
- Formation of National Liberation Committee
- Russian influence: Yalta, Potsdam, the Oder–Niesse line and the rise of the Polish Workers' Party

↓

Khrushchev and Poland
- The impact of de-Stalinisation
- Wladyslaw Gomulka as leader of Poland

3 Russification

▶ *How successful was the Russification process from 1855 to 1964?*

Russification was the process whereby non-Russian regions were drawn more securely into the framework of the empire. The procedure for this to happen involved administrative integration to be implemented followed by an inculcation process. The latter was characterised by the transmission of Russian language, religion and culture to the peoples of national minorities. Subsequently, the traditions of minorities became 'subsidiary, colourful ethnic remnants' rather than forces for social change in their own right. Such 'social Russification' was linked to economic integration; moves towards a common language went hand in hand with more general improvements to telecommunications and transport.

The origins of Russification

The start of Russification is usually seen as the Polish Revolt of 1863 (see pages 182–3). The Milyutin Plan acted as a kind of blueprint for other attempts to resolve regional conflicts and to expand Russian authority. But Milyutin's liberal policy was criticised at the time. The influential newspaper editor of the *Moscow Bulletin*, Mikhail Katkov, claimed that empowering the nobility at regional level through civic reforms such as the introduction of the *Zemstva* was asking for trouble. Katkov believed that in a multinational empire, liberalism would lead to inter-regional strife and separatism. He stated that 'freedom does not mean freedom to arm the enemy'. Katkov and his supporters demanded that an alternative be considered. Regions could be brought under control through the persuasive and forceful transmission of Russian values (that is, Russification).

Under Alexander III and Nicholas II, Russification spread through areas that were deemed to accept it without much opposition. Thus, the Ukraine, the Baltic provinces and the Caucuses were all targeted as regions that could easily be annexed. This was about incorporating other regions to create a unified Russian Empire. Russification was continued by Lenin, Stalin and Khrushchev, mainly through constitutional changes (see below). The main difference from tsarist policy was that the communists aimed to create a federal system of government (that is, one whereby each national minority had a certain amount of autonomy but together they formed a federation of states to be guided centrally from Moscow).

Constitutions and national minorities

The differences between the constitutions created by the communists were as follows (see Figure 4.4, page 201, to locate the different republics):

- 1918: a constitution created the RSFSR (that is, Russia, but also including parts of Central Asia, most notably Kazakhstan, Uzbekistan and Turkmenia).
- 1924: a new constitution formally created the Federal Union of Soviet Socialist Republics (USSR). By this time, via a treaty of 1922, the Republics of the Ukraine, Belorussia and Transcaucasia (Azerbaijan, Armenia, Georgia) had joined with the RSFSR (see pages 32–4). Each republic was allowed its own government and other symbols of sovereignty such as national flags. However, such governments were still answerable to *Sovnarkom* (see page 33).
- 1936: the 'Stalin Constitution' added Kirghizia and Tajikistan to the list of states given full republic status. It also created a system that appeared to allow greater representation of the interests of separate nation states in the centralised government of the USSR. It also gave, in theory, the right of members to secede from the Union. Figure 1.3 on page 35 shows the newly created structure.

In reality, under Stalin, very tight control was kept on minorities, more so than under the tsars. The fact that Khrushchev partly reverted to the model of treatment of national minorities established in the mid-1920s under Lenin suggests that the Stalinist approach was considered inappropriate.

Repression and national minorities

The tsars and communists used repression to keep national minorities in check. A difference between the two, though, was one of scale in the repressive measures used. Under the tsars, minorities were controlled through a mixture of reforms to appease and military force (such as in Poland in the mid-1860s). Under the communists, especially Stalin, there was a tendency to promise reforms but then to focus more on repression to gain obedience. For example, when Germany invaded Russia in 1941, Stalin accused a number of national minority governments of collaboration (those of the Crimean Tatars, Volga Germans and some Caucasian groups). As punishment, great swathes of the populations of the areas concerned were deported to remote areas of Central Asia. This kind of treatment was not apparent under the tsars. The only minority group that was treated in a very similar, consistent manner by different regimes was the Jews (see pages 194–5).

Russo-Finnish relations

The tsars before Nicholas II took a fairly liberal stance on Finland, conceding to demands for a separate Finnish parliament (*Diet*) in 1863 and a constitution in 1865. The appointment by Nicholas II of **Nikolei Bobrikov** as governor general marked a change in fortune for the Finns. Under Bobrikov, Finland was fully

 KEY FIGURE

Nikolei Bobrikov (1839–1904)

A general in the Russian army, he was appointed governor-general of Finland in 1898. He was disliked by moderates in Finland, especially the Young Finns, for administering policies such as five years' military service, the introduction of Russian as the official language of administration and the employment of Russian officials into the higher levels of government.

integrated into the Russian Empire and Russified. Finland's separate army was disbanded, the Finnish State Secretariat was abolished, and Russian became the main language. Inevitably, this provoked much opposition, mainly through a policy of passive non-cooperation, but it also led to the assassination of Bobrikov in 1904 by terrorists. In 1905, Finland was given full autonomy only to find that the agreement was quickly reneged on by Stolypin in the same year. As with Poland, it was the Treaty of Brest-Litovsk that enabled Finland to achieve lasting independence.

After the First World War, Finland went about establishing and consolidating a republican-style government under the presidency of Kaarlo Juho Ståhlberg. However, relations with the Soviets remained challenging. A number of border disputes arose, such as the **Pork mutiny of 1922**. Some improvement occurred with signing of the Treaty of Tartu in 1920. This resulted in Finland gaining Petsamo at the expense of allowing East Karelia to become independent. In 1923, Finnish communists established the Karelian Autonomous Soviet Socialist Republic (a Soviet satellite state), which once again heightened tensions. By the 1930s, Stalin had placed Finland under further pressure by hindering its merchant shipping, especially in the seas between Lake Lagoda and the Gulf of Finland.

At the start of the Second World War, Finland refused a request from Stalin to allow the Soviet Union to set up military bases on Finnish territory. This angered Stalin and resulted in his order to bomb the Finnish capital, Helsinki (November 1939). In turn, this action sparked the Winter War between the Soviet Union and Finland (November 1939 to March 1940). The significance of this for the Russian government was that war once again highlighted military weaknesses; there were somewhere near 50,000 Soviet deaths as a result of this very limited military conflict. Nevertheless, Finland ceded border space to the Russians and this set a precedent for the Baltic States to be forced to become part of the USSR by the summer of 1940.

After the end of the Second World War, Finland signed a Treaty of Friendship, Co-operation and Mutual Assistance (1948) with Russia. From this, the Finns gained neutrality status and were, in the main, left alone by the Soviet Union.

The Baltic provinces

The Baltic provinces consisted of Estonia, Latvia and Lithuania. At the start of the period, these provinces were strongly influenced by 'old' German rulers. The states were relatively stable and prosperous, especially given the abundant supplies of raw materials that were essential to a range of industrial activities. The attraction of regular and better-paid employment encouraged many native Russians to migrate to the area, with Riga (in Latvia), in particular, becoming a very important commercial and business centre. As the Russian economic

KEY TERM

Pork mutiny of 1922
The Pork 'mutiny' of February 1922 occurred when a group of Red Guards decided to cross the border between Russia and Finland: the guards looted property before persuading Finnish workers (with guns and money) to join their Soviet battalion. The leader, Frans Myyryläinen, started the process of recruitment by standing on a box that had previously stored pork (hence the name of the incident).

influence increased, Russification followed almost naturally. Thus, the use of the Russian language became more widespread. This was illustrated, for example, by the renaming of various educational institutions.

German influence waned by the end of the nineteenth century, and this coincided with a rise in nationalism among native Estonians, Latvians and Lithuanians. However, this was never strong enough for full independence to be achieved. During the early years of the Second World War (1939–41), the three states were annexed to the federal system of Russian government created under the 1936 constitution. The new members of the RSFRS had the same rights as existing members, including the legal right to secede (that is, to break away from the USSR), but their behaviour was tightly controlled from Moscow. As in other regions, the authorities were not afraid to use severe repressive measures to maintain law and order. The Baltic provinces suffered especially badly during the later parts of the Second World War. There were mass deportations due mainly to a fear that there were many who were collaborating with the Nazis.

After the war, the region became more stable, although it remained under the influence of the Soviet Union.

The Ukrainians

The Ukrainians suffered similar treatment to the Poles during the rule of Alexander II. Although nationalism was not the same force as it was in Poland, the Ukrainians looked to build a separate cultural identity as reflected in literature and the arts in general. In response, Alexander II issued decrees (1863 and 1876) which forbade the publication and import of books written in Ukrainian. This early attempt at Russification was reinforced by Alexander III but, again, as with Poland, the peace treaty that ended Russia's involvement in the First World War also granted the Ukraine full independence. Unfortunately for the Ukrainians, this was very short lived as they were not able to resist the might of the Red Army during the Civil War (1917–21).

Ukraine was a very important grain-producing area for Russia. Ukrainian peasants were fully aware of their importance to the Russian economy and were resistant to changes that they believed were unjust. In particular, Stalin's collectivisation programme was vehemently opposed. Stalin blamed such behaviour on the *kulaks*. The result was that Ukrainian peasants suffered more than any other regional group when it came to the purges.

In theory, the position of Ukraine improved when, under the 1936 constitution, it retained its status (see page 191). However, during and after the Second World War, many Ukrainians were accused of being German collaborators. Those found guilty were either executed or transported to the far north.

The Caucasians

Those living in the Caucasus region of Russia were divided along religious lines. The Armenians and Georgians were Christians, and the Azeris, Chechens, Ossetians and Abkhazians were Muslims. These divisions, coupled with the high level of illiteracy in the region, made Russification relatively easy. Nevertheless, populist movements arose to fight against repression. Of particular note were the Dashnaks and the Georgian Mensheviks, who proved to be very antagonistic towards Nicholas II. The Dashnaks organised their own self-defence militias to be used against intrusions by Russian officials. The Georgian Mensheviks led the nationalist movement in Georgia but also sought to make an ally with Germany.

Georgia gained independence in 1920 but was 'retaken' by the Red Army in 1921. It was then suggested by some communists that Georgia should be amalgamated with Armenia and Azerbaizhan. Georgian communists opposed this, arguing that they should be included in the Soviet Union on the same terms as other regions such as Ukraine. Stalin, in his role as commissar for national minorities, ordered **Ordjonikidze**, his representative in Georgia, to bring the dissidents under control. Unfortunately, Ordjonikidze ended up physically attacking one of the Georgian communist leaders. The incident was made worse when Stalin attempted to defend the actions of Ordjonikidze. Lenin reacted by condemning the authoritarian approach adopted by Stalin, claiming that such actions would lead to further discontent not just in Georgia but throughout the Soviet Union. Ironically, the 1936 constitution gave full republican status to Georgia although, as with the other republics, this was no guarantee of autonomy.

The Jews

Jews were a unique group in that they did not have a homeland in the Russian Empire. Before the time of Alexander II, an artificial place of settlement had been established (the **Pale of Settlement**) but this was restrictive for Jews. Alexander II therefore allowed members of the Pale to migrate to other regions. His son, Alexander III, clamped down on this and generally the period up to the First World War was one during which Russian Jews were persecuted. Jews never seemed to pose much of an active opposition to Russian leaders; it was a perceived threat that resulted in their being treated so badly. Alexander III believed that Jews were behind the infamous **Ignatiev memorandum** along with all of the 'negative and insidious' influences from the West. Partly as a result of this, a mini-**pogrom**, called 'little thunder', occurred in the Pale,

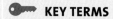

KEY FIGURE

Grigol Ordjonikidze (1886–1937)

Born in Georgia in 1886 into a noble family. After training as a medic he entered radical politics; he was involved in the 1905 'revolution' and served as a commissar in the Ukraine during the Russian Civil War. In 1930, Ordjonikidze became a full member of the Politburo before being promoted to the important post of People's Commissar for Soviet Industry (1932).

KEY TERMS

Pale of Settlement The region within which Jews were allowed to settle. From 1835, it included Lithuania, Poland and the south-western provinces (including Ukraine).

Ignatiev memorandum Nicholas Pavolich Ignatiev (1832–1908) was Russia's ambassador to Constantinople. In 1876, he sent a note to Serbian leaders, without official approval, saying that they could rely on Russian help if they declared war on Turkey.

Pogrom An organised massacre of Russian Jews.

prompted by an **anti-Semitic** group known as the Holy League. Other repressive measures from 1882 onwards included the following:

- the confinement of Jews once more to the Pale of Settlement
- the banning of Jews from trying to purchase land in prosperous rural areas
- restrictions on access to senior positions in the military or medicine
- removal from the electoral register of the *Zemstva*.

Nicholas II continued the anti-Jewish position taken by his father. They were accused of being 'revolutionaries' as some were affiliated to the Social Democrats (SDs; and there was indeed a separate Jewish SD Party called the Bund). Despite Nicholas's dislike of Jews, he made some important concessions by allowing them to sit on the *Duma*.

The communists were just as repressive towards Jews. More 'special' settlements were established in the 1930s, such as that at Khaburovsk. By the Second World War, more oppression took place with a ban being imposed on the Jewish religion, the closure of a range of Jewish institutions (for example, schools and societies) and a ban on specialist publications. This carried on after the war. Of particular note was the **Doctors' Plot** of August 1952, which ended in fifteen Jewish leaders being tried and executed. The perceived threat of Jewish subversiveness and plotting was always apparent throughout the rule of Khrushchev, with a number of prominent Jewish technical specialists being executed for anti-communist activity.

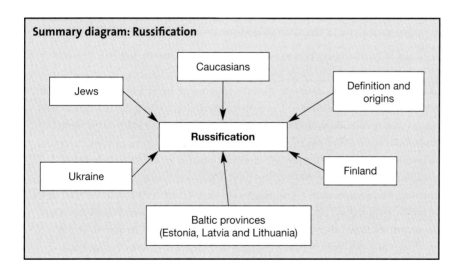

Summary diagram: Russification

KEY TERMS

Anti-Semitic Prejudiced against Jews.

Doctors' Plot
An announcement was made by the Stalinist regime in January 1953 concerning nine doctors who had worked alongside a US Jewish group to murder high-ranking Soviet officials. Seven of the doctors were Jews.

The impact of the First World War and the Treaty of Brest-Litovsk

▶ *To what extent was the Treaty of Brest-Litovsk a turning point in the development of the Russian Empire?*

Once the Bolsheviks had dealt with the issue of the Constituent Assembly, they moved on to address how to withdraw from the First World War (see page 32). Lenin had promised to bring peace to the Russian people ('Peace, Bread and Land') but doing this without it appearing that Russia was surrendering conditionally was a tricky business. Eventually, in March 1918, the Treaty of Brest-Litovsk was signed with Germany.

The origins of the treaty

On 23 October 1917, the Bolshevik and Soviet government issued a Decree on Peace which asked 'All the Belligerent Nations' to start peace talks based on 'no annexations or indemnities'. Coinciding with this, Lenin ordered details of so-called 'secret' treaties made between the Allies to be issued. The Bolsheviks believed that Russia had been let down by the Entente and that the latter were planning to divide up the spoils of war between themselves. Subsequently, the Allies showed minimal interest in the Decree on Peace. Lenin was therefore forced to go it alone to negotiate a separate peace with Germany.

A group of Russian negotiators was sent, on 16 November, to Brest-Litovsk (a town in Belorussia) to meet a German delegation to discuss the possibility of an armistice. The Russian politicians, spurred on by Trotsky, who arrived at Brest-Litovsk in the middle of December, attempted to drag out the talks. They hoped that revolution would break out in the West before a deal was signed; this would have either placed the Soviets in a very strong bargaining position or terminated the need for any kind of treaty (see page 197). The German leadership soon became wary of the Soviet 'game playing' and responded by entering discussions with Ukrainians over support for independence. The latter would be granted in full after a period of German protection. Worried by this development (and other territorial demands made by the Germans), Trotsky broke off talks and returned to Petrograd to convey his view of what had happened to the other Bolshevik leaders.

Trotsky relayed the German demands at a meeting of the Central Committee of the new Russian government that took place on 11 January 1918. Trotsky reiterated his view that talks should be stalled for as long as possible. Lenin disagreed and suggested that a treaty should be signed as soon as possible to protect the gains made from the October Revolution. But a remaining 'Left'

Socialist Revolutionary (SR) faction in the Central Committee, led by Bukharin, opposed the ideas of both Trotsky and Lenin. They demanded that the conflict be prolonged and turned into a **revolutionary war**. Lenin was frightened by this prospect and chose to side with Trotsky; the latter was sent back to Brest-Litovsk to prolong talks for as long as possible.

Germany signed a separate treaty with the Ukrainians on 9 February. On 18 February 1918, the German leadership responded further to Russian dalliance by ordering a force of 700,000 troops to push deep into Russian territory. It took them just five days to advance over 150 miles towards Petrograd. The offensive was met with little resistance, which encouraged Germany, on 23 February, to demand even more stringent conditions for peace. The Central Committee called another meeting to discuss the renewed demands. Lenin wanted the terms to be accepted, Trotsky argued for no response to be given while Bukharin continued to demand for the war to be continued under the banner of the revolution. Lenin got his way and on 3 March the treaty was signed. Bukharin and the Left SRs resigned from Soviet government.

The stipulations of the treaty

The price of peace for Russia was high. Germany insisted on harsh territorial demands, labelled as 'massively punitive [punishing]' by the historian Steve Smith (2002).

Much land was ceded to Germany which contained valuable resources. Russia lost the following (see also Figure 4.3, page 198):

- Poland
- Estonia
- Latvia
- Lithuania
- Ukraine
- Georgia
- Finland.

All of these territories gained a form of independence, initially as German protectorates. This handing over of land amounted to Russia's loss of:

- a third of agricultural land
- a third of all railway track
- a third of the population of the Soviet Republic (about 55 million people)
- two-thirds of coalmines and half of heavy industry (iron and steel)
- nearly all available oil and most cotton textile production.

Lenin knew that these conditions were harsh and not what the Russian people expected. However, there is evidence that he believed that the war would soon be over, that Germany would be defeated and that territory would be recovered. A greater hope was still that a communist revolution would occur in Germany; the conditions there, according to Marxism, were ripe for such an event.

KEY TERM

Revolutionary war
An (international) war fought on behalf of and by workers against capitalists.

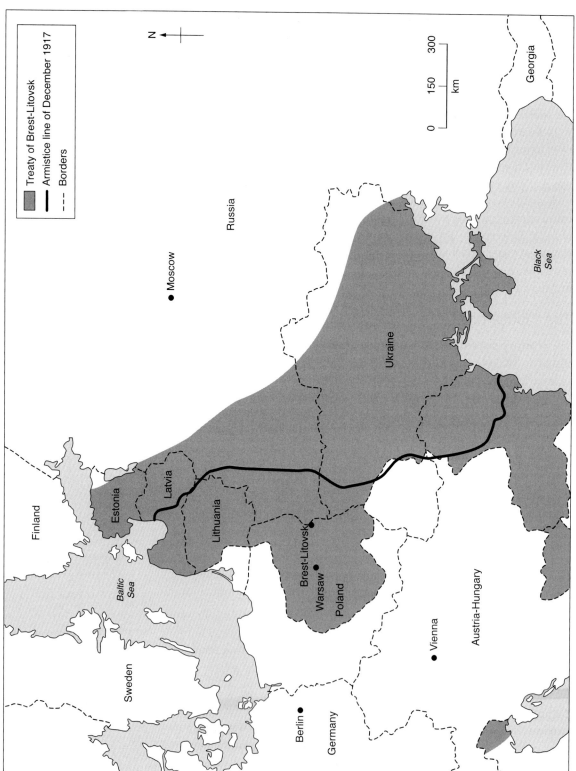

Figure 4.3 Land given up by the Russian delegation in signing the Treaty of Brest-Litovsk.

The agreement also gave the Bolsheviks time to establish a government and to attend to other matters such as the state of the economy.

The consequences of the treaty

The treaty affected Russia in a number of ways:

- The departure of Bukharin and the Left SRs from the Soviet government meant that the Bolsheviks were in sole control of Russia.
- Once the burden of war had been lifted, the Bolsheviks started to implement their policies. Some historians have claimed that this gave Lenin the opportunity to introduce repression to consolidate power. It is believed that Lenin had manufactured the situation to allow him to use violence against opponents, something he believed was inevitable. This view has been countered by historians who argue that the level of violence used has been exaggerated and that when it was used it was simply necessary. The historian Christopher Hill (2007) has stated that: 'there was no wholescale suppression of the opposition press during the six months after the Bolshevik revolution, and no violence against political opponents, because there was no need for it. The death sentence was even abolished at the end of October, though Lenin thought this very unrealistic.'
- Hill's view is partly supported by comments made by Lenin in November 1917: 'We do not use the sort of terror as was used by the French revolutionaries who guillotined unarmed people, and I hope we shall not have to use it.'
- Lenin's sentiments appeared sincere when members of the Provisional Government who had been arrested were 'pardoned' having promised 'not to take arms against the people any more'.
- By early 1918, Lenin appeared to renege on his 'promise'. The *Cheka* was used to arrest and punish hoarders of grain. The Bolsheviks argued that harsh treatment of certain groups in society, especially *kulaks*, was needed if the population as a whole was to avoid famine.
- The treaty had exacerbated the problem of food shortages; this was due to the loss of Ukraine, a major food-producing area.
- Opponents of the Bolsheviks used the crisis of food shortages to gain support. This was coupled with attacks on senior Bolshevik members, including Lenin. On 30 August 1918, a member of the SRs assassinated the head of the Petrograd *Cheka* and on the same day Lenin was shot and wounded by Fanya Kaplan, a member of the SRs.

Thus, it appears that the treaty added to the problems faced by the Bolsheviks and did not work quite in the way that Lenin intended. However, it is possible that the new Russian leader was happy to see opposition gather momentum with the likelihood of this leading to civil war. It would have given him the opportunity to risk an all-out offensive against those who openly revealed themselves as opponents. If his gamble paid off, he would be in a much more secure position to deal with other political and economic challenges he faced.

> **Summary diagram: The impact of the First World War and the Treaty of Brest-Litovsk**
>
> > **The First World War and the origins of the Treaty of Brest-Litovsk**
> >
> > - October 1917: Decree on Peace
> > - November 1917: Russian negotiators sent to Brest-Litovsk
> > - January 1918: Central Committee meeting; discussed German demands
> > - February 1918: Germany threatened new military offensive against Russia
> > - March 1918: Treaty of Brest-Litovsk signed; debates had divided revolutionaries
>
> > **Stipulations of the Treaty of Brest-Litovsk**
> >
> > - 'Massively punitive'?
> > - Russia lost territory: Poland, Estonia, Latvia, Lithuania, Ukraine, Georgia and Finland
> > - Territorial losses resulted in: loss of agricultural land, railway track, raw materials for industry
>
> > **Political consequences**
> >
> > - Bukharin and SRs' refusal to agree with Treaty left Bolsheviks in charge of Russia
> > - Bolsheviks implemented policies to consolidate power
> > - Bolsheviks used repression in the form of the *Cheka*
> > - Possibility of civil war emerged

Expansion in Asia

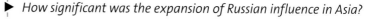

▶ *How significant was the expansion of Russian influence in Asia?*

Russian expansion in Asia consisted of:

- attempts to turn Central Asia into a kind of colony that would provide Russia with raw materials for industry (especially cotton textiles)
- attempts to spread Russian influence over the Far East, especially eastern China, Japan and Korea.

Most of the expansion in Central Asia was over by the late 1880s but Russia's efforts to exert influence continued until the end of the period.

Expansion in Central Asia

By the start of Second World War, the Soviet government had influence over the following parts of Central Asia (see Figure 4.4, page 201):

- Kazakhstan
- Turkmenistan
- Uzbekistan

Figure 4.4 A map of the Russian Empire c.1900: it shows how far into Central Asia and the Far East the empire had spread.

- Kyrgyzstan
- Tajikistan
- Azerbaijan.

Much of the Central Asian territory had been taken under control by the 1880s through the use of force. In contrast to the tsars, the communists consolidated their control in the region through more peaceful means: the constitutions (see pages 190–1). The main motives for expansion and control were uniform throughout the period:

- Central Asia was to provide living and working space for large numbers of peasants from European Russia (and, hence, to quell the demands of such peasants for more land).
- The region was developed for cotton cultivation to serve the raw material needs of the textile factories in European Russia.
- The Central Asian territories bordered Afghanistan, India and China, creating the prospect of further expansion and influence in these areas.

Central Asia largely avoided Russification; the tsars and communists seemed to think that, given the complexity of societies there and the difficulties with communication and transport, Russification was not achievable (or desirable). However, other measures had to be carried out if Russian leaders were to achieve their goals:

- The Steppe Statute of 1891 was passed which granted 40 acres of land to peasant settlers, enough to establish a successful farm unit (although it was of no use to the native nomadic peoples).
- In 1910, Stolypin pushed for even greater migration to the area to accommodate rising peasant demands for land in European Russia. This surge in movement resulted in land belonging to natives being expropriated, a move that was to cause much resentment.
- Islam had evolved as a major religion in Central Asia. The tsars showed some respect for Muslims. Under Nicholas II the All-Russian Muslim League appeared and gained representation in the first *Dumas* (although after the 1907 electoral law, Asian Muslim representation in the *Duma* was disallowed). Under the communists there was condemnation of any repression that Muslims had experienced under the tsars and guarantees that their rights would be protected.
- From 1915 to 1917, the Russian government attempted to draw on peoples from Central Asia to help with the war effort. However, they were deemed, in general, not fit for combat duties and were given other jobs. The largely Muslim population resented the fact that attempts at conscription had started during the Ramadan period and, coupled with the disrespectful judgements about their military prowess, this was enough for them to rebel. The 'conscription revolt' indicated how sensitive the population of Central Asia was to over-involvement of Russian rulers in their affairs.
- The Soviet regimes appeared more sensitive to the wants and needs of Central Asia, as was revealed in the construction and implementation of the constitutions (see pages 190–1). But the more remote, harsh areas of the region were still used as dumping grounds for groups from other parts of the Soviet Union that needed punishing. For example, the Crimean Tatars were deported to south Kazakhstan in 1945 having been accused of collaborating with Germany. Many of them died in the severe conditions they found themselves in.
- In 1957, Khrushchev issued a decree titled 'On the Rehabilitation of Deported Peoples'. This allowed many groups who had been deported in the period from 1941 to 1945 to return to their homelands. Some groups were excluded though, such as the Volga Germans and Meskhetians.
- Khrushchev also involved himself in the affairs of Central Asia through his Virgin Land policy (see page 96). As with the migration policies of the tsars, this did not go down well with indigenous people as they felt swamped by immigrants looking to take even more land.

Thus, Central Asia became a highly valued part of the Russian Empire and the Soviet Union but, unlike other regions, it was allowed to keep its identity.

Russian involvement in the Far East

Attempts to spread Russian influence in the Far East were largely governed by developments in transport and communications. Before the completion of the Trans-Siberian Railway in 1903 (see pages 79–80), the main route towards the Pacific coast was a dirt track. By the end of the nineteenth century, it could still take up to three months to travel from Moscow to Sakhalin.

Despite the logistical problems of expanding into the Far East, territorial gains dated back to the seventeenth century. By 1905, a series of events led to Russia gaining a foothold as far as the Amur basin and Manchuria:

- The Amur basin was secured by 1860 as a result of the efforts of Nikolai Muraviev, governor-general of eastern Siberia. Using his personal army (the Transbaikal Cossack Host), Muraviev forced the Chinese to sign two treaties which gave Russia not only the territory around the Amur river but also access to the Pacific coast. In 1860, the town of Vladivostok was established and was to become the naval base for Russia's Pacific fleet.
- By the 1890s, it was evident that Russia had a rival in the Far East: Japan. In 1894, Japan attacked China; the Russian government exploited the turmoil this created in the region by concluding a defensive treaty with China (see pages 139–40 on the long-term origins of the Russo-Japanese War). The treaty resulted in the Russians being allowed to construct the Chinese–Eastern Railway, which gave them access to the mineral deposits to be found in Manchuria. By 1897, Russia had also negotiated a deal to lease Port Arthur (at the end of the Liaodong peninsula), an ice-free trading port and extra base for the Russian navy.
- The Chinese Boxer Rebellion of 1899–1900 provided the Russian government with an opportunity to consolidate its presence in Manchuria (see page 139). The Japanese were understandably upset by this development and attempted to broker a deal with Russia. In return for being allowed to influence affairs in Korea, the Japanese were willing to let Russia maintain its interest in Manchuria. The Russians declined the offer and the Japanese reacted by torpedoing Russian ships in Port Arthur. The Russo-Japanese War (1904–5) was the end product of the dispute.

After the Russo-Japanese War, Russian involvement in the Far East was influenced by further wars and conflicts. The First World War, the Russian Revolution and the Russian Civil War diverted the attention of Russian leaders from issues in the Far East. After the end of the Civil War, the communists returned to the region to address issues related to spheres of influence, occupation and conflict.

China

From 1917 to 1937, the Chinese government was dominated by the Kuomintang (KMT, National People's Party). Even though the party was non-communist (and by the 1930s openly opposed communists), the Soviet Union provided it with financial aid. For Lenin and Stalin, the KMT seemed the only viable option to restore unity in China after upheavals caused by the First World War. In 1924, the Soviets signed a formal peace treaty with Sun Yat-sen, the leader of the KMT. When Sun died in 1925 he was replaced by General Chiang Kai-shek. Chiang was far more conservative than Sun and took a harder line against opponents, especially the Chinese Communist Party (CCP, founded in 1921). Initially, Chiang formed a loose alliance with the communists but by the mid-1920s he decided they had become too powerful. In 1927, Chiang ordered the 'extermination' of trouble makers: communists, trade unionists and peasant leaders. Further purges happened in 1930 and 1934; under their leader, Mao Zedong, the Chinese communists reacted by regrouping and setting up a base at Yenan in Shensi province (north-eastern China). From 1934 until 1937, the communists gained considerable support and fought back against Chiang. The conflict was temporarily halted by the outbreak of war with Japan in 1937.

The Soviet Union continued to support the KMT, particularly when Chiang struggled to resist Japanese advances. Japan used Manchuria (which it had occupied since 1931) as a base from which to launch attacks in east China, and by the end of 1937 most of that area was under their control. The CCP called a truce with the KMT to help fight the common enemy. The CCP were very effective in adopting guerrilla tactics against the Japanese in the north, a move which gained them even more support from the Chinese people. Stalin supported their efforts in 1941 by establishing Soviet air units at Nanking, Hankow, Chunking and Lanchow. The collective actions of the KMT, CCP and Soviet Union stopped the Japanese from making inroads further west.

After the defeat of Japan at the end of the Second World War, fighting between the KMT and CCP resumed. US intervention resulted in the KMT having jurisdiction over the territory that had been taken by the Japanese with the exception of Manchuria, which had been recaptured by Russia. Despite US aid, Chiang's forces proved no match for the Chinese communists and in 1949 Mao gained control of the whole of mainland China. In October 1949, the People's Republic of China was created with Mao as president.

Although the Soviets had supported the KMT, Mao initially acknowledged the hegemony (leadership) of Stalin when it came to attempts to spread communism in the post-war era. In November 1949, Mao and Stalin signed a Treaty of Friendship, Alliance and Mutual Assistance; until Stalin's death, relations between the two remained cordial. Under Khrushchev, the friendship rapidly deteriorated (see pages 221–2) and by the 1960s border disputes were emerging. Something of a 'honeymoon period' between China and Russia had ended.

Manchuria

Manchuria was under Japanese influence from 1905 to 1931, and then from 1931 to 1945 the Japanese went a step further and occupied the territory. The occupation meant control over Port Arthur, a base that would be of strategic importance to the Japanese merchant and shipping fleets. In 1945, Soviet troops liberated Manchuria and Stalin handed it back to China. However, the Soviet Union kept jurisdiction of Port Arthur until the death of Stalin in 1953.

Korea

Korea came under Japanese control in 1910. With the defeat of Japan in 1945, Korea was divided into two zones: the North (the area above the 38th parallel) was to be overseen by Russia and the South by the USA. The plan was to help Korea to reconstruct and develop a new system of government, but animosity between the two protecting powers caused the division between North and South to become entrenched. In June 1950, the North Korean leader Kim Il Sung (probably encouraged by Stalin and Mao Zedong) decided to invade the South with the aim of reuniting the two halves. A full-blown war ensued, with China backing the North and the USA supporting the South. The Korean War ended in 1951 but the dispute over the border between North and South was not resolved until 1953. In July 1953, the dividing line was established at the 38th parallel, which was where it had been placed at the end of 1945. The Soviet Union played no direct role in the war but it was still blamed by the US president, Truman, for influencing the initial invasion by Kim. This heightened Cold War tensions and undoubtedly encouraged Khrushchev, when he gained power, to introduce his policy of 'peaceful coexistence' (see page 171).

Sinkiang, Tanu Tuva and Mongolia

Russian influence was also strong in regions to the north and north-west of China:

- Sinkiang province (north-west of China) was part of the Chinese Empire from 1760 until 1920. In 1921, it came under Soviet influence and partial occupation until 1949. It was returned to the Chinese after the formation of the People's Republic of China.
- Tanu Tuva (north of Mongolia) was made a Russian protectorate in 1914 but became an independent 'People's Republic' in 1921. In 1944, its status changed once more when it was annexed to the Soviet Union.
- Mongolia was under Chinese jurisdiction from 1697 until 1911, when it gained its autonomy. In 1945, it was occupied by Soviet forces but in the following year it became the Mongolian People's Republic. Although an independent state, it remained under strong Soviet influence.

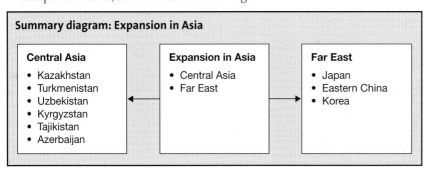

Summary diagram: Expansion in Asia

Central Asia	**Expansion in Asia**	**Far East**
• Kazakhstan	• Central Asia	• Japan
• Turkmenistan	• Far East	• Eastern China
• Uzbekistan		• Korea
• Kyrgyzstan		
• Tajikistan		
• Azerbaijan		

Communist advances into Europe after the Second World War

▶ *Why did Russia advance into Eastern and Central Europe after the Second World War?*

The end of the Second World War

By the time of the Yalta Conference in February 1945, it was evident that Germany was losing the war and the meeting therefore considered what would happen to Europe after Germany's defeat. The Russian approach to affairs in Eastern Europe after the Yalta Conference is often presented as being based on expansionism. However, it should be remembered that Russia had been invaded twice in the twentieth century and was seriously concerned about its own security. On a more pragmatic note, the Red Army had suffered heavy losses in driving Germany out of Russia and Eastern Europe and now occupied, or as the Russians argued, had liberated much of that land. By July 1945, Russian troops effectively controlled the Baltic States, Finland, Poland, Czechoslovakia, Hungary, Bulgaria and Romania. Germany surrendered in May 1945 and the Allies met again at Potsdam in July, but the conference did not go smoothly. Most notably, there were disagreements over Germany, as Stalin wanted to cripple it so that it was never a threat again and also began to follow through the agreement reached at Yalta over establishing pro-Soviet governments in Eastern Europe. However, this brought him into conflict with the new US president, Harry Truman, who adopted a much tougher line than Roosevelt towards what he saw as Soviet expansion.

Stalin interfered in the governance of a number of Eastern European countries by supporting the installation of pro-communist regimes. In some cases, such as with Hungary, free elections were put in place. However, such elements of democracy were limited by threats of force and imprisonment if voters and politicians did not toe the Soviet line. For example, elections in Hungary saw the communists gain just twenty per cent of votes but they still managed to dominate the Cabinet. Similar situations arose in Poland, Bulgaria, Albania and Romania; by the end of 1947, all of these states had communist governments (see Figure 4.5, page 207).

The notion that the Russians wanted to continue to expand the influence of communism was reinforced by the rhetoric of Stalin:

- In a speech made in February 1946, Stalin stated that communism and capitalism were totally incompatible; war between those who supported the opposing ideologies was seen as inevitable. For Stalin, the outcome was not in doubt; communism would come to dominate the world.

Figure 4.5 Map showing communist advance into Eastern and Central Europe after the Second World War.

- But it is claimed that the speech was misreported (especially by George Kennan); Stalin was not necessarily threatening war but was simply stating his concerns about the security of Russia in the future.
- In March 1946, Churchill made a speech at Fulton, Missouri, USA, which reiterated a view he had held for some time: 'From Stettin in the Baltic to Trieste in the Adriatic, an iron curtain has extended across the continent.' Churchill believed that Russia was determined to go for 'indefinite expansion of their power and doctrines' and that the only way to stop this was for an alliance in the West to act as a barrier. Stalin claimed that Churchill was exciting war. He proclaimed that Russian intentions were only to expand influence in Eastern Europe so that there was a communist barrier against possible attack from the West (primarily Germany) in the future.

In response to the continuing increase in Russian influence in Eastern Europe, the wartime alliance between Russia and the West, particularly the USA, broke down. Distrust between Russia and the USA was such that there was talk of the threat of war between the two. Fearful of the spread of communism, President Truman announced, under the Truman Doctrine, that he was prepared to send money, advice and equipment to any country which, in the view of America, was under threat from communism, with the aim of preventing its further spread. This policy became known as containment and was given a practical boost when, in 1947, the USA offered financial aid to help rebuild Europe's economy and prevent the further spread of communism, which it was believed developed where there was poverty and hardship.

These developments were viewed with suspicion by Stalin. He forbade any Eastern European state to accept US aid as he believed it would weaken Russian control, while allowing the USA to increase its influence in the region. Russia had already established Cominform to promote ideological unity among Communist parties in Europe, although its main aim was to complete the Sovietisation of the satellite states. Then, following the introduction of Marshall Aid and developments in Germany (see pages 163 and 214–15), the Soviet Union set up Comecon to integrate the economies of Eastern Europe. Although there was no real integration until after 1959, the communist states did follow a communist economic model:

- Five-Year Plans were established.
- Centralised economies were set up.
- Agriculture was collectivised.

Control of Eastern Europe was reinforced by the summoning its leaders to Moscow, and Soviet ambassadors in these states often intervened directly in the states' affairs. This development was further strengthened by military measures, with the armed forces of the Eastern bloc having the same equipment as the Soviet Union, having a completely integrated system centred in Moscow and by the establishment of the Warsaw Pact in 1955 in response to the Western powers allowing the Federal Republic of Germany to join the North Atlantic Treaty Organisation (NATO). Further control over the Eastern bloc was achieved through a network of bilateral treaties of friendship, cooperation and mutual assistance signed between the Soviet Union and individual satellite states, each of which contained:

- a ban on joining hostile alliances
- a mutual defence agreement
- recognition of equality, sovereignty and non-interference in each other's affairs, although this did not stop the Russians.

These developments were supplemented by the cult of Stalin, who was celebrated in all the countries as the builder of socialism and the liberator of Eastern Europe from fascism.

Despite this, there were exceptions to the quick spread of Russian-influenced communist governments in Eastern Europe. In both Yugoslavia and Czechoslovakia there was resistance to Russian pressure.

The case of Yugoslavia

At the end of the Second World War, Yugoslavia was still a relatively new country. It had been established in 1920 as a result of the Treaty of St Germain. A result of this treaty was that Austria lost Dalmatia, Bosnia and Herzegovina to Serbia. The latter was then co-joined with Montenegro to form Yugoslavia. The politicians of the newly established state were determined to create a sense of national identity and to maintain independence from external influences.

In 1945, new elections were held in Yugoslavia. The outcome was the installation of a communist government led by Marshall Tito. At the time there was no reason to expect that Russia would treat Yugoslavia any differently from any of the other Eastern European states. However, Tito wanted to continue consolidating Yugoslavian autonomy and therefore resisted attempts by Stalin to interfere. As the liberator of Yugoslavia from German occupation during the Second World War, Tito had immense support from the Yugoslav population.

Tito objected to Stalinist communism. In particular, he objected to the over-centralisation of government associated with Stalin. Tito was also aware that under Russian influence Yugoslavia's freedom to trade with whoever it wished would be curtailed. As a result of Tito's non-compliance, Yugoslavia was expelled from the Cominform in 1948. In conjunction with this, Russia withdrew economic support; Stalin's hope was that this would result in a rapid decline in the living standards of Yugoslavs, who would then blame Tito for their plight. The envisaged destabilisation of the Yugoslavian government would make it easy for Stalin to step in and restore order.

Tito maintained his stance and continued to govern according to his own brand of communism. Economic relations with the West were strengthened and the Yugoslav leader even managed to gain financial aid from the International Monetary Fund (IMF). These manoeuvres reassured the people of Yugoslavia that Tito was the right person to govern.

With public support behind him, Tito progressed to make radical changes. These included:

- The handing over of ownership and control of industry from the state to workers' councils.
- The establishment of communes (consisting of 5000–100,000 people) and a Commune Assembly. The communes, under the guidance of the assembly, organised their own welfare, health, education and cultural programmes. The assembly was also responsible for administering economic policy.

The communes appeared to be popular with most Yugoslavs, as they provided them with opportunities to play an active role in improving living and working standards. As it was in stark contrast to Stalin's policy of centralisation, Tito's model did not sit well with the Russians. Some Marxist commentators at the time argued that Tito's communism was how Marx thought it would emerge. Others, though, were soon to find fault with the system. It was pointed out, for example, that the model leaned towards capitalism which, in turn, led to inequalities between workers. Some were rewarded more than others, depending on their economic role.

Relations between Yugoslavia and Russia remained frosty until after the death of Stalin. In 1955, Khrushchev visited Tito to make friends and offer help for the future development of Yugoslavia. More cordial relations were strengthened by Khrushchev's abandonment of Cominform in 1956. Tito continued to govern successfully until his death in 1980. However, in his bid to create a unified Yugoslavia he had kept tight control of national minorities in the state. The rise of Croatian and Serbian nationalism in the 1980s, in particular, signalled the start of the break-up of Yugoslavia.

The case of Czechoslovakia

Like Yugoslavia, Czechoslovakia was created as a new state under the Treaty of St Germain. Initially, it consisted of Bohemia and Moravia; Slovakia and Ruthenia were added under the Treaty of Trianon in 1920. Thus, in comparison with Yugoslavia, Czechoslovakia became a multinational state. More specifically, it consisted of:

- 6.5 million Czechs
- 2.5 million Slovaks
- 3 million Germans (most of who lived in Bohemia, Moravia and a region on the old German–Austrian borderlands known as the Sudetenland. The Germans became the most unsettled of the national minorities; they had been proud to belong to the Habsburg Empire but now found themselves living among Slavic peoples, who, they mistrusted)
- 700,000 Hungarians
- 500,000 Ruthenians
- 100,000 Poles
- pockets of Romanians and Jews.

The government of Czechoslovakia was modelled on a Western type of liberal democracy consisting of an elected parliament of two houses and an elected president. The first president, **Tomáš Masaryk**, kept his position until 1935, illustrating how stable the political system appeared to be. This is further supported by the fact that, until the Depression years of the 1930s, there were very few instances of conflict between the national minorities and even fewer challenges to the government.

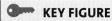

KEY FIGURE

Tomáš Masaryk (1850–1937)

A Czechoslovak politician, philosopher and sociologist. He was the first president of Czechoslovakia (1918) and went on to serve in this position on three further occasions (1920, 1927 and 1934). He is probably best known for instigating the formation of the Czech Legion during the First World War (a resistance group to Austro-Hungarian control) and the creation of an independent Czechoslovakia.

Under Foreign Minister Edvard Beneš, the new Czech government sought to form alliances with other countries. Subsequently, 'peace' treaties were signed with Yugoslavia and Romania (1920–1, known as the 'Little Entente'), Italy (1924) and France (1924 and 1925, the latter as part of the Treaty of Locarno). With the coming to power of Hitler and the formation of a Czech Sudeten German political party under **Konrad Henlein**, Beneš became concerned that Czechoslovakia might be invaded by Germany. In 1935, the Czech foreign minister approached Stalin for help. The Russian leader agreed to defend Czechoslovakia on condition that:

- support was mutual
- France also intervened to support the Czechs in the face of any Nazi invasion.

By March 1939, with help from Henlein and the Sudeten Germans, Hitler had invaded and secured the whole of Czechoslovakia. The French, and therefore Russia, stood by and watched. Britain too refused to help. Until 1945, Czechoslovakia remained as a German protectorate but with Slovakia being allowed by Hitler to break away to become independent.

After the Second World War, free elections were held in Czechoslovakia (1946). They resulted in the formation of a coalition government consisting mainly of left-wing parties including communists. In fact, the communists gained over a third of the votes, seats in parliament and Cabinet positions. A communist, **Klement Gottwald**, was elected as prime minister but other key positions were allocated to non-communists (for example, Beneš became president and Masaryk was foreign minister). The coalition appeared unified enough to enable Czechoslovakia to remain independent of outside influences. The new government pushed ahead with economic policies designed to develop trade with the West and to gain a share of Marshall Aid.

Just before new elections, scheduled for May 1948, the communists in Czechoslovakia dramatically turned face and seized power through a military coup. The reasons for this appear to be that:

- They were losing support from the people, who blamed them for the eventual rejection of Marshall Aid. American financial help was seen by many Czechs as essential to improving living standards.
- They had also lost the cooperation of many non-communist Cabinet members. The latter had protested at the demotion of eight senior police officers who had resisted being manipulated by communist politicians. But the non-communists were not united in their attempts to prevent their opponents gaining more influence over the institutions used to control law and order. The non-communists took advantage of the disunity before political opposition grew.
- They had established control over the police, military and trade unions. Taking power by force would therefore have been something of a formality.

KEY FIGURES

Konrad Henlein (1898–1945)

A prominent Sudetan German politician. After the German invasion and occupation of the Sudetenland, Henlein joined the Nazi Party and served in the SS. He also became the official *Reichsstatthalter* (governor) of the Sudetenland from 1939 until the end of the Second World War.

Klement Gottwald (1896–1953)

By the mid-1920s, Gottwald had become the leader of the Communist Party of Czechoslovakia. After the Second World War, and as part of the Sovietisation process, Gottwald was chosen to be prime minister (1946–8) and then president (1948–53), a position he served in until his death.

- They were prompted by Stalin to take over; Russia was concerned at the attempt to accept American aid (or 'dollar imperialism' as they called it) and more generally the stronger ties that had started to develop between Czechoslovakia and the West.

The coup resulted in the resignation of all non-communist members of the coalition except the president and foreign minister. Beneš was forced to select a new Cabinet which agreed to bow down to orders sent from Stalin. Beneš waited until the results of the May election before standing aside (to be replaced by Gottwald) and Masaryk supposedly killed himself (it was later revealed that he was murdered). Unsurprisingly, the May elections were rigged. Under Russian guidelines, voters were given a list of candidates to vote for (the National Front list), all of whom were communists. In turn, the candidates were obliged to carry out policies approved by the Russian government.

The communist takeover in Czechoslovakia caused consternation in the West. It had been the last of the Eastern European democracies. Churchill's 'Iron Curtain' (see pages 162–3) was fully drawn across Europe. The takeover subsequently caused a backlash from the West. In March 1948, Belgium, Britain, France, Luxembourg and the Netherlands signed the Brussels Pact in direct response to the February coup. The pact involved the signatories agreeing to defend any member against attack from an external aggressor. It also paved the way for a 'special' agreement to be made with the USA; the result of this was the formation of NATO. Thus, Stalin's intent to spread Soviet influence in the East seemingly heightened the political tensions that emerged in the early years of the Cold War.

The case of Hungary

Hungary emerged as an independent republic from the old Austro-Hungarian Empire in November 1918. Two developments characterised the history of Hungary in the inter-war period:

- After the First World War, Hungary lost territory to its neighbours. Initial losses were confirmed by the Treaty of Trianon; territory housing three-quarters of Hungary's population was divided up and given to Yugoslavia, Czechoslovakia and Romania. The neighbours had taken advantage of Hungary's weaknesses which had resulted from its association with Austria. From 1920 until 1939, Hungary's main foreign policy aim was to regain the lost land, even if that meant siding with Germany and Italy.
- The concept of republicanism in Hungary was unpopular with conservatives. The first two presidents, **Mihaly Károlyi** and **Béla Kun**, struggled to establish their authority. Elections held in January 1920 led to the formation of a right-wing government and calls for the restoration of the monarchy under King Karl. However, not all Hungarians were happy about this and Karl was forced to remain in exile. The conservatives still held sway though; the new government was headed by **Admiral Horthy**, who also acted as regent until

KEY FIGURES

Mihaly Károlyi (1875–1955)

During the period of the Hungarian Democratic Republic (1918–19), he served as Hungary's leader. More specifically, he was initially prime minister (1–16 November 1918) before becoming president (16 November 1918–21 March 1919).

Béla Kun (1886–1938)

He replaced Károlyi as leader of Hungary in March 1919; the new government was based on the Russian Soviet model but lasted only for 133 days. Kun then moved to the Soviet Union to serve as the head of the Crimean Revolutionary Committee.

Admiral Horthy (1868–1957)

An admiral in the Hungarian navy and a statesman: he was Regent of the Kingdom of Hungary during the inter-war period (1920–39) and greater part of the Second World War. He could best be described as a 'national conservative'; his political views were typified by his alliance with Hitler in the 1930s and the resultant joint invasion of the Soviet Union in 1941.

the time was right for King Karl to return. In fact, Horthy remained leader of right-wing regency-based governments until Hungary was occupied by Germany in 1944.

At the end of the Second World War, there was a significant change in the governance of Hungary. As with other East European states, 'free' elections were held in Hungary but despite gaining less than a fifth of the votes, the communists ended up dominating the Cabinet. Clearly, Stalin had influenced the setting up of the new regime. The Hungarian communists were not all pro-Stalin; however, those who opposed Russia suffered as a result. For example, the interior minister, **János Kádár**, was imprisoned and tortured, and the foreign minister, **László Rajk**, was hanged. By the end of 1949, nearly a quarter of a million Communist Party members had been expelled.

Until Stalin's death, Hungary was governed in a repressive manner by the Stalinist leader **Mátyás Rákosi**. Even when a more moderate head of government was installed, **Imre Nagy**, Rákosi continued to influence government affairs. In 1955, he managed to gain enough support to instigate the overthrow of Nagy. However, the Hungarian people became increasingly dissatisfied with the Stalinists. As a response to this, Khrushchev, with Tito's backing, persuaded the Hungarian Communist Party to replace Rákosi with a more liberal-minded leader, Ernő Gerő. Tito was interested to intervene as he believed that a Hungary more detached from Soviet influence would prove to be a useful ally.

The appointment of Gerő raised hopes and inevitably led to even more demands for change along the lines of what had occurred in Yugoslavia. By October 1956, unrest developed into a major uprising.

The Hungarian uprising 1956

The uprising unfolded as follows:

- On 23 October, a huge demonstration in Budapest took place; calls were made for reforms to be accelerated.
- Khrushchev reacted by deciding, without consulting Gerő, to send 30,000 troops, artillery and tanks to Hungary to quell the unrest.
- A new government was then formed; Gerő was replaced with Nagy. On 30 October, Khrushchev promised Nagy and other Eastern European leaders more freedom to negotiate agreements over the level of Soviet influence. Khrushchev also ordered Soviet troops to withdraw from Hungary.
- Nagy took advantage of the more liberal stance adopted by the Russian leader by advocating that Hungarian communists should share power with groups of other political persuasion. In addition, he expressed a desire to take Hungary out of the Warsaw Pact.
- The Suez Crisis resulted in the prospect of Russia losing influence in the Middle East. The significance of this was that it coincided with the problems

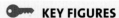

KEY FIGURES

János Kádár (1912–89)

Best known as a Hungarian communist leader and general secretary of the Hungarian Socialist Workers' Party. He governed Hungary from 1956 until his retirement, due to ill-health, in 1988.

László Rajk (1909–49)

A Hungarian communist who rose to importance as minister of the interior and then minister of foreign affairs. Rajk was keen to protect the Hungarian Communist Party from Stalinist influence; as a result of his views he was put on 'show trial' and executed.

Mátyás Rákosi (1892–1971)

A Hungarian communist who led the Hungarian Communist Party (renamed the Hungarian Working People's Party in 1948) from 1945 to 1956. He was a ruthless leader guided by Stalinist principles; he called himself 'Hungary's greatest pupil and disciple of Stalin'.

Imre Nagy (1896–1958)

A Hungarian communist who held the position of leader of Hungary on two occasions: 1953–5 and 1956. Nagy opposed intrusion from Russia and after the failed Hungarian Revolution of 1956 he was put on trial for treason, found guilty and finally executed in 1958.

in Hungary. Khrushchev believed that the situations in Egypt and Hungary indicated to the West that Soviet power was on the wane. On 4 November, he therefore ordered troops, artillery and tanks back into Hungary. Nagy was replaced with the pro-Soviet politician János Kádár.

The result of the uprising was three-fold:

- Khrushchev had sent a clear message to Eastern European leaders that he was unwilling, despite de-Stalinisation, to lessen Soviet involvement in their countries.
- The West, especially the USA, realised that Khrushchev was willing to risk a more global conflict occurring by maintaining his authority over Hungary. Therefore, there was a reluctance from the West to intervene.
- After some prevarication, communist China under the leadership of Mao supported Khrushchev's actions. This temporarily eased some of the tension that had emerged over ideology between the Soviet and Chinese governments.

The case of Germany

The question of what do about Germany at the end of the Second World War was broached at the Yalta (February 1945) and Potsdam (July–August 1945) Conferences. At Yalta, the 'Four-Power Control of Zones' principle was established. As a result, each of the Allied powers was allotted a zone within Germany to administer (Berlin was divided into four separate zones), until a foundation for future peace could be laid. At Potsdam, Britain, the USA and the USSR reached a consensus over the punishment of war criminals, the demilitarisation of Germany and **denazification**. However, there was disagreement over other issues, especially how Germany was to be governed in the short term and over reparations.

The challenge of governance was resolved by the setting up of an Allied Control Council. It consisted of senior military officials from each of the allied nations with each, under the insistence of Stalin, being responsible only for their own zone. Stalin believed that this would prevent the Western Allies from ganging up on Russia to limit its influence. Thus, the exercise of power lacked cohesion and initially proved to be ineffective.

With respect to reparations, the USSR demanded that a very harsh treatment be meted out on Germany. Britain and the USA were against this as they believed it would damage Germany's ability to purchase imports. This, in turn, would have a detrimental impact on the economies of the world's major exporters (Britain and the USA in particular). An agreement was eventually reached whereby the parties concerned would be allowed to take reparations only from the zones under their control.

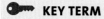

KEY TERM

Denazification The process adopted by the Allies to eradicate the influence of Nazism in post-Second World War Germany and Austria. Particular attention was paid to politics, government, education, culture, the media, social institutions and economic policies.

As a concession to the Russians, Britain and the USA agreed to pay ten per cent of their reparations to the Stalinist regime and an extra fifteen per cent in exchange for any food and raw materials that Stalin authorised to be moved out of the Soviet zone. But this compromise did not bode well for future cooperation between the Allies over how to support and mould economic policy in Germany.

The initial agreements made over Germany were undermined by a series of events that resulted in the formal division of Germany into East and West:

- From June 1945 to November 1946, Stalin shifted his position on Germany: he moved from accepting that there would be 'two Germanies' (West and East) to claiming 'all Germany must be ours'.
- On 1 January 1947, the USA and Britain announced that they were integrating the economies of their zones in Germany to create Bizonia. The hope was that this would lead to greater wealth from inter-zonal trade and that subsequently the French and Russian zones would be enticed to form a united German economy.
- At the Moscow Conference of Foreign Ministers in March to April 1947, the Soviet Union rejected the idea of Bizonia, suspecting that it was a ruse to take away its influence in Germany. A follow-up conference in London in November to December 1947 failed to resolve differences. The Soviets pushed for the formation of a central German government to reunify the nation (and which they hoped to influence), whereas the USA and Britain opposed this and seemed to head towards wanting a formal division between West and East Germany.
- In June 1948, the Western Allies introduced a new currency to their zones, the Deutschmark. The Soviets countered this by producing the Ostmark to be used in their zone. They also blockaded West Berlin to prevent the East from being influenced by the evils of capitalism. The blockade was a serious development for West Berlin as it was reliant on rail and road links that went through the Soviet-controlled territory for supplies.
- The West responded by flying in food and raw materials to West Berlin. By the end of January 1949 it was apparent the blockade had failed, as the West was able to supply some 8000 tonnes of goods per day. Stalin, unwilling to go to war over Berlin, made a concession that he would lift the blockade if a meeting of the Council of Foreign Ministers was called. The talks did not solve the problems but the blockade was lifted.
- The West German constitution was approved in the spring of 1949 and elections to a new parliament followed in August.
- This resulted in the USSR establishing East Germany in October 1949.

Other Eastern European states

Communist regimes were also established in the other countries of Eastern Europe:

- *Romania*: the expulsion of the Nazis was followed by a coalition government, but this was dominated by communists. In February 1945, the Soviet Union forced the king to appoint a communist prime minister and within a few months, communists controlled the country, which enabled them to abolish the monarchy in 1947.
- *Bulgaria*: as with Romania, a coalition government was initially set up, but in a rigged election in 1945 they won a majority, executed other political leaders and a year later abolished the monarchy.
- *Albania*: this was unlike other countries in Eastern Europe, as the communists gained power relatively easily with little opposition.
- *Greece*: this was the one exception to communist success. A civil war between royalists and communists broke out. Britain and the USA supported the royalists and Stalin kept his promise not to aid the communists. As a result, by 1949 the communists in Greece were defeated.

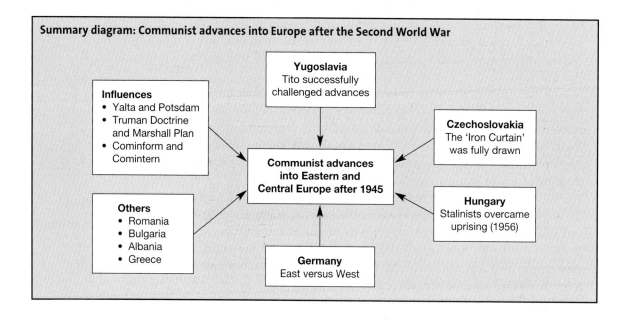

Summary diagram: Communist advances into Europe after the Second World War

Chapter summary

The Russian Empire grew considerably throughout the period and for a variety of economic, social and political reasons. The tsars were keen to expand to give the impression to the rest of the world that Russia was a power to be reckoned with. However, such a policy was not always successful, especially the components concerned with Russification. The latter caused resentment that grew into rebellion and this was difficult for Russian leaders to control without resorting to repression.

Under the communists, territorial expansion was continued alongside the policy of gaining 'spheres of influence'. This approach was also met by opposition, particularly after the Second World War with Stalin's Sovietisation of Eastern Europe. The constitutions of the communists attempted to deal with the issues of governing national minorities but were something of a sham as promises of autonomy and independence were tempered by the resort to repression if the minorities demanded too much freedom.

Refresher questions

Use these questions to remind yourself of the key material covered in this chapter.

1 Who were the national minorities in the Russian Empire?

2 What were the causes and consequences of the Polish Revolt of 1863?

3 What was the impact of the First World War on Russo-Polish relations?

4 What were the causes and consequences of the Russo-Polish War of 1920?

5 Why were Russo-Polish relations tense from 1933 to 1941?

6 What was the impact of the Second World War on Russo-Polish relations?

7 What was Russification?

8 How did relations between Russia and Finland develop from 1855 to 1964?

9 How did the 1936 constitution affect the Baltic provinces, the Ukraine and the Caucuses?

10 How were Jews in Russia treated from 1855 to 1964?

11 What was the importance of the Treaty of Brest-Litovsk of 1918?

12 Why and how did Russia expand into Central Asia and the Far East from 1855 to 1964?

13 Why and how did Stalin advance communism into Eastern and Central Europe after the Second World War?

14 Why did the German question cause Russia so many problems after the Second World War?

In-depth studies and debates

The examination requires you to study three topics in depth and for this unit they are:

- Alexander II's domestic reforms
- The Provisional Government
- Khrushchev in power 1956–64.

This section will go into more detail about how the Russian Empire, nationalities and satellite states were dealt with by three separate Russian regimes. Some of the key debates about the impact of policies on the Russian Empire, nationalities and satellite states will be considered so that you will have enough depth of knowledge to be able to evaluate passages that are set on any of the depth study topics.

Key debate 1: how far were issues relating to the empire and minorities neglected by Alexander II?

Many of the more general texts on tsarist Russia (and even some of the more specialist ones such as Edvard Radzinsky's *Alexander II*, 2005) pay scant attention to the impact of the reign of Alexander II on the Russian Empire and minorities. There appears to be an underlying assumption that the tsar's domestic reforms affected all of the empire in a similar way. A good example is the emancipation of the serfs. Some historians give the impression that a Russian peasant was the same kind of rural worker regardless of the region in which they lived. Micro-studies have revealed that this was clearly not the case, and that freedom from serfdom impacted on rural folk differently according to time and place.

Alexander II's domestic reforms are usually analysed with respect to how successful they were in achieving their aims. Most discussion revolves around the connection between the emancipation edict and reforms that followed, especially those to regional government. The break-up of serfdom took away authority from the nobility to administer and govern at a local level. The introduction of the *Zemstva* to take over the running of local affairs is seen as a major step towards liberalising the empire. Although some historians have pointed out some of the long-term failings of the *Zemstva*, few have paid attention to how they were viewed in particular parts of the empire and by minorities.

In connection with the above, the following points tend to be glossed over or ignored:

- The Polish rebellion of 1863 was the result of a complex interplay of factors including the access to land, the proposed policies of the Polish leaders, Michael Gorchakov and Aleksander Wielopolski, and the role of the Catholic Church in Polish society. Alexander II tried very hard to compromise with the

Polish government by allowing it to frame its own land-reform programme. Extremists in Poland opposed the proposals (along with those to do with conscription) and rebellion erupted. Of particular note is that peasants divided their allegiance; some supported the insurgents while others backed the Russians. After the rebellion was ruthlessly suppressed in 1864, the tsar imposed reforms which benefited the majority of peasants to the detriment of the nobility.

- The Polish rebellion was quite obviously the start of the Russification process (although this is usually attributed to Alexander III). This supports the argument that Alexander II was very concerned to maintain order across the whole of the empire.
- Other hints of 'separatism' that appeared after 1864 were given much attention. For example, an official commission was set up in 1876 to investigate separatist activity in the Ukraine.
- Alexander II continued his father's liberal policy towards the Baltic Germans (the upper-class people of Latvia and Estonia). This was done in the face of rising nationalism in both of the states, mainly from the middle-class intelligentsia. Estonian nationalist fervour, for example, revealed itself in the publication of literature written in Estonian. The newspaper *Sakala* published by K.R. Jakobson campaigned for social and economic equality between all Estonians, although it made clear that it supported the tsarist regime in Russia. This again shows how the tsar was concerned about maintaining regional stability but it also reveals the complexity of this challenge.
- The tsar took some practical measures to improve the lot of Jews. For example, some categories of Jews (merchants and doctors in particular) were allowed to live outside the Pale of Settlement.
- During the rule of Alexander II, there was significant Russian expansion into Central Asia (see pages 200–2).

Alexander II was well aware of the need to monitor developments across the whole of the empire in response to his programme of reforms. He also listened to the demands of national minorities and in general reacted in a responsible manner. It is therefore important to bear in mind the ethnic make-up of the empire when evaluating the tsar's achievements.

Key debate 2: to what extent did opposition from national minorities lead to the fall of the Provisional Government?

Opposition towards the Provisional Government from national minorities is a factor that is often overlooked when analysing the reasons for its demise. This is mainly due to the emphasis placed on the impact of the First World War and other problems inherited by the Provisional Government. One line of thought on this matter is that as the Provisional Government's main aim was to maintain the cohesiveness of the state until a Constituent Assembly could be instigated, it should have been a priority to assert authority across the whole of the empire. Instead, the Provisional Government focused mainly on urban political, economic and social issues, especially in Petrograd and Moscow. Some historians have stressed that this was a mistake as:

- Minorities became frustrated that their wants and needs were not being addressed. The Provisional Government's slowness in creating an assembly in which the minorities could express their views caused resentment and calls for autonomy.
- Minorities were spurred on by the successes of workers, soldiers and sailors in establishing committees to demand more rights from employers and the government.
- Minorities took advantage of the 'principles' adopted by the Provisional Government on which administration of the state was to be based (particularly the abolition of police units and provincial governors).

As a result, certain national minorities started to organise their own forms of provincial government, thus creating the possibility of the disintegration of the empire:

- A central *Rada* (council) was formed in Kiev in Ukraine; its main aim was to press for Ukraine to have autonomy.
- Similarly, in Finland, politicians campaigned for the establishment of their own *Sejm* (parliament) free from the influence of central Russian government.

It has been pointed out that such moves were not ignored by the Provisional Government. For example, demands for self-rule in the Transcaucasus were met with the formation of a Special Transcaucasian Committee. The problem with such initiatives though, as in other regions such as Estonia and Latvia, was that they were often undermined by the formation of local soviets. This is evidence to show how more general issues of autonomy for regions was tied up with the more particular concerns of workers and peasants. When bodies such as the *Rada* and *Sejm* stated that they would deal with local social and economic problems such as land distribution, they became 'a tier of unofficial opposition to policies announced in Petrograd'.

On the one hand, it seems reasonable to emphasise that the fortunes of the Provisional Government rested on how well they dealt with the challenges of a lack of the legitimacy, the land question, urban unrest and the First World War. However, it also seems important to consider the strength of opposition from national minorities to the government and how the latter seemed to underestimate the strength of feeling at regional level. Given that, for example in Georgia, Estonia and Ukraine, the majority of the population were peasants, it seems naïve for the Provisional Government not to have prioritised dealing with the land transference issue. Not getting a grip on the rise of nationalism in the regions of the empire undoubtedly caused the Provisional Government further problems as it enabled more left-wing parties at a local level to gain support.

Key debate 3: how valid is 'courageous failure' as an assessment of Khrushchev's policy towards minorities, satellite states and Asia?

Khrushchev has been viewed as a 'courageous failure' when it comes to his domestic (see page 121) and foreign policies. With respect to minorities, satellite states and Asia, the 'courageous' label stems from de-Stalinisation and the policy of 'peaceful coexistence'. Critics of Khrushchev have highlighted the following failures of his 'courageous' policies:

- Khrushchev attempted to resolve conflict with Tito and Yugoslavia through appeasement. It is argued that by allowing Tito a certain amount of autonomy, other Eastern European states were encouraged to follow the Yugoslavian model. This created instability in the Soviet bloc and may even have contributed to the final collapse of communism in 1991.
- The Hungarian crisis of 1956 is said to have ended in disaster for two reasons. First, it appeared that, by using force, Khrushchev had resorted to Stalinist tactics to deal with opposition. De-Stalinisation and, therefore, the prospect of further liberal reforms in Eastern Europe suffered a major setback. Second, communist parties in the West lost support, which dented the prospect of communism spreading outside the Soviet Union.
- With respect to the German question, Khrushchev's approach resulted in the construction of the Berlin Wall. As with the Hungarian uprising, this suggested that Khrushchev was too willing to resort to repression when his more liberal policies failed.
- De-Stalinisation seemed to worsen relations with China as Khrushchev struggled to deal with the criticisms from his Chinese counterpart. According to the historian Martin McCauley (2002), from as early as 1954, 'the wily Mao bamboozled Khrushchev', suggesting that the Soviet leader was no match for his Chinese counterpart. By the 1960s, the Chinese were claiming that they, rather than Khrushchev's Soviet Union, were the real upholders of Marxism–Leninism. This caused communist parties throughout the communist world to start to take sides and divide the movement, something that would not have been conceivable under Stalin.

Defenders of Khrushchev have argued that he was more of a 'courageous success' than a failure when it came to his dealings with minorities, satellite states and Asia. In particular, they believe that the following achievements are often sidelined:

- Khrushchev managed to gain support from Tito over the Hungarian uprising.
- Khrushchev also got the backing of other socialist states (Poland, Czechoslovakia, Romania and Bulgaria) as well as China for his handling of the Hungarian crisis. Also, the West failed to intervene, which meant that Khrushchev had scored something of a propaganda victory.

- The Soviet leader's stance on Germany prevented the West from taking total control of the country and its capital, Berlin.
- Mao's attempt to manipulate the Soviets failed. Khrushchev held his own against Mao and on more than one occasion showed the Chinese that he was prepared to take a strong position against them. For example, in 1958, the Soviet Union declined to provide China with military support in its conflict with Taiwan and the USA.

Study skills: thematic essay question

How to write a conclusion to a thematic essay

You may have already considered the importance of a conclusion when studying units 1 and 2 of the OCR course. As with those units, a conclusion needs to make a judgement based on what you have already written and should be briefly supported so that it is not an assertion. It should *not* introduce new ideas – if they were important they should have been in the main body of the essay. It is also important *not* to offer a contrary argument to the one you have pursued throughout the rest of your essay. This will be avoided if you have planned and thought through your essay before you started writing (see pages 70–3 for guidance on planning).

It might be that you are largely restating the view that you offered in the opening paragraph. In stronger answers there might be a slight variation to that judgement so that you confirm your original view, but suggest, with a brief example, that there were occasions when this view was not always correct.

As with unit 1 and 2 answers, if the question has a named factor, then you should give a supported judgement about that factor's relative importance, explaining why it is or is not the most important and the role it played in the events you have discussed. If the question asks you to assess a range of issues, the conclusion should explain which you think was the most important and why, and give some brief support for your claim. Remember, a claim is simply an assertion unless there is some evidence to support it and will therefore not score highly.

Consider the question below and the sample conclusions in Responses A and B that follow. Response A is an example of a weak conclusion and Response B an example of a strong conclusion.

> 'The armistice of 1920 was the most important turning point in Russo-Polish relations from 1855 to 1964.' How far do you agree?

The focus of the answer should initially have been on the importance of the 1920 Russo-Polish armistice in determining the course of relations between the two. It then needed to compare the armistice with other potential turning points such as the Polish Revolt of 1863 and the signing of the Treaty of Brest-Litovsk in 1918. The main body of the essay should look to compare and contrast other potential turning points with the 1920 armistice so that any links between the developments can be demonstrated and also so that the evaluation of the various events is comparative.

The following issues are likely to have been considered in the essay:

- How potential turning points can be compared (for example, by looking at their political, economic and social impact on Russia and Poland).
- The impact of the Polish Revolt of 1863 on Russo-Polish relations.
- The rise of socialism in Poland in the early 1890s and how that affected Russo-Polish politics.
- The Russian Civil War and the 1920 armistice.
- Hitler's accession to power in 1933 and how this affected Russia's policy towards Poland.
- The discovery in 1943 of the bodies of Polish officers in the Katyn Forest.
- The Yalta and Potsdam conferences of 1945.
- The change in the leadership of Poland in 1956 when Wladyslaw Gomulka took control.

Response A

The armistice between Poland and Russia signed in October 1920 was the most important turning point in Russo-Polish relations from 1855 to 1964. Under the agreement, Polish independence was confirmed and it was decided that western Ukraine and western Belorussia should come under Polish authority. The freedom and territory gained in 1920 were to remain in place until after the Second World War. This was the longest period of Polish independence from Russian control across the whole period. But there were other turning points of significance. The 1863 Polish revolt led to the Milyutin plan and the attempted Russification of Poland. Russification was overturned to some extent by the First World War and the Treaty of Brest-Litovsk. Poland was freed from Russia but this was not consolidated until the end of the Civil War with the armistice. Hitler's rise to power was also a turning point, but Poland's status was not greatly affected by this until 1939. Finally, the conferences at Yalta and Potsdam in 1945 were not quite as important, although they did seem to stimulate a move by Russia to Sovietise Eastern Europe including Poland.

Analysis of Response A

- A clear judgement is reached. It explains why the 1920 armistice was the most important turning point, but does not explain why it was more important than other potential turning points.
- There is some awareness of continuity and change, which is a strong point.
- There is no relative judgement about the importance of the turning points; there is simply a list of alternatives.

Response B

The armistice between Poland and Russia signed in October 1920 was an important turning point in Russo-Polish relations from 1855 to 1964. Under the agreement, Polish independence was confirmed and it was decided that western Ukraine and western Belorussia should come under Polish authority. The freedom and territory gained in 1920 were to remain in place until after Second World War. This was the longest period of Polish independence from Russian control across the whole period. In contrast, the 1863 Polish revolt led to Russification and less Polish autonomy, and freedoms granted under the Treaty of Brest-Litovsk were not consolidated until the end of the Civil War. Hitler's lebensraum policy only affected Polish sovereignty from 1939 until 1945. However, more important than the 1920 armistice were the conferences at Yalta and Potsdam in 1945. They laid a foundation for Russia to Sovietise Eastern Europe including Poland. Despite the appointment in 1956 of Wladyslaw Gomulka, a more liberal leader, Poland remained a satellite state of Russia until 1989. Thus, in comparison to the 1922 armistice, the conferences of 1945 had a greater long-term and negative impact, from a Polish point of view, on Russo-Polish relations.

Analysis of Response B

- A clear judgement is reached that the 1945 conferences were the most important turning point and why they were more significant.
- The importance of 1922 armistice in comparison to the 1945 conferences is explained.
- There are links made between the factors and some support for the claim is made; the result is a judgement about the relative importance of the factors concerned.
- The response shows awareness of the link between factors and this is explained.

Activity

You should now try and write a conclusion to some of the questions below. Ensure that you reach a clear, supported judgement and that when you have to discuss more than one factor your evaluation of the importance of the factors is comparative.

Essay questions

1 To what extent were national minorities treated more favourably by the communists than the tsars in the period from 1855 to 1964?
2 'The pace and extent of Russification varied considerably across the period from 1855 to 1964.' How far do you agree with this judgement?
3 Assess the reasons for the changing attitudes of Russian leaders towards expansion in Asia from 1855 to 1964.

Study skills: depth study interpretations question

How to reach a judgement

This section looks at how to reach a judgement about the two passages. In the first paragraph you will have explained the two interpretations and placed them in the context of the wider historical debate about the issue, and in the second and third paragraphs you will have evaluated the strengths and weakness of the two interpretations. However, in order to reach the higher mark bands you must reach a supported judgement as to which passage's view about the issue in the question you think is more convincing.

A good conclusion will:

- reach a clear judgement as to which passage's view about the issue in the question is more convincing
- explain why a particular passage is more convincing and why the other is less convincing
- suggest that there are some parts in both passages which are more or less convincing
- briefly support the judgement so that it is not simply an assertion.

Read the question and Passages A and B below about the response of China to Russia's invasion of Hungary in 1956 and then the example conclusions (Responses A and B) that follow:

> Evaluate the interpretations in both of the passages and explain which you think is more convincing as an explanation of the importance of the response of the Chinese leader Mao to Russia's invasion of Hungary in 1956.

PASSAGE A

1956 was the year that the new Soviet leader, Nikita Khrushchev, shook the communist world by launching an extraordinary attack on his predecessor, Joseph Stalin, who had died three years earlier. Khrushchev denounced Stalin and his 'cult of personality'. Mao could see how easily this charge could be made against him in China. His apparent encouragement of criticism from within the Party, was, therefore, a way of taking the sting out of the suggestion and preventing the comparison being made between him and Stalin. However, if Mao had indeed launched the **100 Flowers Campaign** *out of fear of being compared with Stalin, the fear temporarily lessened in 1956. In November of that year Khrushchev sent Soviet tanks into Budapest to crush the Hungarian Uprising. That was the Soviet leader's way of making it clear that de-Stalinization did not mean the lessening of the grip of the Communist Party over the USSR or the weakening of Soviet control over the Eastern bloc.*

Mao fully approved of the Soviet action for two reasons. In the first place, he believed it was the kind of tough line that communist governments should take

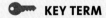 **KEY TERM**

100 Flowers Campaign
The Maoist policy, established by 1957, of allowing Chinese leadership to be discussed and criticised.

in order to maintain their authority. In the second, he was relieved by the knowledge that the Soviet Union had merely been flirting with liberal ideas. This meant that he did not need to compete with Khrushchev in the defence of hardline communism. Neither leader had any intention of relaxing his political control over the people.

(*Michael Lynch*, Origins and Development of Authoritarian and Single-party States, *Hodder Education, 2013, p. 126.*)

PASSAGE B

Early on October 24 thousands of Soviet troops and tanks entered Budapest. But instead of pacifying the city, they deepened the crisis. When armored vehicles were surrounded by Molotov cocktail-wielding youths, Hungarian security forces offered little support, and some went over to the rebels. By midafternoon at least twenty-five protesters had been killed, and more than two hundred injured. By October 30 hundreds of Hungarian civilians and Soviet soldiers had died. The situation seemed more dire than ever yet the Presidium in Moscow decided to accept it. General Zhukov, for example, stated that 'we should withdraw our troops from Budapest and from all of Hungary if that's demanded'. Khrushchev seemed to agree with the idea of 'a peaceful path, the withdrawal of troops and negotiations' although he was clearly uncomfortable with it. Apart from the possibility of losing Hungary Khrushchev agonized about rebellion spreading to its neighbors. Student demonstrations in Romania had led Bucharest authorities to close their border with Hungary. Czechoslovakia and East Germany seemed vulnerable as well. The Soviet bloc threatened to crumble.

Beginning on October 23 Khrushchev had sought the advice of the Chinese. Initially, Mao urged that 'the working class of Hungary should be allowed to regain control of the situation and put down the uprising on its own'. But by October 30, having heard about the lynching of a Hungarian secret policeman in Budapest, Mao changed his mind. That Khrushchev needed advice from Mao confirms his crisis of confidence. However, with or without Chinese sanction (the issue of when and how Khrushchev learned of Mao's change of position remains unclear), Khrushchev reversed his stance on October 31. He told the Presidium 'we must ... not pull troops out of Budapest. We must take the initiative and restore order in Hungary. If we leave Hungary, that will encourage the Americans, English and French, the imperialists. They will perceive it as a weakness and go on the offensive'.

(*Adapted from William Taubman,* Khrushchev: The Man and his Era, *The Free Press, 2003, pp. 295–7.*)

Response A

In conclusion, Passage B offers a more convincing view of Mao's response to Khrushchev's decision to invade Hungary in 1956. The passage offers a balanced answer considering both Mao's view of the invasion and Khrushchev's response independent of the advice given by the Chinese leader. It is accurate in the details given about the timing, extent and immediate impact of the invasion. In particular, it highlights the possibility that unrest might escalate and spread throughout Eastern Europe, which prompted the final responses of both Mao and Khrushchev. Interpretation A glosses over the details of the invasion (and is misleading about the timing of it), which are important in aiding understanding about the changing views held by the Chinese and Russian leaders.

Response B

Both passages correctly acknowledge that Mao's response to Khrushchev's actions over the Hungarian uprising was important in that it was supportive. However, they differ with respect to the motives and timing of Mao's response. Passage A implies that Mao's response came after Khrushchev sent troops and tanks to Hungary whereas Passage B makes the important point that Khrushchev consulted Mao before making his decision. But Passage A is more explicit about Mao's reasoning; by the mid-1950s the Chinese leader was indeed concerned that its 'ally' was drifting from hardline communism. Passage B, however, infers that Mao's interest in Hungary was based on his wish to preserve the freedoms of workers, which would have been in line with communist ideology. Finally, Passage A gives the impression that relations between China and Russia were fairly cordial and that they were following a similar path; they were both concerned to present the image that communist control over 'the people' would not be relaxed. This view ignores the fact that the two states were becoming increasingly antagonist towards each other. Passage B gives a hint of this by highlighting how Khrushchev was willing to consult Mao initially but in the end he made up his own mind as to how to respond to the Hungarian crisis. Therefore, overall, Passage B provides the more convincing explanation of the importance of Mao's response to Khrushchev's decision-making.

Analysis of Responses A and B

Both conclusions offer a judgement and both support their claims. However, Response B is the stronger conclusion:

- Response A focuses almost exclusively on Passage B, with mention of Passage A only towards the end.
- Response B compares the two interpretations in reaching its judgement and is more balanced.
- Response B, although it argues that Passage B is stronger, does not dismiss the valid points made in Passage A.

Activity

Revisit the questions on the passages in Chapters 1–3 (pages 74, 125 and 173) and write a conclusion for those questions.

Timeline

1855	Accession of Alexander II – the 'Tsar Liberator'
1856	Russia's defeat in the Crimean War
1861	Emancipation of the serfs
1863	Polish Revolt; start of Russification
1864	*Zemstvo* law and legal reforms
1865	Censorship regulations eased
1866	First assassination attempt against Alexander II
1874–81	Growth of opposition groups: *Narodniks*, Land and Liberty, People's Will
1877–8	Russo-Turkish War
1881	Constitutional proposals; assassination of Alexander II; the 'Reaction'
1883	Peasant Land Bank created
1887	Failed attempt to assassinate Alexander III
1889	Introduction of land captains
1891	Famine in 17 of Russia's 39 provinces
1892–3	Witte's 'Great Spurt'
1894	Accession of Nicholas II
1898	Formation of Social Democrats (SDs)
1901	Formation of Socialist Revolutionaries (SRs)
1903	SDs split into Bolsheviks and Mensheviks
1904–5	Russo-Japanese War
1905	Bloody Sunday; 1905 Revolution; October Manifesto

1906	Fundamental Laws passed
1906–11	Stolypin's reforms
1906–14	Four *Dumas* met
1914–18	First World War
1917	February Revolution; formation of Provisional Government
1917–21	Russian Civil War; War Communism
1918	Constituent Assembly; Treaty of Brest-Litovsk; constitution
1920	Russo-Polish War
1921	Kronstadt rising; famine and economic collapse (about 8 million died of starvation and disease 1918–21)
1921–7	New Economic Policy (NEP)
1924	Lenin's death (struggle for power 1922–9); constitution
1918–53	Stalin in power
1928–9	Introduction of First Five-Year Plan and of collectivisation
1932–4	Famine (about 5 million died of starvation and disease)
1934–40	The Great Terror (reprised after Second World War)
1936	Stalin Constitution
1941–5	Second World War
1945	Yalta and Potsdam conferences
1946	Censorship tightened; famine in Ukraine (1946–7)
1947–9	Cold War
1948	Military coup in Czechoslovakia

1948–9	Berlin Blockade
1949	Leningrad purge; formation of Comecon; formation of People's Republic of China; formation of East Germany
1950–3	Korean War
1953	Discovery of Doctors' Plot announced; death of Stalin
1954–6	Khrushchev's rise to power; launch of Virgin Land campaign
1955	Creation of Warsaw Pact

1956	Denunciation of Stalin by Khrushchev ('Secret Speech'); Hungarian uprising
1959	Khrushchev's maize-growing campaign launched
1962	Workers' riots in Novocherkassk; Cuban Missile Crisis
1963	Agricultural crisis generated by soil erosion on the 'virgin lands'
1964	Fall of Khrushchev

Glossary of terms

100 Flowers Campaign   The Maoist policy, established by 1957, of allowing Chinese leadership to be discussed and criticised.

Agents provocateurs   Those who tempt others to commit a criminal act so that they can then be charged.

All-Russian Congress of Soviets   A meeting of delegates from soviets throughout Russia to decide on the policies to be adopted by the soviets.

American Relief Administration   A US relief mission to aid Europe, including Russia, after the First World War. The director of the organisation was Herbert Hoover, future US president.

Anschluss of Austria   The union of Germany and Austria that was officially announced on 13 March 1938.

Anti-Semitic   Prejudiced against Jews.

Appeasement   Foreign policy based on coming to a mutual agreement to resolve disputes, usually through the making of concessions.

April Theses   Lenin's outline of policies to be followed by the Bolsheviks after his return from exile in April 1917.

Armistice   An agreement to stop fighting.

Article 87   A section of the 1906 Fundamental Laws that allowed for proposed legislation to be submitted directly to the tsar for his approval.

Attrition warfare   Where no progress is made by either side during a war but both sides continue to wear each other down until one gives way.

Autocracy   A system of government in which one person has total power.

Balkan League   An alliance, put together between the spring and autumn of 1912, between Serbia, Bulgaria, Greece and Montenegro.

Baltic Germans   The upper-class inhabitants of Estonia and Latvia who had links with Germany.

Battle of Britain   An aerial battle between Germany and Britain that took place from 12 August to 30 September 1940.

Berlin Blockade   In June 1948, the Western powers combined to introduce a new currency in the zones under their control. Russia saw this as an attempt to show how capitalism could bring prosperity to Berlin and retaliated by blocking all communication links with the Western part of the city. The blockade was eventually lifted in May 1949.

Berlin Wall   A wall erected in 1961 by Russia in Berlin to formally separate the East from the West. The aim was to stop people escaping to the Western zones. The wall was taken down in November 1989.

Black Earth regions   The area from the south-western borderlands into Asiatic Russia.

Black Repartition   A vision held by peasants of a time when all land would be shared out equally.

Bloody Sunday   On 9 January 1905, a group of demonstrators marching on the Winter Palace, and led by Father Gapon, were shot at by soldiers. Over 200 people were killed and about 800 injured.

Bonus schemes   Where extra payments were made to workers for exceeding individual production targets.

Bourgeois   Anything associated with the wealth and status of the middle classes.

Boxer Rebellion   A seven-week siege of foreign embassies in Peking (now Beijing) by Chinese rebels.

Break bulk   The carriage of low-value, high-density goods in large quantities. That is, heavy, bulky goods such as coal and iron ore.

Capitalist economy   An economy based on making as much profit as possible from industrial and commercial activity.

Census   An official count of the number of people in the population.

Central Committee   The chief decision-making group of the Russian Communist Party.

Civil marriage   Legal marriage whereby civilians are allowed to choose their partners.

Cold War   A state of tension and hostility between the Soviet bloc and Western powers after the Second World War. However, the hostility did not spill over into actual fighting between the two power blocs.

Collective leadership   Rule by a group whereby responsibilities are equally shared out.

Collectivisation   A communal system of farming whereby peasants shared resources to produce food, which was then distributed to ensure that local populations were adequately fed. Surpluses were sent to urban populations.

Comintern   The Communist International body was established in March 1918 with the aim of spreading communism overseas.

Command economy   An economy that is controlled totally by the state.

Communism   A form of rule which allowed for the control, by the 'people', of the means of production, distribution and exchange.

Consolidation   The joining together of resources. In this context, smallholdings were granted that were equivalent to the area of the strips farmed under the old way of farming.

Constitutional government   A government that is organised and administered according to a set of written or unwritten rules.

Containment policy   The policy of attempting to stop communism spreading throughout the world.

Council of Ministers   Senior politicians who drafted domestic policies.

Cult of personality   The use of propaganda to build a positive image of a leader so that the population offers total obedience to that leader.

De facto   Rule as a matter of fact or circumstance rather than rule gained by legal means.

De-Stalinisation   The denunciation, by Khrushchev, of Stalin's policies.

Democratic centralism   Under the Bolsheviks, the people would agree to being led by a cadre (group of key personnel) based in Moscow, until a genuine workers' government could be put in place.

Denazification   The process adopted by the Allies to eradicate the influence of Nazism in post-Second World War Germany and Austria. Particular attention was paid to politics, government, education, culture, the media, social institutions and economic policies.

Détente   A relaxation in tensions between states during the period of the Cold War, although it is usually applied to the period from 1963 to the late 1970s.

Dialectical   Relating to the ongoing changes in society from one stage to another.

Dictatorship   Absolute rule, usually by one person, with no legal, political, economic or social restrictions.

Dictatorship of the proletariat   In theory, when the workers controlled political power. Lenin argued that before this could happen, workers would have to be ordered what to do by the Bolsheviks as they did not have the knowledge, understanding and skill to take full control of governing Russia.

Diktat   An order given by those in power; something that is non-negotiable.

Dissidents   Those who disagreed with the aims and procedures of the government.

Doctors' Plot   An announcement was made by the Stalinist regime in January 1953 concerning nine doctors who had worked alongside a US Jewish group to murder high-ranking Soviet officials. Seven of the doctors were Jews.

Duopoly   Power in the hands of two people.

Eastern Front   Where the German and Austrian-Hungarian forces met the Russian forces in Eastern Europe.

Eastern question   The issues that arose over the decline of the Turkish Ottoman Empire.

Economic autarky   When a country can provide all of the resources it needs without having to trade.

Emancipation of the serfs   An announcement in 1861 that peasants would be freed from being owned, like any other property, by wealthy landowners and the state.

Expansionist foreign policy   Foreign policy that involved the acquisition of territory from other countries (or sometimes expanding influence over such territory).

Factionalist   One who went about pursuing his or her own interests to the detriment of party unity.

First secretary of the party   The most important administrative officer in the Communist Party.

Five-Year Plans   These involved setting production targets which were to be achieved on a five-year cycle.

Fundamental Laws   Basic laws that reinforced the ideology underpinning tsarist rule.

Fundamental Laws of 1906   Regulations that reinforced the position of the tsar. Law 5, for example, stated that 'Supreme autocratic power belongs to the Emperor of all Russia'.

'Georgian affair'   The mishandling of Georgian nationalism by Ordjonikidze, the commissar for national affairs in Georgia. His actions were defended by Stalin.

GNP per capita   Gross national product per head of the population. This is often used as a measure of living standards.

Gold standard   The fixing of a country's currency to a specific quantity (and therefore value) of gold.

Gosplan   A group originally set up in 1921 to plan for industrialisation and economic growth.

Government bonds   A way of investing in the government by buying bonds (loan certificates) and cashing them in at a later date with interest.

Grand Alliance   The wartime alliance of Britain, France, Russia and the USA.

Great Powers   Britain, France, Russia, Germany (Prussia before 1871) and Austria-Hungary before 1914.

Great Purge   The period from 1936 to 1938 when thousands of people were arrested, convicted and executed for committing 'counter-revolutionary' crimes.

Great Russia   Also known as Muscovy, the old Russian principality that had Moscow at its centre.

Great Russian Bear   A term used by the West to describe the perceived military threat posed by Russia.

Great Terror   The period from 1936 to 1938 when the terrorisation of the Russian people reached a peak.

Green armies   Mainly peasant groups who opposed Bolshevik rule.

Gross national product (GNP)   The total value of all the goods and services produced in a country.

Guesstimates   Estimates of what happened but based on guesswork, usually as a result of flimsy or missing evidence.

Gulags   Labour camps that were used mainly to house political dissidents and those suspected of being anti-communist.

Holy Sepulchre   The cave outside Jerusalem in which the body of Christ is believed to have lain between his burial and Resurrection.

Home Front   What was happening domestically during the war, especially with respect to the wartime work civilians were involved in.

Housing cooperatives   Organisations formed by employees who belonged to the same work enterprise or professional union. They were given first pickings over new state housing as long as they could meet government-set prices.

Ignatiev memorandum   Nicholas Pavolich Ignatiev (1832–1908) was Russia's ambassador to Constantinople. In 1876, he sent a note to Serbian leaders, without official approval, saying that they could rely on Russian help if they declared war on Turkey.

In kind   Payment other than by using money, such as the exchange of goods and services.

Incendiary   Setting fire to rural property, usually farm buildings and hayricks.

Iron Curtain   An imaginary border between Russian-dominated Eastern and Western Europe.

July Days   From 3 to 6 July 1917, there were widespread demonstrations in Petrograd against the Provisional Government. The rebellion proved to be disorganised and was easily put down by troops still loyal to the government. The rising showed the weaknesses of opposition to the government at this point, particularly the Bolsheviks.

Justices of the peace   Landowners appointed as officials to maintain law and order at a local level. They worked in conjunction with the police.

Kadets   The Constitutional Democrats, a liberal political group founded in 1905.

Katyn Forest massacre   The execution of around 5000 Polish officers by the Red Army in the forest of Katyn, Smolensk, on the eve of the German invasion.

Kolkhozy   A farm owned and partly organised by the state but worked on by peasant farmers not directly employed by the state. Members could own a house, a small plot of land and a few animals.

Komsomols   Members of the youth organisation known as the Young Communist League.

Kronstadt   A Baltic naval base.

Kulaks   The Bolsheviks popularised this term to indicate the existence of a class of allegedly rich, exploiting peasants. Some historians point out that it was a term used after the 1861 Emancipation Edict and was derived from the Russian *Kulaki* (meaning 'fists').

Kurile Islands and South Sakhalin   The Kurile Islands, in Russia's Sakhalin Oblast region, are a volcanic archipelago that stretches approximately 1300 km north-east from Hokkaido, Japan, to Kamchatka, Russia, separating the Sea of Okhotsk from the North Pacific Ocean.

Labour camps   Punishment camps where political opponents were set to hard labour. They were placed in the more inhospitable parts of Russia such as Siberia.

Labour Code   Rules for the deployment and control of labour.

Labourists   Those who were specifically interested in improving the working conditions of the proletariat.

Land and Liberty   A pressure group consisting of intellectuals who believed that it was important to live among peasants so as to understand their plight.

Land captains   Landowners who were appointed, from 1889 onwards, mainly to supervise the work of the regional councils, or *Zemstva*, that had been introduced by Alexander II.

Leading cadres   The 'top' members of the Communist Party responsible for organising and educating the masses.

League of Nations   An international body set up in 1919 to keep international peace through the settlement of disputes by arbitration.

Lebensraum   In German, *lebensraum* means 'living space'. In the 1930s, it was a term the Nazis used to describe their expansionist foreign policy.

Legitimism   The policy based on the idea that what was being done was right and just in the eyes of the majority.

Lend–lease   The US Congress passed an Act in March 1941 that allowed the president to lend or lease equipment to countries 'whose defense the president deems vital to the defense of the USA'.

Lenin Enrolment   A campaign that aimed to encourage peasants to join the Bolshevik Party.

Leningrad affair   A purge of the friends and colleagues of Zhdanov after his death in 1948.

Liberal democracy   A political ideology that promotes the right of the people to exercise freedom of choice. This would include the freedom to speak what one believes in, and the freedom to choose a representative in government.

Liquidate the *kulaks* as a class   Stalin's policy to eliminate wealthier peasants (*kulaks*) as part of the class war in the countryside. *Kulaks* were considered to be bourgeois.

Marshall Plan   A programme to help European recovery after the Second World War which was put forward by the US Secretary of State General George Marshall (1880–1959). He believed that the USA should 'assist in the return of normal economic health in the world without which there can be no political stability and no assured peace'.

Marxism–Leninism   Lenin's interpretation of Marxism which argued that the move to worker control of the means of production, distribution and exchange could be speeded up.

Marxism–Leninism–Stalinism   Stalin's version of Marxism–Leninism.

Medele'ev tariff of 1891   Named after Dimitry Medele'ev, who put together a 700-page book of tariffs (taxes) that should be applied to all imports of goods.

Megalomania   An individual's belief that they are very powerful and important.

Militarisation of labour   Workers were forced to work as either labourers or soldiers.

Mir A group of elders who were responsible for governing the behaviour of members of rural communities or villages.

Mobilisation order The order by the government for the military to be organised to go to war. A part mobilisation refers to some of the military being prepared for a limited conflict. Full mobilisation means that all of the military would be in a state of readiness to go to war.

Monopoly capitalism The profit-making motives that dominated the economies of Western Europe.

Monopoly concessions Being given the right to be the only seller of a particular product.

Munich Peace Conference A meeting between Germany, Italy, France and Britain that resulted in Germany being allowed to occupy the Sudetenland as long as it guaranteed not to go into the rest of Czechoslovakia.

MVD The secret police that was the successor of the NKGB and the predecessor of the KGB.

Nation-state An organised political community (or country) consisting of people sharing the same language, culture and history.

National Liberation Committee (NLC) Set up in Chelm (south-east of Lublin) in July 1944 by the Polish State National Council to oppose the National Government in exile in London. The NLC was supported and controlled by Russia.

Nationalisation The state control of industry and commerce by taking ownership of the means of production, distribution and exchange of goods and services.

Natural rate of growth The relationship between birth rates and death rates and how this affected population growth. If the birth rate increased and the death rate fell, the natural rate of growth would have been relatively high.

Nepman The 'new' type of businessman that emerged as a result of the NEP.

New Soviet Man The ideal Soviet citizen: hard working, law abiding, moral and supportive of the Communist Party.

New work discipline Factory owners introduced strict rules and regulations that were required for employees to work safely and efficiently with machines. This was especially important for recruits from the countryside who were used to working according to 'nature's clock'.

Nomenklatura 'Approved' officers, administrators and managers in the communist regime who possessed specialist skills.

North Atlantic Treaty Organisation (NATO) Members of this group agreed to support each other if they were attacked by an aggressor. Those who belonged were anti-communist and it was obvious that NATO was designed to combat the perceived threat from the Soviet Union.

October Manifesto Nicholas II's blueprint for a new form of elective government that revolved around the *Duma*.

Octobrists Supporters of the tsar and, in particular, his proposals made in the October Manifesto.

Okhrana The tsarist secret police (that replaced the Third Section) whose main job was to search for those who were determined to undermine the work of the government.

Old Believers Those who believed in the most traditional form of the Russian Orthodox Church. They also thought that they were more Russian than other Russians.

'Opium of the people' The view that religion was like a drug that took people's minds off worrying about economic and social problems. It was coined by Karl Marx in *Contribution to the Critique of Hegel's Philosophy of Right* (1843–4).

Oppositionists Those who opposed the communist revolution.

Orthodox and non-Orthodox religion Orthodox religion was the established and traditional beliefs of the Russian Orthodox Church, which had its roots in the Greek Orthodox Church. Non-Orthodox refers to any set of beliefs that differed from those of the Russian Orthodox Church.

Orthodoxy, Autocracy and Nationality The slogan used by the tsars and Pobedonostsev to justify and explain the conservative nature of tsarist rule.

Ottoman Turks   Those who were part of the dynasty originally founded by Osman (*c*.1300) which governed the Turkish Empire until 1922.

Pale of Settlement   The region within which Jews were allowed to settle. From 1835, it included Lithuania, Poland and the south-western provinces (including Ukraine).

Pan-Slavism   The movement to unite all Slavic peoples as one nation.

Paternalistic   Protecting the people.

Patriarchy   A male-dominated form of organisation and rule.

Peasant Land Bank   A bank especially set up by the government to allow peasants to borrow money at relatively cheap rates to allow the purchase of land.

Peasant vigilantism   Rural people taking the matter of law and order into their own hands.

People's Will   A terrorist group consisting of members of the educated classes who were upset by Alexander II's refusal to continue with his reform programme after the mid-1860s.

Petrograd   St Petersburg was renamed Petrograd in August 1914. The tsar ordered the renaming as he thought St Petersburg (Sankt-Peterburg) sounded German. And, of course, war had just broken out between Russia and Germany.

Plenipotentiaries   Officials who had 'total' power at a local level.

Pogrom   An organised massacre of Russian Jews.

Polish Home Army   The Polish resistance army that originated from the Union of Armed Struggle (established in September 1939). The Home Army coordinated the activity of over 150 resistance sub-groups; by 1944, the groups probably consisted of over 300,000 men and women. It was answerable to the commander-in-chief in London.

Polish question   The question as to whether the Poles would be allowed self-rule.

Polish Workers' Party (PPR)   Founded in 1942 and led by Wladyslaw Gomulka. By December 1945, it had around 65,000 members, only about a tenth of the membership of its rival, the Polish People's Party (PSL). In December 1948, the PPR changed its name to the

Polish United Workers' Party and, with the backing of Stalin, monopolised party politics.

Pork mutiny of 1922   The Pork 'mutiny' of February 1922 occurred when a group of Red Guards decided to cross the border between Russia and Finland: the guards looted property before persuading Finnish workers (with guns and money) to join their Soviet battalion. The leader, Frans Myyryläinen, started the process of recruitment by standing on a box that had previously stored pork (hence the name of the incident).

Potemkin   A battleship on which a mutiny occurred. The incident was later made famous through the silent film *Battleship Potemkin* (1928).

Presidium   A small group of ministers rather like the Cabinet in the British political system.

Principalities   Territories ruled over by a member of a royal family, usually a prince.

Progressive Bloc   A group within the fourth *Duma* consisting of members of the Kadets, Octobrists, Nationalists and Party of Progressives, who challenged the authority of Nicholas II.

Proletariat   Those who worked in industry and lived in urban areas.

Protectorates   States that were temporarily protected by another, usually more powerful state.

Prussia   The most important German state before the unification of Germany in 1871.

Putilov works   The biggest private factory in Russia by the start of the twentieth century. It specialised in iron production and became very important during the First World War in providing artillery.

Rabkrin   The Workers' and Peasants' Inspectorate, a highly bureaucratic and overstaffed organisation.

'Reaction'   Alexander III reacted to the liberal reforms put together by his father by reversing them and introducing more repressive measures.

Real wages   Wages after the impact of inflation is taken into account. That is, the amount of money available that allows the purchase of goods and services.

Red Guard   A general term to denote armed supporters of the Bolsheviks, especially in the second half of 1917.

Red Terror   Fear engendered by the Bolsheviks through the threat of arrest, imprisonment, exile and/or execution.

Redemption payments   The repayment of loans that had to be taken out to purchase land that was redistributed after 1861.

Reds   A general term for those who actively supported the Bolsheviks during the Civil War.

Reparations   Payments that constitute compensation for the damage done during a war.

Revolutionary defencism   Defence and protection of everything achieved by the revolution of March 1917.

Revolutionary war   An (international) war fought on behalf of and by workers against capitalists.

Russian Orthodox Church   A branch of Christianity that was very traditional and that was independent from outside authorities such as the papacy. It taught the people to obey the tsar as he was said to be anointed by God.

Russian peoples   The Russian peoples are usually considered to be those originating from and living in Muscovy (Muscovites or 'Great Russians'), the Ukraine ('Little Russians') and Belarus ('White Russians').

Russian Soviet Federative Socialist Republic (RSFSR) This resulted from the 1918 constitution. It constituted Russia and parts of Central Asia, most notably Kazakhstan, Uzbekistan and Turkmenia.

Russification   A policy aimed at transforming the different peoples of the Russian Empire into 'pure' Rus (the supposedly original inhabitants of Russia).

Schlieffen Plan   The plan put together in 1905 by the chief of the German General Staff, General Count Alfred Von Schlieffen (1833–1913), to act partly as a blueprint for a German attack in the West.

Scorched earth policy   Stalin ordered that all material objects of worth should be destroyed as the Russian forces retreated, to stop them falling into the hands of the enemy.

Sectarians   Anyone who belonged to a group that held extreme, and often unusual, religious views.

Slavophiles   Those who believed that Orthodox Slavs were superior to Western Europeans.

Social control   Control, usually by politicians, of the beliefs, attitudes and actions of members of society through the careful organisation and administration of particular institutions, for example, education, religion and the media.

Socialist realism   The 'official' way of representing, through writing and the visual arts, the heroic efforts of workers and peasants to ensure the success of communism.

Sovkhozy   Farms owned by the state and worked on by state employees.

Stakhanovite movement   Based on the extraordinary efforts of the Donbas miner Alexei Stakhanov, who produced way above the normal quantity of coal per man-shift. He was turned into a 'model' worker for others to copy. Those who did were given special rewards such as red carpets and holidays in Moscow.

State pricing mechanism   The government policy of providing official prices for goods and services.

Straits The stretch of sea from the Dardanelles into the Bosphorus.

Subsistence farming   Ensuring that just enough was produced to keep members of a community fed over a given period.

Sudetenland   An area in Czechoslovakia that contained about 3 million Germans in 1938.

Suez Crisis   The Suez Canal was nationalised by President Nasser in 1956. France and Britain, alarmed by Egypt's growing ties with communists, planned to take control of this important shipping route.

Sultan   Muslim head of the Ottoman Empire.

Supreme Soviet of the USSR   The main law-making body in Soviet government.

Taxation exemptions   Being allowed to pay lower tax in return for lending money to the government.

Tenements   Similar to blocks of flats.

Treaty of Berlin   Germany and Russia agreed to remain neutral if either was attacked by a third power.

Tripartite Pact   A military alliance between Germany, Italy and Japan.

United Nations   An organisation that formally came into being in June 1945 that was designed to maintain world peace.

USSR   This resulted from the 1924 constitution. By this time, via a treaty of 1922, the Republics of the Ukraine, Belorussia and Transcaucasia (Azerbaijan, Armenia and Georgia) had joined with the RSFSR. Each republic was allowed its own government and other symbols of sovereignty such as national flags. However, such governments were still answerable to *Sovnarkom*.

Vanguard   In this context, a leading group of people whose mission was to lay the base for a proletarian takeover of the governance of Russia.

Vera Zasulich case   Zasulich was a revolutionary who shot and wounded the governor of St Petersburg, General Trepov, in 1878. Trepov was a tyrant known for flogging political prisoners. Zasulich was put on trial but the jury found her not guilty as her actions were considered just. Some argued that this verdict showed that the 1864 legal reforms allowed revolutionary activity to flourish.

Viceroy   A person sent by a ruler (usually a monarch) to govern part of a region or an empire.

Vyborg Manifesto   A set of demands from militant *Duma* MPs asking the people of Finland not to pay taxes or serve in the armed forces until the *Duma* was restored.

War Bonds   Government savings certificates issued during wartime to the public with a promised fixed rate of return after the war. They had the important psychological impact of making people feel that they were making a valid contribution to the war effort.

War indemnity   A sum of money paid by one nation to another as a result of losing a war.

Westernisers   Those who wanted to modernise Russia in the same way as Western Europe.

Whites   A general term for those who actively opposed the Bolsheviks during the Civil War.

Winter Palace   Official residence of the tsars in St Petersburg.

Workers' insurance system   Insurance against being injured in the workplace. Other schemes, against ill-health, old age and unemployment, were also introduced through the 1924 and 1936 constitutions.

Working-class consciousness   An awareness among workers that they were experiencing similar living and working conditions, and therefore belonged to a single class of worker.

World revolution   The idea that communism would not be confined to the Soviet Union but would be spread throughout the world.

Further reading

Edward Acton, *Russia: The Tsarist and Soviet Legacy* (Longman, 1995)

Edward Acton and Tom Stableford, *The Soviet Union: A Documentary History, Volume 1, 1917–1940* (University of Exeter Press, 2005)

Edward Acton and Tom Stableford, *The Soviet Union: A Documentary History, Volume 2, 1939–1991* (University of Exeter Press, 2007)

Anne Applebaum, *Gulag: A History of Soviet Camps* (Penguin, 2003)

Robert Conquest, *The Great Terror: A Reassessment* (Oxford University Press, 1990)

Helen Dunmore, *The Siege* (Penguin, 2002)

Orlando Figes, *A People's Tragedy: The Russian Revolution 1891–1924* (Jonathan Cape, 1996)

Orlando Figes, *The Whisperers: Private Life in Stalin's Russia* (Penguin, 2007)

Orlando Figes, *Revolutionary Russia, 1891–1991* (Pelican, 2014)

Sheila Fitzpatrick, *Everyday Stalinism: Ordinary Life in Extraordinary Times: Soviet Russia in the 1930s* (Oxford University Press, 1999)

Martin Gilbert, *The Routledge Atlas of Russian History* (Routledge, 2007)

Vasily Grossman, *A Writer at War: With the Red Army 1941–45* (Pimlico, 2006)

Geoffrey Hosking, *Russia and the Russians: From Earliest Times to 2001* (Penguin, 2001)

Lindsey Hughes, *The Romanovs: Ruling Russia 1613–1917* (Hambledon Continuum, 2008)

Catriona Kelly, *Comrade Pavlik: The Rise and Fall of a Soviet Boy Hero* (Granta Books, 2005)

Stephen Kotkin, *Stalin: Paradoxes of Power 1878–1928* (Penguin, 2015)

Dominic Lieven, *Towards the Flame: Empire, War and the End of Tsarist Russia* (Allen Lane, 2015)

Michael Lynch, *Reaction and Revolution: Russia 1894–1941* (Hodder Education, 2015)

Martin McCauley, *The Khrushchev Era 1953–64* (Routledge, 1995)

Catherine Merridale, *Ivan's War: The Red Army 1939–45* (Faber & Faber, 2005)

Walter G. Moss, *A History of Russia. Volume I: To 1917* (Anthem Press, 2003)

Walter G. Moss, *A History of Russia. Volume II: Since 1855* (Anthem Press, 2005)

Peter Oxley, *Russia 1855–1991: From Tsars to Commissars* (Oxford University Press, 2001)

Richard Pipes, *Russia Under the Old Regime* (Penguin, 2005)

Edward Radzinsky, *Alexander II: The Last Great Tsar* (Free Press, 2006)

Christopher Read, *Lenin* (Routledge, 2005)

Christopher Read, editor, *The Stalin Years. A Reader* (Palgrave Macmillan, 2005)

Simon Sebag Montefiore, *Stalin: The Court of the Red Tsar* (Phoenix, 2004)

Victor Serge, *Memoirs of a Revolutionary* (University of Iowa Press, 2002)

Robert Service, *A History of Modern Russia: From Nicholas II to Putin* (Penguin, 2003)

Hugh Seton-Watson, *The Russian Empire 1801–1917* (Oxford University Press, 1967)

Aleksandr Solzhenitsyn, *One Day in the Life of Ivan Denisovich* (Penguin, 2000)

John Steinbeck, *A Russian Journal* (Penguin, 2000)

Geoffrey Swain, *Russia's Civil War* (History Press, 2008)

Ian D. Thatcher, *Trotsky* (Routledge, 2003)

William Taubman, *Khrushchev: The Man and his Era* (Simon & Schuster, 2003)

J.N. Westwood, *Endurance and Endeavour: Russian History 1812–2001* (Oxford University Press, 2002)

Alan Wood, *The Origins of the Russian Revolution* (Methuen, 1987)

Index